The Life and Teachings
of Jesus

The Life and Teachings of Jesus

A Restatement of the Gospels

Dedicated to the students of Einstein School in
an effort to provide them with a clear and
trustworthy guide for living

By Preston Thomas
with the invaluable assistance
of Larry Watkins and Joshua Thomas

THE LIFE AND TEACHINGS OF JESUS

Copyright © 1992, 2000, 2013 by:

Center for Quality Education (CQE), 180 Townwood Drive, Charlottesville, VA 22901

Library of Congress Control Number: 2012954796
ISBN 978-0-9632517-2-5

Printed in China through Four Colour Print Group, Louisville, Kentucky

10 9 8 7 6 5 4 3 2 1

First Edition May 1992
Second Edition November 2000
Third Edition March 2013

Table of Contents

Chapters

Sections

Organization

Introduction

This book is a restatement of the life and teachings of Jesus as recorded in the New Testament books of Matthew, Mark, Luke, and John. As with an earlier effort by Thomas Jefferson, who produced *The Jefferson Bible* in the early 1800s, the purpose here is to distill from the scriptures only those verses truly portraying the life and teachings of Jesus. The following passage, quoted from Douglas Luxton's foreword to *The Jefferson Bible*, is presented here because it also provides an excellent introduction to the present work:

> During his first term in the White House, the Father of American Democracy revealed his dream of separating the sayings which were indisputably the words of Jesus from what he considered to be extraneous matter in the Holy Library of 66 volumes, 1189 chapters, 773,000 words. Others failing to do the work, Jefferson, in evenings of escape from affairs of the nation, prepared a preliminary extraction which it was his custom to read nightly before retiring.
>
> In one of his letters to [John] Adams in 1813 the great statesman gave this description of his work: "We must reduce our volume to the simple Evangelists; select, even from them, the very words only of Jesus, paring off the amphibologisms [misinterpretations] into which they have been led, by forgetting often, or not understanding, what had fallen from Him, by giving their own misconceptions as his dicta, and by expressing unintelligibly for others what they had not understood themselves. There will be found remaining the most sublime and benevolent code of morals which has ever been offered to man. I have performed this operation for my own use, by cutting verse by verse out of the printed book, and arranging the matter which is evidently his and which is as easily distinguishable as diamonds in a dunghill. The result is an octavo of forty-six pages."
>
> Three years later, in 1816, Jefferson wrote from Monticello to Charles Thompson: "I too have made a wee little book from the same materials, which I call the philosophy of Jesus; it is a paradigm of his doctrines, made by cutting the texts out of the book, and arranging them on the pages of a blank book, in a certain order of time and subject. A more beautiful or precious morsel of ethics I have never seen; it is a document in proof that I am a *real Christian*, that is to say a disciple of the doctrines of Jesus."

I would like to introduce *The Life and Teachings of Jesus* by commenting on a number of points contained in this quotation from the foreword to *The Jefferson Bible*.

his dream of separating the sayings which were indisputably the words of Jesus from what he considered to be extraneous matter

My idea for this project had its roots in an event that took place many years ago. My grandmother was dying; she was bedridden, but alert. I searched for good words, meaningful words, that I could read to her in an effort to help her be prepared to leave this life and enter into the next. I settled on a small book called *The Sayings of Jesus*. It contained only the teachings of Jesus; I knew that his words would be the best words I could find.

A number of years later, after I had started a small private school, the idea came back to me of having a book of Jesus' teachings, this time to give to departing students. At the school we attempted to help the whole child, to provide guidance in developing character; and the idea for *The Life and Teachings of Jesus* really took root in me when I saw students who had been with us for many years leaving and realized I had nothing to give them. I wanted something to leave with them that they could read and comprehend, and that would provide a trustworthy and helpful guide for living. It was then that I really decided to find such a book, or perhaps produce one myself.

Since undertaking work on this project, the hope has grown in me that this restatement would also prove useful and uplifting to many others. I believe that, of all human knowledge, the most valuable is to know the life and teachings of Jesus. Therefore I offer this restatement in the hope that it will contribute to the expansion of this knowledge of his inspirational life and incomparable teachings.

it was his custom to read nightly before retiring

My hope also is that this book will be used and read often in search of the help, guidance, and inspiration that only Jesus' matchless life and teachings can provide. My suggestion is to read only a small portion (one chapter or one section) each day. Let the words sink in, and make it a priority to maintain regular daily readings. Simply running these words and teachings through our minds can have a very positive effect. Following Jesus' guidelines for living provides direction and stability, while transforming our lives.

Good words like these are precious. They are our heritage as dwellers on planet earth. They should be valued and studied. Through them we may come to know the true teachings of Jesus and the inspirational life he lived.

> *select from them [the simple Evangelists] the very words only of Jesus, paring off the amphibologisms [misinterpretations] into which they have been led, by forgetting often, or not understanding, what had fallen from Him, by giving their own misconceptions as his dicta, and by expressing unintelligibly for others what they had not understood themselves.*

Certainly the disciples were human, with their own weaknesses, limitations, and misconceptions. They, like we, were far from perfect; rather they were very imperfect beings in association with a God-man, who was himself engaged in living a perfect life here on earth. They could not hope to fully comprehend the significance of Jesus and his teachings. Much of what he said and did was little understood by them.

The goal of this work, like that of Jefferson's, is to separate out those teachings that are truly Jesus' from the associated teachings of his followers.

But while Jefferson was concerned only with Jesus' *teachings*, the goal of this work is also to truly depict Jesus' *life*. Jesus lived his teachings; he is our best and ideal example. His life in all its facets, his actions and reactions, his perfection of character and ideal personality development, his life of love and service, his faith and single-minded determination to do his Father's will, are all of immense value to us.

> *I too have made a wee little book . . . which I call the philosophy of Jesus.*

As with Jefferson's effort, the thrust of this work is to reveal the true teachings *of* Jesus and to separate them from the teachings *about* Jesus. The goal is to illuminate and distinguish his personal teachings from the teachings and interpretations of his followers.

Jesus is distinct from and greater than any truth teacher ever to live on our world. We do well to give his life and teachings the special respect and study they deserve. It is most important to learn what Jesus taught and how he lived, and to clearly distinguish his spirit and teachings from all others. His teachings are supreme. He is our touchstone to truth. *All other teachings may be rightly judged by their harmony with the true teachings of Jesus.*

> *made by cutting the texts out of the book, and arranging them on the pages of a blank book, in a certain order of time and subject*

The effort here is analogous. I have sought to divide the events of Jesus' life into the smallest possible units and then connect them together in chrono-logical sequence. In this fashion the book traces Jesus' life and teachings from his birth through to his death and resurrection. For such a project I have relied on a number of reference works, including: *The Gospels Paralleled*, *Halley's Bible Handbook*, *Jesus and His Times*, *The Master Study Bible*, *The Oxford Annotated Bible*, *The Paramony*, *The Urantia Book*, and *The Word: The Bible From 26 Translations*. These and other resources are listed in the bibliography.

> *There will be found remaining the most sublime and benevolent code of morals which has ever been offered to man. . . . A more beautiful or precious morsel of ethics I have never seen.*

Here Jefferson expresses his recognition of the importance of the morals and ethics offered by Jesus. This is the immediate goal of this work—to pro-vide a trustworthy guide for living. As Jefferson recognized, Jesus provides us with the highest and best moral and ethical teachings ever presented to mankind. These teachings are of supreme value to us. They show and teach us how to be, and how to live.

Jesus did indeed lead a life without sin; he lived a perfect life here on earth. His life is our best example of the high moral and ethical behavior he taught. He shows us the perfection of man: what man can be at his best. We cannot go wrong if we go his way.

> *it is a document in proof that I am a* **real Christian***, that is to say a disciple of the doctrines of Jesus.*

Christianity is founded on the life and teachings of Jesus. If one truly desires to know Jesus, and follow in the way of his personal religion, this book can be of great value, for herein is presented Jesus' life and teachings in purity and wholeness.

In summary, this work represents one person's attempt to bring together and order, by time and subject, the best of the gospels. It is a human work and therefore quite subject to error. It was prepared in the hope of restating the life and teachings of Jesus in such a way as would prove useful and helpful to those who read and study it, particularly young people. Its higher goal is to contribute to a revival of Jesus' original gospel of the kingdom—the saving truth that we are all sons and daughters of a loving heavenly Father—and to an expansion of the inner kingdom he taught: the rule of God in the hearts of individual believers.

PART 1
BIRTH AND YOUTH

I. John's Introduction[a]

1. "The Word Was Made Flesh"

[1]In the beginning was the Word, and the Word was with God, and the Word was God. [2]He was in the beginning with God; [3]all things were made through him, and without him was not anything made that was made. [4]In him was life, and that life was the light of men.

[6]There was a man sent from God, whose name was John.[b] [7]He came for testimony, to bear witness to the light, that all men through him might believe. [8]He was not the light, but came to bear witness to the light.

[9]The true light that lights every man was coming into the world. [10]He was in the world, and the world was made by him, and yet the world knew him not. [11]He came to his own and his own received him not. [12]But to as many as received him, who believed in his name, to them he gave power to become sons of God, [13]born not of blood, nor of the will of the flesh, nor of the will of man, but of God.

[14]And the Word was made flesh, and dwelt among us full of grace and truth; we have beheld his glory, glory as of the only Son from the Father. [15]John bore witness to him and cried, "This was he of whom I said, 'He who comes after me ranks before me, for he was before me.'" [16]And from his fullness have we all received, and grace upon grace. [17]For the law was given by Moses, but grace and truth came through Jesus Christ. [18]No one has seen God; but God's only Son, who is in the bosom of the Father, he has made him known.

(Jn. 1:1–4, 6–18)

---

a   "John's Introduction"—These are the words of John Zebedee, the apostle who wrote the New Testament book of John, which is the source of this introduction.

b   "There was a man sent from God, whose name was John."—John the Baptist. (See Section IV.)

Jn. 1:7   all men through him might believe. (KJV) / all might believe through him. (RSV)
Jn. 1:9   that lights every / that enlightens every (RSV)
Jn. 1:10   made by him, (KJV) / made through him, (RSV)
Jn. 1:11   own and his own received (KJV) / own home and his own people received (RSV)
Jn. 1:12   to as many as received (KJV) / to all who received (RSV) • become sons of (KJV) / become children of (RSV)
Jn. 1:13   born, (KJV) / who were born, (RSV)
Jn. 1:14   Word was made flesh (KJV) / Word became flesh (RSV)
Jn. 1:16   received, and grace (KJV) / received, grace (RSV)
Jn. 1:17   given by Moses, but grace (KJV) / given through Moses; grace (RSV)
Jn. 1:18   has seen God; but God's only (KJV) / has ever seen God; the only (RSV)

For an explanation of the numbers in the text and the verse notes, see "How to Read the Numbers and Reference Notes" on page 227.

Jesus by M. Hook

3

II. The Birth of Jesus

2. Gabriel's Announcement to Mary

[26]The angel Gabriel was sent by God to a city of Galilee named Nazareth [27]to Mary. [28]And he came unto her and said, "Hail, O favored one, the Lord is with you!"

[29]But she was greatly troubled at the saying and considered in her mind what sort of a greeting this might be.

[30]And the angel said to her, "Fear not, Mary, for you have found favor with God. [31]You will bear a son and you shall call his name Joshua (Jesus).[a] [32]He will be great and will be called the Son of the Most High; [33]and of his kingdom there will be no end. [36]Your kinswoman Elizabeth has also conceived a son. [35]And the power of the Most High will overshadow you."

[38]And Mary said, "I am the handmaid of the Lord; let it be to me according to your word." And the angel departed from her.

(Lk. 1:26–33, 36, 35, 38)

---

a "Joshua (Jesus)."—The name *Jesus* is the Greek translation of the Hebrew *Yeshua*. *Yeshua* is the contracted form of *Yehoshua*, and the English translation of *Yehoshua* is *Joshua*.

Lk. 1:26   The / In the sixth month, the (RSV)
Lk. 1:27   to Mary. / to a virgin betrothed to a man whose name was Joseph, of the house of David; and the virgin's name was Mary. (RSV)
Lk. 1:30   her, "Fear not, Mary, (KJV) / her, "Do not be afraid, Mary, (RSV)
Lk. 1:31   You will bear / And behold, you will conceive in your womb and bear (RSV) • name Joshua (Jesus). (See fn. *a*.) / name Jesus. (RSV)
Lk. 1:36   Your / And behold, your (RSV) • Elizabeth has / Elizabeth, in her old age, has (RSV)
Lk. 1:35   And / And the angel said to her, "The Holy Spirit will come upon you, and (RSV)
Lk. 1:38   said, "I / said, "Behold, I (RSV) (122:3/1346)

4

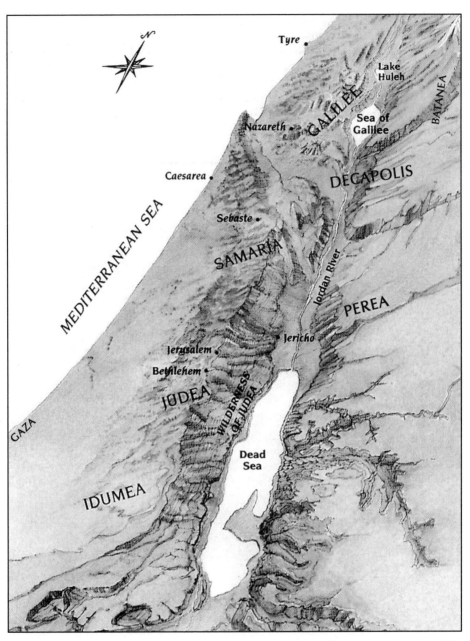

"The angel Gabriel was sent by God to a city of Galilee named Nazareth."

3. Mary's Visit to Elizabeth

[39]In those days Mary arose and went with haste into the hill country, to the City of Judah, [40]and she entered the house of Zacharias and greeted Elizabeth.

[41]And when Elizabeth heard the greeting of Mary, the babe leaped in her womb; and Elizabeth was filled with the Holy Spirit [42]and she exclaimed with a loud cry, "Blessed are you among women and blessed is the fruit of your womb! [45]And blessed is she who believed that there would be a fulfillment of what was spoken to her from the Lord."

[46]And Mary said, "My soul magnifies the Lord, [47]and my spirit rejoices in God my Savior, [48]for He has regarded the low estate of his handmaiden. For behold, henceforth all generations will call me blessed; [49]for He who is mighty has done great things for me, and holy is his name."

[56]And Mary remained with her about three months and then returned to her home.

(Lk. 1:39–42, 45–49, 56)

Lk. 1:39   to the City / to a city (RSV)
Lk. 1:40   of Zacharias and (KJV) / of Zechariah and (RSV) (122:2/1345–6)

4. Birth and Youth of John the Baptist

[57]Now the time came for Elizabeth to be delivered and she brought forth a son. [58]And her neighbors and kinsfolk heard that the Lord had shown great mercy to her, and they rejoiced with her. [59]And on the eighth day they came to circumcise the child; and they would have named him Zacharias after his father, [60]but his mother said, "Not so; he shall be called John."

[80]And the child grew and became strong in spirit. And he was in the wilderness till the day of his public manifestation to Israel.

(Lk. 1:57–60, 80)

Lk. 1:57   she brought forth a (KJV) / she gave birth to a (RSV)
Lk. 1:59   him Zacharias, after (KJV) / him Zechariah, after (RSV) (135:0,1/1496–7)

5. The Birth of Jesus

¹In those days a decree went out from Caesar Augustus that all the world should be enrolled.[a] ²This was the first enrollment, when Quirinius was governor of Syria. ³And all went to be enrolled, each to his own city.

⁴And Joseph went up from Galilee from the city of Nazareth, to Judea, to the city of David which is called Bethlehem, because he was of the house and lineage of David, ⁵to be enrolled, with Mary, who was with child.

⁶And so it was that while they were there the days were accomplished that she should be delivered. ⁷And she gave birth to her first born son, and wrapped him in swaddling cloths,[b] and laid him in a manger, because there was no place for them in the inn.

²¹And at the end of eight days when he was circumcised he was called Joshua (Jesus),[c] the name given by the angel. (Lk. 2:1–7, 21)

---

a   "In those days a decree went out from Caesar Augustus that all the world should be enrolled."—Dated papyri in Egypt tell of a 14-year cycle of census inaugurated by the Roman emperor Caesar Augustus (27 BC–AD 14), and record one in AD 20. Counting back 14 years, we come to AD 6, the date of the preceding census; this census is referred to in Acts 5:37. Counting back 14 more years (and remembering that instead of starting at year zero our calendar begins at Jan. 1, AD 1), we come to the first census, the one originally decreed by Caesar Augustus, at 8 BC. This was the census attended by Joseph and Mary. However, because of Jewish opposition to "being numbered" (and paying taxes to Rome), Herod is thought to have been slow in instituting this first census of the Roman world. (*Master Study Bible*, p. 1330) But it is not likely that Herod would have long delayed this census of "all the world," which was decreed by the Emperor himself. If we assume that Herod held the census the next year, we can date Jesus' birth at 7 BC.

This date of 7 BC is also consistent with two other recorded events associated with Jesus' birth. Herod (Ch. 7, fn. *a*), who was alive at the time of Jesus' birth, died in 4 BC. (Ch. 9, fn. *b*) Also, the three extraordinary conjunctions of Jupiter and Saturn, which would explain the new "star" in the sky noticed by the Magi (Ch. 7, fn. *b*), took place in 7 BC.

The modern calendar is based on calculations made by Dionysus Exegines, a Roman abbot who lived more than 500 years after the time of Jesus. Because of insufficient historical data, the monk erred in fixing the time of birth and this error persists in our calendar to this day.

b   "swaddling cloths,"—Narrow strips of cloth wrapped around an infant to restrict movement.

c   "Joshua (Jesus),"—*Joshua* is the English form and *Jesus* the contracted Greek form of the Hebrew *Yehoshua*. (See Ch. 2, fn. *a*.)

Lk. 2:5   Mary, who / Mary, his betrothed, who (RSV)
Lk. 2:6   And so it was that while (KJV) / And while (RSV) • the days were accomplished that she should be (KJV) / the time came for her to be (RSV)
Lk. 2:21   called Joshua (Jesus), the (Ch. 2, fn. *a*) / called Jesus, the (RSV) • angel. / angel before he was conceived in the womb. (RSV) (122:7,8/1350–1)

6. Angels Sing Anthems of Glory over Bethlehem

[8]And there were in the same country shepherds abiding in the field, keeping watch over their flock by night.[a]

[13]And there was a multitude of the heavenly host praising God, and saying, [14]"Glory to God in the highest, and on earth peace, good will toward men."

(Lk. 2:8, 13–14)

---

a   "keeping watch over their flock by night."—During the wintertime, from November until April, when pasturage became slim and rain and cold weather threatened, sheep could no longer be kept outdoors and were placed under cover. Since the sheep were out at night it is likely that Jesus' birth occurred in or around the warmer summer months. Thus we may conclude that Jesus was born around the middle of the year 7 BC, rather than early or late in that year.

Lk. 2:8   (KJV)
Lk. 2:13   (KJV) • And there / And suddenly there (KJV) • was a / was with the angel a (KJV)
Lk. 2:14   (KJV) (122:8/1352)

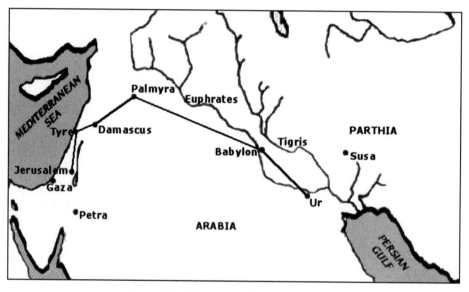

Possible Route of the Wise Men

7. Visit of the Wise Men

¹Now when Jesus was born in Bethlehem of Judea in the days of Herod the King,ᵃ behold, wise men from the East came to Jerusalem, saying, ²"Where is he who has been born King of the Jews? For we have seen his star in the East,ᵇ and have come to worship him."

³When Herod the King heard this he was troubled; ⁴and assembling all the chief priests and scribes of the people, he inquired of them where the Messiahᶜ was to be born. ⁵They told him, "In Bethlehem of Judea; for so it is written by the prophet: ⁶'And you, O Bethlehem, in the land of Judah, are by no means least among the rulers of Judah; for from you shall come a ruler who will govern my people Israel.'"

(Mt. 2:1–6) *(continued)*

---

a "Herod the King,"—Also called Herod the Great. Herod was the son of the governor of Idumea (the area south of Judah). He rose to a high position in the government of Judah during the reign of the aging high priest, Hyrcanus II. During this time Hyrcanus' younger nephew, Antigonus, rebelled against his uncle's rule. Antigonus raised an army in Syria and, after securing the help of many Judeans unhappy with Hyrcanus' rule, as well as the Parthians to the east, he overthrew Hyrcanus in 40 BC. Herod fled to Rome, taking his case directly to Mark Anthony, who received Herod as an old family friend. And, through the assistance of the Roman rulers Anthony and Octavian, he was proclaimed king of Judah by the Roman Senate in 40 BC. He captured Jerusalem in 37 BC from Antigonus and ruled from Jerusalem until his death in 4 BC. His kingdom eventually expanded beyond Judea and Idumea to include Samaria, Galilee, Gaza, Perea, and the territory east of the Sea of Galilee. (See map on page 5.)

b "we have seen his star in the East,"—The most likely explanation of this new star in the sky concerns the extraordinary triple conjunction of Jupiter and Saturn in the constellation of Pisces that took place on three separate nights in 7 BC. This new bright light in the sky, which would naturally have been described as a new "star," appeared on the nights of May 29, September 30, and December 5, 7 BC.

"This is by far the most popular explanation for the star of Bethlehem. Johannes Kepler, after seeing the Jupiter–Saturn conjunction in Pisces a few days before Christmas in 1603, calculated backward and discovered the 7 BC event. But Kepler was certainly not the first to call attention to it. In 1977, David H. Clark and two colleagues quoted a similar assertion in English church annals dating from AD 1285." (*Sky and Telescope*, December 1986, p. 632, "Computing the Star of Bethlehem")

c "Messiah"—See Ch. 13, fn. *c*.

Mt. 2:3   troubled; / troubled, and all Jerusalem with him; (RSV)
Mt. 2:4   the Messiah was (Ch. 13, fn. *c*) / the Christ was (RSV)
Mt. 2:6   Micah 5:2 (122:8,10/1352–4)

7. Visit of the Wise Men (continued)

[7]Then Herod summoned the wise men secretly and ascertained from them what time the star appeared;[d] [8]and he sent them to Bethlehem, saying, "Go and search diligently for the child, and when you have found him bring me word that I too may come and worship him."

[9]When they had heard the king they went their way; and lo, the star which they had seen in the East was before them. [10]When they saw the star they rejoiced exceedingly.[e] [11]And going into the house they saw the child with Mary his mother and they fell down and worshiped him. Then, opening their treasures, they offered him gifts, gold and frankincense and myrrh.

[12]And being warned in a dream not to return to Herod, they departed to their own country by another way.

(Mt. 2:7–12)

---

d "ascertained from them what time the star appeared;"—The first conjunction of Jupiter and Saturn took place the night of May 29, 7 BC. (See fn. *b* above.)

e "When they saw the star they rejoiced exceedingly."—This implies that, around the time the wise men left Herod and found Jesus, the star *reappeared*. Knowing the dates of the conjunctions, we may reason that the Magi first saw the star the night of May 29, 7 BC (the first conjunction). They then made the long journey (probably from Babylon in the East) to Jerusalem; it is estimated that this trip would have taken around three months traveling by camel. (See map on page 8.) The reappearance of the star after the audience with Herod would then correspond to the second conjunction on September 30.

Since the second appearance of the star was associated with the discovery of the baby Jesus, we may use the date of the second conjunction (September 30) to approximate Jesus' birth to late August or early September, 7 BC. This date is consistent with the fact that shepherds still had sheep out at night, which could only happen during the warmer months. (See Ch. 6, fn. *a*.)

Mt. 2:9 East was before / East went before (RSV) • them. / them, till it came to rest over the place where the child was. (RSV)
Mt. 2:10 exceedingly." / exceedingly with great joy;" (RSV) (122:10/1353–4)

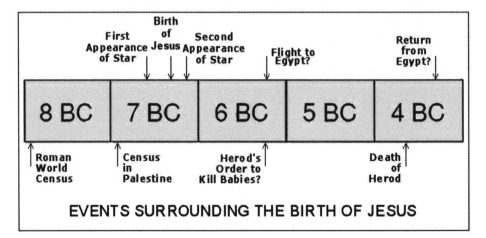

EVENTS SURROUNDING THE BIRTH OF JESUS

8. Presentation in the Temple

[22]And when the time came for their purification according to the law of Moses, they brought him up to Jerusalem to present him to the Lord [23](as it is written in the law, "Every male that opens the womb shall be called holy to the Lord") [24]and to offer a sacrifice according to what is said in the law, "a pair of turtledoves, or two young pigeons."

[25]Now there was a man in Jerusalem whose name was Simeon, and this man was righteous and devout, looking for the consolation of Israel, and the Holy Spirit was upon him. [26]And it had been revealed to him by the Holy Spirit that he should not see death before he had seen the Lord's Messiah.[a]

[27]And inspired by the Spirit, he came into the temple; and when the parents brought in the child Jesus to do for him according to the custom of the law, [28]he took him up in his arms and blessed God and said:

[29]"Lord, now let your servant depart in peace, according to your word,

[30]For my eyes have seen your salvation,

[31]Which you have prepared in the presence of all peoples;

[32]A light for revelation to the gentiles

And for glory of your people Israel."

[33]And his father and his mother marveled at what was said about him.

[36]And there was a prophetess, Anna, the daughter of Phanuel, of the tribe of Aser. [38]She did not depart from the temple, worshiping with fasting and prayer night and day. And coming up at that very hour she gave thanks to God, and spoke of him to all who were looking for the redemption of Jerusalem.

(Lk. 2:22–33, 36, 38)

---

a   "the Lord's Messiah."—The long-awaited Jewish deliverer, who would reign in righteousness and bring about the kingdom of God on earth. (See Ch. 13, fn. c.)

Lk. 2:23   Exodus 13:2 • law, "Every / law of the Lord, "Every (RSV)
Lk. 2:24   Leviticus 5:11; • law, "a / law of the Lord, "a (RSV)
Lk. 2:26   Lord's Messiah (Ch. 13, fn. c) / Lord's Christ (RSV)
Lk. 2:29   now let your servant (NAB) / now lettest thou thy servant (RSV) • to your word (NRSV) / to thy word (RSV)
Lk. 2:30   For my eyes (NRSV) / For mine eyes (RSV) • seen your salvation (NRSV) / seen thy salvation (RSV)
Lk. 2:31   Which you have prepared (NRSV) / Which thou hast prepared (RSV)
Lk. 2:32   glory of your people / glory to thy people (RSV) (122:9/1352–3)

III. The Youth of Jesus

9. Flight to Egypt and Return to Nazareth

[14]And Joseph rose and took the child and his mother by night and departed to Egypt,[a] and remained there until the death of Herod.

[16]Herod, when he saw that he had been tricked by the wise men, was in a furious rage. He gave orders and had killed all the male children in Bethlehem who were two years old or under, according to the time which he had ascertained from the wise men.

[21]When Herod died[b] Joseph took the child and mother, and went to the land of Israel. [22]But when he heard Archelaus reigned over Judea[c] in place of his father Herod, he was afraid to go there and withdrew to the district of Galilee.[d] [23]And he went and dwelt in a city called Nazareth.

(Mt. 2:14, 16, 21–23)

---

a "departed to Egypt,"—Alexandria was the location of a large Jewish settlement in Egypt and would have been a natural place for them to live during their sojourn there.

b "When Herod died"—The Jewish historian Josephus (who lived in the latter half of the first century AD) records the death of Herod (at age 70) shortly before April 12, 4 BC.

c "Archelaus reigned over Judea"—Herod died in the spring of 4 BC. By Herod's final will his son Archelaus was named as ruler over Judea, Samaria, and Idumea. Most of the remainder of Herod's kingdom was divided among his other two sons: Herod Antipas was made ruler over Galilee and Perea, while Herod Philip became ruler over the Transjordan lands of Batanea and Trachonitis. (See map on page 5.)

Herod Antipas was the man who later ordered the death of John the Baptist. In AD 6, Caesar Augustus replaced Archelaus with a series of military prefects. The most famous of these rulers was Pontius Pilate, the man who ordered Jesus' death.

d "withdrew to the district of Galilee."—If Jesus were born around August, 7 BC (Ch. 5, fn. *a*; Ch. 7, fns. *b* and *e*), he would have been around three years old when the family returned to Nazareth after the death of Herod in April, 4 BC.

Mt. 2:14   And Joseph rose / And he rose (RSV)
Mt. 2:16   Herod / Then Herod (RSV) • rage. He gave orders and had killed / rage and he sent and killed (RSV) •
           Bethlehem who / Bethlehem and in all that region who (RSV)
Mt. 2:21   When Herod died Joseph took (Mt. 2:19, 21) / And he rose and took (RSV)
Mt. 2:22   and withdrew / and being warned in a dream he withdrew (RSV)   (122:10/1353–4)

10. Youth in Nazareth; Visit to Jerusalem

⁴⁰And the child grew and waxed strong in spirit, filled with wisdom; and the grace of God was upon him.

⁴¹Now his parents went to Jerusalem every year at the feast of the Passover.*a*

⁴²And when he was twelve years old,*b* they went up to the feast according to custom; ⁴³and when the feast was ended, as they were returning, the boy Jesus stayed behind in Jerusalem. His parents did not know it, ⁴⁴but supposing him to be in the company, they went a day's journey, and they sought him among their kinsfolk and acquaintances. ⁴⁵And when they did not find him they returned to Jerusalem seeking him. ⁴⁶After three days they found him in the temple, sitting among the teachers, listening to them and asking them questions. ⁴⁷And all who heard him were amazed at his understanding and his answers. ⁴⁸And when they saw him they were astonished; and his mother said to him, "Son, why have you treated us so? Behold, your father and I have been looking for you anxiously."

⁴⁹And he said to them, "How is it that you sought me? Did you not know that I must be in my Father's house?" ⁵⁰And they did not understand what he was saying to them.

⁵¹And he went down with them and came to Nazareth and was obedient to them; and his mother kept all these things in her heart.

⁵²And Jesus increased in wisdom and in stature, and in favor with God and man.

(Lk. 2:40–52)

---

a "the feast of the Passover."—Hundreds of years after the time of Abraham, his descendants, on the occasion of an unusually severe famine, entered Egypt as laborers on the Egyptian public works. As time passed they found themselves falling into economic slavery as common and downtrodden laborers of the Nile valley.

The Passover feast commemorated the time when Moses delivered the Hebrews out of their economic bondage in Egypt. It began on the 15th day of Nisan, a date that fell somewhere in March or April each year. The Passover was the most important of the yearly Jewish religious festivals.

b "when he was twelve years old,"—If Jesus were born in late summer 7 BC (Ch. 5, fn. *a*; Ch. 7, fns. *b* and *e*), he would have turned 12 around August, AD 6, and this Passover would have occurred around April, AD 7.

Lk. 2:40   waxed strong in spirit, filled (KJV) / and became strong, filled (RSV) • the grace of (KJV) / the favor of (RSV)
Lk. 2:50   understand what he was saying to them. / understand the saying which he spoke to them. (RSV) (123–7/1355–1406)

11. The Great Temptation

[12]The Spirit drove him out into the wilderness.[a] [13]And he was in the wilderness forty days, tempted by Satan; and he was with the wild beasts; and the angels ministered to him.   (Mk. 1:12–13)

---

a   "The Spirit drove him out into the wilderness."—Each of the four gospels (Matthew, Mark, Luke, and John) treat the temptation of Jesus somewhat differently. Mark recounts the event in two short verses (quoted above). Matthew and Luke tell a detailed story but differ in the order of temptations. The gospel of John does not mention the event at all.

The gospel writers recount the temptation as taking place immediately following Jesus' submission to baptism by John. However, since John's baptism marked the actual beginning of Jesus' public ministry, it is more likely that the 40 days following John's baptism was a time of communion with God and planning the proclamation of the kingdom. Perhaps Jesus' temptation occurred just before his baptism and the two events were combined in the gospel record. This would be consistent with the Father's expression of approval at Jesus' baptism—"This is my beloved son in whom I am well pleased." (Ch. 14, Mt. 3:17)—which would naturally occur after Jesus had met and overcome his "great temptation."

Mk. 1:12   Spirit drove / Spirit immediately drove (RSV)   (134:7,8/1492–4)

Jesus by L. Mullins

PART 2
THE SON OF MAN

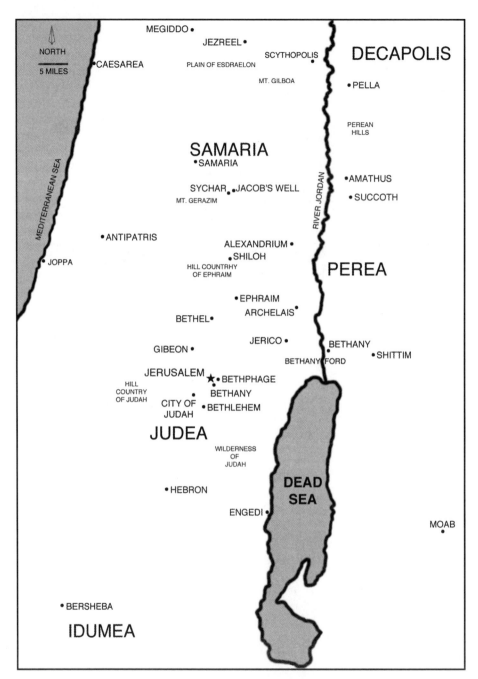

"Then went out to him Jerusalem and all Judea and all the region about the Jordan, and they were baptized by him in the river Jordan." (at Bethany Ford)

16

IV. John the Baptist

12. Coming of John the Baptist

²It is written in Isaiah the prophet: "Behold I send my messenger before you, who shall prepare your way, ³the voice of one crying in the wilderness, 'Make ready the way of the Lord, make straight a highway for our God.'" ⁴And so John the Baptist appeared in the wilderness, preaching a baptism of repentance for the forgiveness of sins.

¹In the fifteenth year of the reign of Tiberius Caesar*a*—when Pontius Pilate was governor of Judea, Herod tetrarch of Galilee,*b* his brother Philip tetrarch of the region of Ituraea and Trachonitis, and Lasanias tetrarch of Abilene—

²in the high priesthood of Annas and Caiaphas, the word of God came to John, the son of Zacharias, in the wilderness.

¹In those days came John the Baptist preaching in the wilderness of Judea, saying, ²"Repent, for the kingdom of heaven is at hand."

⁴Now John wore a garment of camels' hair, and a leather girdle around his waist;*c* and his food was locusts and wild honey. ⁵Then went out to him Jerusalem and all Judea and all the region about the Jordan, ⁶and they were baptized by him in the river Jordan, confessing their sins.

(Mk. 1:2–4; Lk. 3:1–2; Mt. 3:1–2, 4–6)

---

a   "In the fifteenth year of the reign of Tiberius Caesar"—Augustus Caesar adopted Tiberius Caesar as his son and made him co-emperor in the provinces in the latter part of AD 11, two and one-half years before his (Augustus') death in AD 14. Therefore the fifteenth year of Tiberius' rule in the province of Palestine would have been AD 25–26. In this way we may date John's ministry at AD 25–26.

b   "Herod, tetrarch of Galilee"—Herod Antipas was made ruler of Galilee at his father's (Herod the Great) death in the spring of 4 BC. (See also Ch. 9, fn. *c*.)

c   "Now John wore a garment of camels' hair, and a leather girdle around his waist;"—Compare John's mode of dress with the description of the legendary Elijah as found in 2 Kings 1:8: "He wore a garment of haircloth, with a girdle of leather about his loins." John not only dressed like Elijah; he also adopted Elijah's method of direct and blunt attack upon the sin and evil of his generation.

Elijah appears to have been John's ideal of a prophet; and Jesus, in speaking of John, once referred to him as Elijah. (See also Ch. 15, fn. *a*; Ch. 65; and fns. *b* and *c* of Ch. 65.)

Mk. 1:2   Isaiah 40:3 • It / As it (RSV) • before you, who / before thy face, who (RSV) • prepare your way / prepare thy way (RSV)
Mk. 1:3   Isaiah 40:3 • 'Make ready the / 'Prepare the (RSV) • make straight a highway for our God'" (Is. 40:3) / make his paths straight'" (RSV)
Mk. 1:4   And so John (NIV) / John (RSV) • the Baptist appeared / the baptizer appeared (RSV)
Lk. 3:1   Caesar—when Pontius Pilate was governor / Caesar, Pontius Pilate being governor (RSV) • Judea, Herod tetrarch / Judea, and Herod being tetrarch (RSV) • Galilee, his / Galilee and his (RSV)
Lk. 3:2   of Zacharias, in (KJV) / of Zechariah, in (RSV)
Mt. 3:1   Judea, saying, "Repent / Judea, "Repent (RSV) (135:6/1501–2)

17

13. John's Teachings

[19]The Jews sent priests and Levites[a] from Jerusalem to ask him, "Who are you?" [22]They said to him then, "Who are you? Let us have an answer for those who sent us. What do you say about yourself?"

[23]He said, "I am the voice of one crying in the wilderness, 'Prepare ye the way of the Lord, make straight a highway for our God,' as the prophet Isaiah said." [28]This took place in Bethany beyond the Jordan where John was baptizing.

[7]But when he saw many of the Pharisees and Sadducees[b] come for baptism, he said to them: "You brood of vipers! Who warned you to flee from the wrath to come? [8]Bring forth fruit that befits repentance. [9]And do not presume to say to yourselves, 'We have Abraham as our father.' For I tell you God is able from these stones to raise up children to Abraham. [10]Even now the ax is laid to the root of the trees. Every tree therefore that does not bear good fruit is cut down and thrown into the fire."

[10]And the multitudes asked him, "What then shall we do?"

[11]And he answered them, "He who has two coats let him share with him who has none; and he who has food, let him do likewise."

[12]Tax collectors also came to be baptized, and said to him, "Teacher, what shall we do?"

[13]And he said to them, "Collect no more than is appointed you."

[14]Soldiers also asked him, "And we, what shall we do?"

And he said unto them: "Rob no one by violence or by false accusation, and be content with your wages."

(Jn. 1:19, 22–23, 28; Mt. 3:7–10; Lk. 3:10–14)

(continued)

---

a "Levites"—The descendants of Levi who maintained the temple and provided the temple music. They were also in charge of providing the money changing that took place in the temple courts.

b "Pharisees and Sadducees"—The *scribes* and *rabbis* taken together formed a religious party known as the *Pharisees*. Although they were sticklers for living according to the "law," they were more progressive than the other Jewish religious groups. They held many beliefs not clearly taught in the Hebrew Scripture, such as belief in the resurrection of the dead—a doctrine only mentioned by the later prophet Daniel.

The *Sadducees* were composed of the *priests* and *certain wealthy Jews*. They were a Jewish religious party that dominated Judea's highest ruling body—the Sanhedrin. It was principally the Sadducees who plotted and brought about the death of Jesus.

Jn. 1:19   The / And this is the testimony of John when the (RSV)
Jn. 1:23   Isaiah 40:3 • wilderness, 'Prepare ye the way of the Lord, make straight a highway for our God,' as (Is. 40:3) / wilderness, 'Make straight the way of the Lord,' as (RSV)
Mt. 3:8   Bring forth fruit (NAS) / Bear fruit (RSV) (135:6/1502–3)

13. John's Teachings (continued)

[15]The people were all waiting expectantly, and all were wondering in their hearts if John might possibly be the Messiah.[c] [16]John answered them all: "I baptize you with water; but he who is mightier than I is coming, the thong of whose sandals I am not worthy to untie. He will baptize you with the Holy Spirit.[d] [17]His winnowing fork is in his hand to clear his threshing floor and to gather the wheat into his granary; but the chaff he will burn up with unquenchable fire."

(Lk. 3:15–17)

---

c   "Messiah."—In ancient times oils were expensive and were used for ceremonial purposes, as well as to cleanse and protect the skin. Kings were *anointed* with holy oil at their coronation to show that they were consecrated to God. The term "messiah" comes from the Hebrew "mashi'ah" and means literally *anointed one*.

The Jews held many conflicting ideas about an expected deliverer, but they all agreed he was to be the *Messiah*, the *Anointed One*. The rabbis had gathered many passages from scripture that they believed were prophetic of a coming Messiah who would *deliver them from bondage*.

To the Jews the Messiah was more than a prophet—one who taught God's will or proclaimed the necessity for righteous living. The Messiah was to bring about the establishment of the *kingdom of God* on earth. This was to be a righteous kingdom in which God, through the Messiah, ruled the nations on earth just as he already ruled in heaven. For the Jews, the coming of the Messiah signified the establishment of a divine world rule on earth, with its capital at Jerusalem.

The gospels were written in Greek and the Greek word for *Messiah* is *Christ*. In this restatement the word *Christ* is rendered as *Messiah*, *Deliverer*, or *Christ*, depending on the context.

d   "He will baptize you with the Holy Spirit."—Here John contrasts his baptism with water, an outward rite, to Jesus' baptism with the Holy Spirit, an inner change of mind and heart.

Lk. 3:15   NIV • the Messiah. (Ch. 13, fn. *c*) / the Christ. (NIV)
Lk. 3:16   Spirit. / Spirit and with fire. (RSV) (135:7/1503)

14. The Baptism of Jesus

[13]Then Jesus came from Galilee to the Jordan to be baptized by him. [14]But John tried to prevent him, saying, "I have need to be baptized by you. Why do you come to me?"

[15]But Jesus answered him, "Let it be so now, for it is fitting." Then he consented.

[16]And when Jesus was baptized,[a] behold, the heavens were opened and he saw the Spirit of God descending like a dove, and lighting upon him; [17]and lo, a voice from heaven saying, "This is my beloved Son in whom I am well pleased."

[1]Then Jesus was led up by the Spirit into the wilderness.

(Mt. 3:13–17; 4:1)

---

a   "And when Jesus was baptized,"—John's ministry took place "in the fifteenth year of the reign of Tiberius Caesar," which would be AD 25–26. (Ch. 12 and fn. a) If Jesus were baptized in AD 26 and if he were born in August–September 7 BC (Ch. 5, fn. a; and Ch. 7, fns. b and e), Jesus would have been around 32 years old when he received John's baptism. This conclusion is consistent with Luke's statement (Ch. 17, Lk. 3:23) that Jesus was about 30 years old when he began his ministry (which followed soon after his baptism).

Mt. 3:14   NAS • you. Why do / you, and do (NAS)
Mt. 3:15   for it / for thus it (RSV) • fitting." / fitting for us to fulfill all righteousness." (RSV)
Mt. 3:16   baptized, behold, / baptized, he went up immediately from the water and behold, (RSV) • and lighting upon (KJV) / and alighting upon (RSV)
Mt. 3:17   Son in whom (KJV) / Son with whom (RSV)
Mt. 4:1   wilderness. / wilderness to be tempted by the devil. (RSV) (135:8/1503–4)

15. Testimony of John

¹⁹And this is the testimony of John when the Jews sent priests from Jerusalem to ask him, "Who are you?"

²⁰He confessed, "I am not the Messiah."

²¹And they asked him, "What then? Are you Elijah?"

He said, "I am not."*ᵃ*

"Are you the prophet?"*ᵇ*

And he answered, "No."

²⁴Now they had been sent from the Pharisees. ²⁵They asked him, "Then why are you baptizing, if you are neither the Messiah, nor Elijah, nor the prophet?"

²⁶John answered them, "I baptize with water; but among you, though you do not know him, stands one who is to come after me, the thong of whose sandal I am not worthy to untie."

(Jn. 1:19–21, 24–26)

---

a "Are you Elijah?" He said, "I am not."—Here John denies that he is Elijah. But why then did he dress in the manner of the legendary Elijah? (See Ch.12, fn. *c*.)

Just as the Jews believed that the Messiah would come to deliver them (Ch. 13, fn. *c*) they also believed that Elijah the prophet would come to prepare the way for the promised deliverer. They looked to the prophecy of Malachi: "Behold, I will send you Elijah the prophet before the coming of the great and dreadful day of the Lord; and he shall turn the hearts of the fathers toward their children and the hearts of the children toward their fathers, lest I come and smite the earth with a curse." (Mal. 4:5–6) John must have reasoned that, if this prophecy applied to Jesus as the Messiah, then he, as Jesus' advance messenger, must be the Elijah of the prophecy. Perhaps this led him to style himself after Israel's first great prophet.

And indeed Jesus later on *affirms* that John is the second Elijah in his role as the forerunner of Jesus. (See Ch. 29, fn. *a* and Ch. 65, fn. *c*.)

b "Are you the prophet?"—The prophet promised by Moses: "The Lord your God will raise up for you a prophet like me from among you, from among your brethren—him you shall heed." And the Lord said to me, "I will put my words in his mouth, and he shall speak to them all that I command him." (Dt. 18:15, 17–18)

Jn. 1:19   priests from / priests and Levites from (RSV)
Jn. 1:20   confessed, "I / confessed, he did not deny, "I (RSV) • the Messiah." (Ch. 13, fn. *c*) / the Christ." (RSV)
Jn. 1:24   the Messiah, nor (Ch. 13, fn. *c*) / the Christ, nor (RSV)
Jn. 1:26   you, though you do not know him, stands one who is to come after / you, stands one whom you do not know, even he who comes after (RSV) (135:9/1505)

21

16. Return of Jesus; Further Testimony of John

[29]John saw Jesus coming[a] toward him and said, [30]"Behold the Lamb of God, who takes away the sin of the world! This is he of whom I said, 'After me comes a man who ranks before me, for he was before me.' [31]For this cause I came baptizing with water that he might be revealed to Israel." [32]And John bore witness, "I saw the Spirit descend as a dove from heaven, and it remained on him. [34]And I have seen and have borne witness that this is the Son of God."[b]

(Jn. 1:29–32, 34)

---

a   "John saw Jesus coming"—Jesus is returning from the wilderness after his baptism by John.

b   "I have seen and have borne witness that this is the Son of God."—At Jesus' baptism John heard the voice of God saying: "This is my beloved Son in whom I am well pleased." (Ch. 14, Mt. 3:17)

Jn. 1:29   John saw / The next day he saw (RSV)
Jn. 1:31   For this cause I / but for this I (RSV) (135:9/1505–6)

V. Choosing and Training the Apostles

17. Choosing the First Apostles

23Jesus, when he began his ministry, was about thirty years of age.*a*

40One of the two who heard John speak,*b* and followed Jesus, was Andrew. 41He first found his brother Simon and said to him, "We have found the Messiah" (which means Christ).*c* 42He brought him to Jesus. Jesus looked at him and said, "You are Simon, the son of John; you shall be called Cephas"*d* (which translated means Peter).

43The next day Jesus decided to go to Galilee. And he found Philip and said to him, "Follow me."

44Now Philip was from Bethsaida, the city of Andrew and Peter. 45Philip found Nathaniel, and said to him, "We have found him of whom Moses in the law and also the prophets wrote, Jesus of Nazareth, the son of Joseph."

46Nathaniel said to him, "Can anything good come out of Nazareth?"

Philip said to him, "Come and see."

47Jesus saw Nathaniel coming to him and said of him, "Behold a true Israelite in whom there is no deceit."

(Lk. 3:23; Jn. 1:40–47)

---

a   "Jesus, when he began his ministry, was about thirty years of age."—If Jesus were born in 7 BC he would have been around 32 years of age at John's baptism, which marked the beginning of Jesus' public ministry. (See Ch. 5, fn. *a*, and Ch. 14, fn. *a*.)

b   "heard John speak,"—Heard John's testimony concerning Jesus. (See Ch. 16.)

c   "Messiah (which means Christ)."—See Ch. 13, fn. *c*.

d   "you shall be called Cephas"—*Cephas* is the Aramaic word for *rock* (its Greek form is *Peter*). Jesus knew the dangers of thoughtless speech and action in the work of the kingdom; perhaps he is seeking to temper Peter's impulsive nature with a name that suggests steadiness and solidity.

Lk. 3:23   age. / age, being the son of . . . (RSV)
Jn. 1:40   followed Jesus, was / followed him, was (RSV)
Jn. 1:42   NAS
Jn. 1:47   "Behold a true Israelite in (NIV) / "Behold an Israelite indeed in (RSV) • no deceit." (TCNT) / no guile." (RSV) (137:1,2/1524–7)

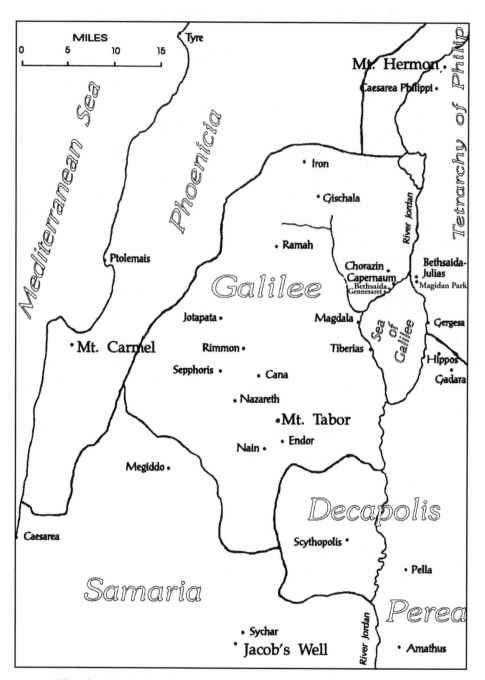

"On the third day there was a marriage at Cana in Galilee.
After this he went down to Capernaum with his disciples."

18. The Wedding at Cana; Tarrying in Galilee

[1]On the third day[a] there was a marriage at Cana in Galilee, and the mother of Jesus was there; [2]Jesus was also invited to the marriage, with his disciples. [3]When the wine gave out, the mother of Jesus said to him, "They have no wine."

[4]And Jesus said to her, "O woman, what has that to do with me? My time has not yet come."

[5]His mother said to the servants, "Do whatever he tells you."

[6]Nearby stood six stone water pots, the kind used by the Jews for ceremonial washing, each holding from twenty to thirty gallons. [9]When the steward of the feast tasted the water, now become wine, and did not know where it came from, the steward of the feast called the bridegroom, [10]and said to him, "Every man serves the good wine first; and when men have drunk freely, then the poor wine; but you have kept the good wine until now."

[11]This, the first of his signs, Jesus did at Cana in Galilee and manifested his glory; and his disciples believed in him.

[12]After this he went down to Capernaum with his disciples.

[13]He went and dwelt in Capernaum by the sea, in the territory of Zebulum and Naphtali.[b] [14]And what was spoken by the prophet Isaiah was fulfilled: [15]"Land of Zebulum and land of Naphtali, the way to the sea, along the Jordan, Galilee of the Gentiles—[16]the people living in darkness have seen a great light; on those living in the land of the shadow of death a light has dawned."

(Jn. 2:1–6, 9–12; Mt. 4:13–16)

---

a   "On the third day"—After the return of Jesus to John's camp. (See Ch. 16.)

b   "Zebulum and Naphtali"—Ancient names for the territory of Galilee.

Jn. 2:4   what has that to / what have you to (RSV)
Jn. 2:6   NIV
Jn. 2:9   from, the / from (although the servants who had drawn the water knew), the (RSV)
Jn. 2:12 his disciples. / his mother and his brothers and his disciples. (RSV)
Mt. 4:13 He / and leaving Nazareth he (RSV)
Mt. 4:14 Isaiah 9:1–2 • And what / that what (RSV) • Isaiah was fulfilled: / Isaiah might be fulfilled: (RSV)
          (137:3–5/1527–31)

19. Calling of Matthew; Banquet at His House

9Jesus saw a man called Matthew sitting at the tax office and he said to him, "Follow me." And he rose and followed him.

10And as he sat at table in the house, behold, many tax collectors and sinners came and sat down with Jesus and his disciples. 11And when the Pharisees saw this, they said to his disciples, "Why does your teacher eat with tax collectors and sinners?"

12But when he heard it, he said, "Those who are whole need not a physician, but those who are sick. 13For I came not to call the righteous, but sinners."

(Mt. 9:9–13)

Mt. 9:9 Jesus saw / As Jesus passed on from there he saw (RSV)
Mt. 9:12 are whole need not a (KJV) / are well have no need of a (RSV) (138:3/1540–1)

20. Choosing of the Twelve

14And he ordained twelve whom also he named apostles,*a* that they should be with him and that he might send them forth to preach. 2The names of the twelve apostles are these: first, Simon, who is called Peter, and Andrew, his brother; James, the son of Zebedee, and John, his brother; 3Philip and Bartholomew (Nathaniel); Thomas and Matthew, the tax collector; James, the son of Alpheus, and Thaddeus (Judas); 4Simon the Zealot, and Judas Iscariot, who betrayed him.

(Mk. 3:14; Mt. 10:2–4)

---

a "And he ordained twelve whom also he named apostles,"—The word *apostle* comes from the Greek *to send*, and refers to the twelve men whom Jesus chose as his personal associates and sent forth as messengers of his gospel of the kingdom.

Mk. 3:14 KJV • twelve whom also he named apostles, that (RSV) / twelve, that (KJV)
Mt. 10:3 Bartholomew (Nathaniel); (John 1:45–47) / Bartholomew; (RSV) • Thaddeus (Judas); (Lk. 6:16) / Thaddeus; (RSV)
Mt. 10:4 Simon the Zealot, and (Lk. 6:15) / Simon the Cananaean, and (RSV) (139/1548–67)

21. Herod Arrests John

[19]But when Herod the tetrarch was reproved by John on account of Herodias, his brother's wife, and on account of all the wicked things which Herod had done, [20]he added this also to them all: he locked up John in prison.

[26]And John's disciples came to him and said, "Rabbi, he who was with you beyond the Jordan, to whom you bore witness, everyone is going to him."[a]

[27]John answered: "No one can receive anything except what is given him from heaven. [28]You yourselves bear me witness that I said I am not the Messiah, but I have been sent before him. [29]He who has the bride is the bridegroom; the friend of the bridegroom who stands and hears him rejoices greatly at the bridegroom's voice. Therefore, this joy of mine is now full. [30]He must increase but I must decrease. [31]He who is of the earth belongs to the earth, and of the earth he speaks; he who comes from heaven is above all. [34]He whom God has sent utters the words of God; for it is not by measure that He gives the spirit. [35]The Father loves the Son and has given all things to his hand. [36]He who believes in the Son has eternal life."

(Lk. 3:19–20; Jn. 3:26–31, 34–36)

---

[a] "everyone is going to him."—(Summary of recent events) John the Baptist began his short but eventful career as a preacher of righteousness around AD 25. He came as a forerunner of Jesus, urging others to "repent, for the kingdom of heaven is at hand."

John attracts great crowds and baptizes many for the remission of sins in the river Jordan. At the height of John's popularity, Jesus leaves Galilee and journeys to where John is baptizing. Jesus would have been around 32 years of age at this time. Jesus is baptized by John who protests, "I need to be baptized by you. Why do you come to me?"

When Jesus is baptized the heavens open and God's spirit descends like a dove and lights on Jesus, and a voice from heaven declares, "This is my beloved son in whom I am well pleased." After his baptism Jesus is immediately led away into the wilderness for a time of communion and the likely planning of his impending public career.

When Jesus returns to John's camp, John sees him and bears witness to his followers: "I saw the spirit descend as a dove from heaven, and it remained on him. And I have seen and have borne witness that this is the Son of God."

Several of John's followers who heard John's testimony become the first disciples of Jesus; they are Andrew, his brother Simon Peter, and probably James and John Zebedee. Jesus and his early followers leave John's camp and return to Galilee; the party comes across Philip and Nathaniel, and they also decide to follow Jesus.

Back in Galilee, Jesus and the first six disciples attend a wedding at Cana. Here Jesus performs his first miracle—the turning of the water into wine.

Jesus next calls Matthew, who becomes the seventh disciple; Jesus chooses five more followers to be with him and preach the gospel; they are known as the 12 apostles. Their early work is well received; when Herod arrests John his disciples come to him in prison and report, "everyone is going to him." John replies, "He must increase but I must decrease."

Following this early work Jesus calls the apostles together and preaches his great "Sermon on the Mount." He then ordains them as preachers of the kingdom (next section).

Lk. 3:19   NASB • by John on / by him on (NASB)
Jn. 3:26   And John's disciples came to him and said, "Rabbi / And they came to John and said to him, "Rabbi •
           witness, everyone is going to him (NIV) / witness, here he is, baptizing, and all are going to him (RSV)
Jn. 3:28   the Messiah, but (Ch. 13, fn. c) / the Christ, but (RSV) (135:10,11/1506–7)

VI. Ordination of the Twelve

22. The Sermon on the Mount

[18]As he walked by the Sea of Galilee he saw two brothers, Simon, who is called Peter, and Andrew, his brother, casting a net into the sea; for they were fishermen. [19]And he said to them, "Follow me, and I will make you fishers of men." [20]Immediately they left their nets and followed him. [21]And going on from there he saw two other brothers, James, the son of Zebedee, and John, his brother, in the boat with Zebedee, their father, mending their nets, and he called them. [22]Immediately they left the boat and their father, and followed him.

[1]Seeing the crowds, he went up on the mountain, and when he sat down his disciples[a] came to him.[b] [2]And he opened his mouth and taught them saying:

[3]"Happy are the poor in spirit[c] [the humble], for theirs is the kingdom of heaven."

[6]"Happy are they who hunger and thirst for righteousness, for they shall be filled."

[5]"Happy are the meek, for they shall inherit the earth."

[8]"Happy are the pure in heart, for they shall see God."

(Mt. 4:18–22; 5:1–3, 6, 5, 8) *(continued)*

---

a   "his disciples"—Here "disciples" refers to Jesus' twelve chosen apostles. The term "disciple" means *student* or *follower*. In the gospels, it is used in two ways: in general it refers to a *follower of Jesus*, but it is also often used to refer specifically to Jesus' *apostles* as in Matthew 10:1, "And he called to him his *twelve disciples* and gave them authority . . ."

b   "Seeing the crowds, he went up on the mountain, and when he sat down his disciples came to him."—In this context *"his disciples"* refers to the twelve apostles. (See fn. *a*, above.)

This verse tells us that Jesus, in order to get away from the crowds, led his apostles up a nearby mountain. Here he imparted special instructions to his chosen followers.

The "Sermon on the Mount" contains much more of Jesus' instruction, and on a wider range of subjects, than any other recorded episode. It may be viewed as *a summary statement of Jesus' personal philosophy of living.*

Such concentrated teaching would hardly have been comprehensible to the general public, and these words are most fittingly viewed as directed exclusively to Jesus' chosen apostles at the time of their ordination as messengers of the gospel of the kingdom. This is confirmed later in this passage when Jesus describes those who are hearing his words (the apostles) in this way: "You are the salt of the earth." "You are the light of the world." (Mt. 5:13–14; page 29)

c   "Happy are the poor in spirit"—This teaching is well illustrated by Jesus' parable of *The Pharisee and the Publican* (Ch. 99). The Pharisee felt rich in spirit—*egotistical*, while the publican felt poor in spirit—*humble*. The publican was approved by God.

Mt. 5:3–8 Happy are (TEV) / Blessed are (RSV)
Mt. 5:3   spirit [the humble], for (AB) / spirit, for (RSV)
Mt. 5:6   are they who (KJV) / are those who (RSV) (140:0,3/1568,70)

22. The Sermon on the Mount (continued)

⁴"Happy are they who mourn, for they shall be comforted."

⁷"Happy are the merciful, for they shall obtain mercy."

⁹"Happy are the peacemakers, for they shall be called the sons of God."

¹⁰"Happy are they who are persecuted for righteousness' sake, for theirs is the kingdom of heaven. ¹¹Happy are you when men shall revile you and persecute you and shall say all manner of evil against you falsely. ¹²Rejoice and be exceedingly glad, for great is your reward in heaven."*d*

¹³"You are the salt of the earth. But if the salt has lost its savor wherewith shall it be salted? It is henceforth good for nothing but to be cast out and trodden under foot of men."

¹⁴"You are the light of the world. A city set upon a hill cannot be hid. ¹⁵Neither do men light a candle and put it under a bushel, but on a candlestick; and it gives light to all who are in the house. ¹⁶Let your light so shine before men that they may see your good works and be led to glorify your Father who is in heaven."

(Mt. 5:4, 7, 9–16) *(continued)*

---

d   These eight beatitudes of Jesus teach *faith* and *love*. They may be divided into two groups.

The first set gives expression to four basic *faith attitudes* taught by Jesus. They involve being poor in spirit (humble toward God), hungering after righteousness (craving spiritual endowments), enduring meekness (cooperating with God—"your will be done"), and being pure in heart (trusting and sincere).

Those who have attained these faith attitudes are able to react to others with *love*—with tenderheartedness and sympathy ("they who mourn"), and with mercy (loving kindness and the urge to relieve suffering), to function as peacemakers (promoting a peaceful resolution of conflicts), and to endure persecutions for righteousness' sake. ("Greater love has no man than to lay down his life for his friends.") This love that Jesus taught is like that of an ideal parent—a *fatherly affection* that is even greater than brotherly love.

The faith and love that Jesus reveals in these beatitudes strengthen moral character and create true happiness.

Mt. 5:4–11   Happy are (TEV) / Blessed are (RSV) • are they who (KJV) / are those who (RSV)
Mt. 5:9   called the sons (KJV) / called sons (RSV)
Mt. 5:11   men shall revile (KJV) / men revile (RSV) • and shall say all manner of evil (KJV) / and utter all kinds of evil (RSV) • falsely. / falsely for my sake. (RSV)
Mt. 5:12   (KJV) • heaven. / heaven for so persecuted they the prophets which were before you. (KJV) (140:3/1570–1)

22. The Sermon on the Mount (continued)

³⁹"Do not resist evil.*^e* If anyone smites you on the right cheek, turn to him the other also. ⁴⁰And if anyone would sue you and take your coat, let him have your cloak as well. ⁴¹And if anyone forces you to go one mile, go with him two miles."

²⁷"I say to you: Love your enemies, do good to those who hate you, ²⁸bless those who curse you, and pray for those who despitefully use you. ³¹And as you wish that men would do to you, do you also to them."

⁴⁵"Your Father in heaven makes his sun to rise on the evil and on the good, and sends rain on the just and on the unjust. ³⁶Be merciful, even as your Father is merciful. ⁴⁸Be you therefore perfect, even as your heavenly Father is perfect."

¹"Judge not, that you be not judged. ²For with what judgment you judge you shall be judged,*^f* and with what measure you mete, it shall be measured to you again. ⁴How can you say to your brother, 'Let me take the speck out of your eye,' when there is a log in your own eye? ⁵First take the log out of your own eye, and then you will see clearly to take the speck out of your brother's eye."

³⁹"Can the blind lead the blind? Shall they not both fall into a pit? ⁶Give not that which is holy to dogs, neither cast your pearls before swine, lest they trample them under their feet and turn again and rend you."

(Mt. 5:39–41; Lk. 6:27–28, 31; Mt. 5:45; Lk. 6:36; Mt. 5:48; 7:1–2, 4–5; Lk. 6:39; Mt. 17:6)

(continued)

---

e "Do not resist evil."—As ambassadors of the Father's kingdom, the apostles are not to forcibly resist evil and injustice.

We may react to evil in three basic ways: We may return evil for evil; this way is active, but not righteous. Or we may choose to suffer evil without complaint; this way avoids doing evil to others, but it is totally passive. Jesus taught a third way—to *return good for evil*, the positive and righteous method. The Master challenges us to overcome evil with the potent force of good.

f "Judge not, that you be not judged. For with what judgment you judge you shall be judged,"—By judging others, we set up a standard to which we will be held. By not judging, we leave our judgment in God's just and merciful hands. When we do judge, we are called to exhibit mercy. ("Be merciful, even as your Father is merciful"—Lk. 6:36.) At the end of our lives, we will all seek merciful judgment from God; therefore are we also required to show mercy to others.

Mt. 5:39 Do / But I say to you, do (RSV) • If anyone smites you / But if anyone strikes you (RSV)
Lk. 6:27 I / But I (RSV) • you: Love / you that hear, Love (RSV)
Lk. 6:28 you, and pray / you, pray (RSV) • who despitefully use you (KJV) / who abuse you. (RSV)
Lk. 6:31 do you also to them (KJV) / do so to them (RSV)
Mt. 5:45 Your Father in heaven (Mt. 5:45) / for he (RSV) • sun to rise (KJV) / sun rise (RSV)
Mt. 5:48 Be you therefore perfect, even as (KJV) / You therefore must be perfect as (RSV)
Mt. 7:2 (KJV) • you (RSV) / ye (KJV)
Mt. 7:4 How / Or how (KJV)
Mt. 7:5 First / You hypocrite, first (RSV)
Lk. 6:39 (KJV) • Can / And he spake a parable unto them, Can (KJV) • into a pit? (RSV) / into the ditch? (KJV)
Mt. 7:6 (KJV) • holy to dogs, neither cast your pearls / holy unto the dogs, neither cast ye your pearls (KJV)
(140:3/1570–1)

22. The Sermon on the Mount (continued)

[15]"Beware of false prophets who will come to you in sheep's clothing, but inwardly are as ravenous[g] wolves. [16]You will know them by their fruits.[h] Do men gather grapes from thorns or figs from thistles? [17]Even so, every good tree brings forth good fruit, but a corrupt tree bears evil fruit. [18]A good tree cannot bring forth evil fruit, neither can a corrupt tree bring forth good fruit. [19]Every tree that does not bear good fruit is hewn down and cast into the fire."

[21]"Not everyone who says to me, 'Lord, Lord,' shall enter the kingdom of heaven, but rather he who does the will of my Father who is in heaven.[i] [22]On that day[j] many will say to me, 'Lord, Lord, did we not prophecy in your name and do many mighty works in your name?' [23]And then will I declare to them, 'I never knew you; depart from me, you who are evil doers!' [24]But everyone who hears these words of mine and does them will be like a wise man who built his house upon the rock."

(Mt. 7:15–19, 21–24)

---

g "ravenous"—1. devouring with voracious eagerness (nations *ravenous* as wolves) 2. urgently eager for food; craving for satisfaction or gratification (*ravenous* appetite). (*Webster's*, p. 1887)

h "You will know them by their fruits."—Some of the fruits of the spirit are: "love, joy, peace, long-suffering, gentleness, goodness, faith, meekness, [and] temperance." (Gal. 5:22–23) (KJV)

i "Not everyone who says to me, 'Lord, Lord,' shall enter the kingdom of heaven, but rather he who does the will of my Father who is in heaven."—Here Jesus reveals the essence of life in the kingdom—*the doing of the Father's will*. In his teachings the kingdom of God *is* the will of God. This is most clearly revealed in the prayer he taught his followers, *"Your kingdom come; your will be done."* (Ch. 28, Mt. 6:10) This major emphasis on the voluntary conformity of our will to God's will (*"your will be done"*) was a new and unique feature of the Master's teachings.

Jesus contrasts this true concept with false ideas of what is required for entrance into the kingdom. It is not enough to call Jesus "Lord," or prophesy and do great works in his name—we must actually choose and do the Father's will.

Jesus' life was devoted to this one great purpose—the doing of his heavenly Father's will—and he faced death with the same prayer that had guided his life: *"Not my will, but yours, be done."* (Ch. 146, Lk. 22:42) (See also Ch. 23, fn. *d*, and Ch. 24, fn. *a*.)

j "On that day"—Judgment Day.

Mt. 7:15 are as ravenous / are ravenous (RSV)
Mt. 7:16 Do men gather grapes from (KJV) / are grapes gathered from (RSV)
Mt. 7:17 (KJV) • tree brings forth / tree bringeth forth (KJV) • tree bears evil fruit (RSV) / tree bringeth forth evil fruit (KJV)
Mt. 7:18 (KJV)
Mt. 7:19 is hewn down and cast into the fire. (KJV) / is cut down and thrown into the fire. (RSV)
Mt. 7:21 but rather he / but he (RSV)
Mt. 7:22 name and / name, and cast out demons in your name and (RSV)
Mt. 7:24 But everyone who / And everyone then who (RSV) (140:3/1571)

23. Further Teachings

[17]"Think not that I have come to abolish the law and the prophets;[a] I have not come to destroy but to fulfill."

[20]"I tell you, unless your righteousness exceeds that of the scribes and Pharisees,[b] you shall never enter the kingdom of heaven."

[21]"You have heard it said: 'You shall not kill; and whoever kills shall be liable to judgment.' [22]But I say to you that everyone who is angry with his brother shall be in danger of judgment."

[27]"You have heard it said, 'You shall not commit adultery.' [28]But I say to you that everyone who looks upon a woman lustfully has already committed adultery with her in his heart."

[1]"Take heed that you do not give your alms before men to be seen by them. [3]When you give alms, let not your left hand know what your right hand is doing. [6]When you pray, go into your room and shut the door and pray to your Father. [7]And in praying use not vain repetitions. [8]Your Father knows what you need before you ask him. [16]And when you fast, be not of a sad countenance that your fasting may be seen by men. [19]Lay not up for yourselves treasures on earth, [20]but lay up for yourselves treasures in heaven, [21]for where your treasure is there will your heart be also."

(Mt. 5:17, 20–22, 27–28; 6:1, 3, 6–8, 16, 19–21)

(continued)

---

a "the law and the prophets;"—In the Hebrew Scriptures *the law* consists of the books of Genesis, Exodus, Leviticus, Numbers, and Deuteronomy. *The prophets* comprise the books of Joshua, Judges, Samuel (1 and 2), Kings (1 and 2), Isaiah, Jeremiah, Ezekiel, and the twelve minor prophets (Hosea, Joel, Amos, Obadiah, Jonah, Micah, Nahum, Habakkuk, Zephaniah, Haggai, Zechariah, and Malachi).

b "the scribes and Pharisees,"—The scribes were a class of men devoted to the study and exposition of the law, serving originally as copyists, editors, and interpreters of Scripture. The Pharisees were a religious party. (See Ch. 13, fn. *b*.)

Mt. 5:17   have not come to destroy but to fulfill." (KJV) / have come not to abolish them but to fulfill them." (RSV)
Mt. 5:20   I / For I (RSV)
Mt. 5:21   heard it said: 'You / heard that it was said to the men of old, 'You (RSV)
Mt. 5:22   be in danger of judgment. (KJV) / be liable to judgment; (RSV)
Mt. 5:27   heard it said / heard that it was said (RSV)
Mt. 6:1   (KJV) • that you do not give your / that ye do not your (KJV)
Mt. 6:3   When / But when (RSV) • alms, let not your (KJV) / alms, do not let your (RSV)
Mt. 6:6   When / But when (RSV) • Father. / Father who is in secret; (RSV)
Mt. 6:7   praying use not vain repetitions. (KJV) / praying do not heap up empty phrases as the Gentiles do; (RSV)
Mt. 6:8   Your / Do not be like them for your (RSV)
Mt. 6:16   fast, be not of a sad countenance that (KJV) / fast, do not look dismal like the hypocrites, for they disfigure their faces that (RSV) • that your fasting / that their fasting (RSV)
Mt. 6:19   Lay not up (KJV) / Do not lay up (RSV) • earth, but / earth, where moth and rust consume, and where thieves break in and steal, but (RSV)
Mt. 6:20   heaven, for / heaven, where neither moth nor rust consumes and where thieves do not break in and steal. For (RSV) (140:6/1576–7)

23. Further Teachings (continued)

22"The eye is the lamp of the body; if therefore your eye is generous, your whole body will be full of light. 23But if your eye is selfish, the whole body will be full of darkness. If then the light in you is turned to darkness, how great is that darkness! 24No man can serve two masters. You cannot serve God and mammon.[c] 25Do not be anxious about your lives; what you shall eat or what you shall drink; nor about your body, what you shall put on. 33But seek first the kingdom of God and his righteousness,[d] and all these things shall be added unto you. 34Therefore, do not be anxious about the morrow. Sufficient for the day is the trouble thereof."

(Mt. 6:22–25, 33–34)

---

c   "You cannot serve God and mammon."—You cannot at the same time follow in God's way and wholeheartedly serve mammon. Mammon is the Semitic word for "money" or "riches."

d   "seek first the kingdom of God and His righteousness,"—What was Jesus' *prime directive* to his disciples? Here is revealed the first priority of the true follower of Jesus—*the kingdom of God.*

Jesus centered his entire teaching mission on this one concept, *the kingdom of God,* which he also referred to as *the kingdom of heaven.*

This kingdom that Jesus taught is the will of his heavenly Father dominant and transcendent in the heart of the believer. Jesus' two favorite prayers, *"your will be done"* (Ch. 28, Mt. 6:10; Ch. 146, Mt. 26:42) and *"not my will, but yours, be done"* (Ch. 146, Lk. 22:42), are our sure guide in the way of the kingdom, and are appropriate in all life situations.

Having gained entrance into the kingdom as a child and by faith, we must progress in righteousness, grow more and more like God; therefore are we directed to seek first the kingdom of God *and His righteousness.* (See also Ch. 22, fn. *i,* and Ch. 24, fn. *a.*)

Mt. 6:22   body; if therefore your (KJV) / body, so if your (RSV) • is generous, your (Mof.) / is sound, your (RSV)
Mt. 6:23   is selfish, the (Mof.) / is not sound, the (RSV) • is turned to darkness, / is darkness, (RSV) • is that darkness! (KJV) / is the darkness! (RSV)
Mt. 6:24   No man can (KJV) / No one can (RSV)
Mt. 6:25   Do / Therefore I tell you, do (RSV)
Mt. 6:33   first the kingdom of God and (KJV) / first his kingdom and (RSV) • be added unto you. (KJV) / be yours as well. (RSV)
Mt. 6:34   about the morrow. (KJV) / about tomorrow, for tomorrow will be anxious for itself. (RSV) (140:6/1577–8)

24. The Consecration of the Twelve

[1]And he called the twelve together and gave them power and authority, [2]and he sent them out to preach the kingdom of God[a] and to heal. [5]These twelve Jesus sent out, charging them, [7]"Preach as you go saying, 'The kingdom of heaven is at hand.' [8]Heal the sick. Freely you have received, freely give."

[9]"Take no gold nor silver, nor copper in your belts, [10]no bag for your journey, nor two tunics, nor sandals, nor a staff. The laborer is worthy of his keep. [16]Behold I send you forth as sheep in the midst of wolves; be you therefore as wise as serpents and as harmless as doves. [17]But beware of men, for they will deliver you up to the councils, and they will castigate you in their synagogues. [18]And you will be brought before governors and kings for a testimony. [19]And when they deliver you up, be not anxious about what you are to say, [20]for what you are to say will be given to you in that hour, for it is not you who speak, but the Spirit of your Father speaking through you. [21]Brother will deliver up brother to death and you will be hated by many for my sake."

[6]And they departed and went through the villages, preaching the gospel[b] and healing everywhere.

(Lk. 9:1–2; Mt. 10:5, 7–10, 16–21; Lk. 9:6)

---

a "he sent them out to preach the kingdom of God"—Jesus has selected and trained his twelve apostles. Now he is sending them out on their first preaching mission. Here is revealed the central and fundamental idea that Jesus directed his apostles to preach to the world—*the kingdom of God*, also known as *the kingdom of heaven*.

This kingdom is the rule of God in the heart of the individual believer. Jesus' kingdom is composed of those individuals who have faith in the heavenly Father and are led to choose and do their Father's will. (See also Ch. 22, fn. *i*; and Ch. 23, fn. *d*.)

b "preaching the gospel"—The special and unique message Jesus sought to leave with us regarding the kingdom of God was known as the *gospel of the kingdom*. This gospel is the good news that *God is our loving heavenly Father.* When we believe this good news that God is our Father and we are his children, the Father's will becomes our will, and we achieve citizenship in the heavenly kingdom.

Lk. 9:1 authority, and / authority over all demons and to cure diseases, and (RSV)
Mt. 10:5 them, / them, "Go nowhere among the Gentiles, and enter no town of the Samaritans, (RSV)
Mt. 10:7 Preach / And preach (RSV)
Mt. 10:8 (KJV) • sick. Freely you have / sick, cleanse the lepers, raise the dead, cast out devils. Freely ye have (KJV)
Mt. 10:10 The / for the (RSV) • laborer is worthy of his (KJV) / laborer deserves his (RSV) • his keep. (NIV) / his food. (RSV)
Mt. 10:16 (KJV) • be you therefore (RSV) / be ye therefore (KJV)
Mt. 10:17 (KJV) • will castigate you / will scourge you (KJV)
Mt. 10:18 (KJV) • And you will be (RSV) / And ye shall be (KJV) • testimony. / testimony against them and the Gentiles. (KJV)
Mt. 10:19 And when / When (RSV) • up, be not anxious about what / up, do not be anxious how you are to speak, or what (RSV)
Mt. 10:21 death and / death and the father his child, and children will rise against parents and have them put to death and (RSV) • by many for / by all for (RSV) • my sake / my name's sake (RSV) (140:9/1583–4)

34

VII. Early Public Work

25. Passover at Jerusalem; Visit with Nicodemus

23Now when Jesus was in Jerusalem at the Passover feast, many believed in his name.*a* 24But Jesus did not trust himself to them, 25because he knew all men and needed no one to bear witness of man; for he himself knew what was in man.

1Now there was a man of the Pharisees, named Nicodemus, a ruler of the Jews.*b* 2This man came to Jesus by night and said to him, "Rabbi,*c* we know that you are a teacher come from God, for no one can do these signs that you do, unless God is with him."

3Jesus answered him: "Verily, verily, I say to you, except a man be born from above, he cannot see the kingdom of God."

(Jn. 2:23–25; 3:1–3) *(continued)*

---

a "Now when Jesus was in Jerusalem at the Passover feast, many believed in his name."— Following his baptism by John, Jesus spends 40 days alone in the wilderness. He then returns to John, who gives public testimony that Jesus is the expected deliverer. Two of John's disciples, Andrew and Peter, become Jesus' first followers. Jesus and his early disciples (Andrew, Peter, James, John, Philip, and Nathaniel) then attend a wedding at Cana. Jesus chooses twelve men as apostles. He then teaches, trains, and ordains them as messengers of his gospel of the kingdom.

The feast of the Passover is the first recorded event of Jesus' public ministry. This feast took place each year in April; since this is the first recorded Passover feast following Jesus' baptism in AD 26 (Ch. 14, fn. *a*), it probably took place the next year, which would be April, AD 27. If Jesus were born in the summer of 7 BC (Ch. 5, fn. *a*), he would have been 32 years old at this time, which marks the beginning of his public work.

b "a ruler of the Jews."—A member of the Sanhedrin, the Jewish Supreme Court.

c "Rabbi"—A term of address meaning "teacher" or "master."

Jn. 2:23 when Jesus was / when he was (RSV)
Jn. 3:3 Verily, verily, I (KJV) / Truly, truly, I (RSV) • [you,] except a man be born (KJV) / you, unless one is born (RSV) • born from above, he (RSV alt. trans.) / born anew, he (RSV) (142:6/1601–2)

25. Passover at Jerusalem; Visit with Nicodemus (continued)

⁴Nicodemus said to him: "How can a man be born again when he is old? Can he enter a second time into his mother's womb and be born?"

⁵Jesus answered: "I say to you, except a man be born of the spirit, he cannot enter the kingdom of God. ⁶That which is born of the flesh is flesh and that which is born of the spirit is spirit. ⁷Do not marvel that I said to you, you must be born from above. ⁸The wind blows where it wills and you hear the sound of it, but you do not know whence it comes and whither it goes—so it is with everyone born of the spirit."

⁹Nicodemus said to him, "How can this be?"

¹⁰Jesus answered him, "Are you a teacher in Israel and yet you do not understand this? ¹¹We speak of what we know and bear witness to what we have seen. ¹²Can you believe if I tell you of these heavenly truths?"ᵈ

(Jn. 3:4–12)

---

d "Can you believe if I tell you of these heavenly truths?"—Jesus tells Nicodemus, "except a man be born from above, he cannot see the kingdom of God." But Nicodemus cannot understand the meaning of this declaration and asks Jesus, "How can a man be born again?"

This is a good question and Jesus answers it in three parts. First, he again declares, "except a man be born of the spirit he cannot enter the kingdom of God." That is to say, the "birth of the spirit" is real and is *required* for entrance into the kingdom of heaven. This is the truth of first import that Jesus seeks to impress upon Nicodemus.

Next, Jesus explains the "birth of the spirit" by contrasting it with natural birth. He tells Nicodemus, "That which is born of the flesh is flesh and that which is born of the spirit is spirit." Here Jesus is teaching Nicodemus that there are two realms of life, two levels of reality—the world of the flesh and the world of the spirit. We began life in the physical world at birth; we live and grow up in this material world of everyday life, and learn the ways of the flesh. However, there is another and higher world, the world of the spirit, and we may also be born into this world, be "born of the spirit."

Jesus concludes by describing the unseen action of the spirit on our minds by analogy with the wind. "The wind blows where it wills and you hear the sound of it, but you do not know whence it comes and whither it goes—so it is with everyone born of the spirit." In other words, just as we can hear the sound of the wind even though we cannot actually see it, so also, when we are born of the spirit, we can witness the manifestations of the spirit, even though we are unable to see the spirit itself.

The "birth of the spirit" is the change of mind by faith that occurs when we wholeheartedly choose to do the Father's will and follow his spiritual guidance. This submission of our will to God's will results in a new orientation of personality whereby we increasingly give forth the fruit of the spirit in our daily life, the result of the action of spirit working in and through us. Paul, in his letter to the Galatians, lists some of the fruit of the spirit as "love, joy, peace, patience, kindness, goodness, faithfulness, gentleness, [and] self-control." (Gal. 5:22)

Jn. 3:5   I / Truly, truly, I (RSV) • you, except a man be born (KJV) / you, unless one is born (RSV) • of the spirit, / of water and of the spirit, (RSV)
Jn. 3:11   We / Truly, truly, I say to you, we (RSV)
Jn. 3:12   Can / If I have told you earthly things and you do not believe, how can (RSV) (142:6/1602)

26. Going through Samaria; The Woman at the Well

[1]The Pharisees heard that Jesus was gaining and baptizing more disciples than John, [2]although in fact it was not Jesus who baptized, but his disciples.[a] [3]When the Lord learned of this he left Judea[b] and went back once more to Galilee. [4]He had to pass through Samaria.[c] [5]So he came to a city of Samaria called Sychar,[d] near the field that Jacob gave to his son Joseph. [6]Jacob's well was there, and so Jesus, wearied as he was with his journey, sat down beside the well. It was about the sixth hour.[e] [7]There came a woman of Samaria to draw water. Jesus said to her, "Give me a drink." [8](For his disciples had gone away into the city to buy food.)

[9]The Samaritan woman said to him, "How is it that you, a Jew, ask a drink of me, a woman of Samaria?" (For Jews have no dealings with Samaritans.)[f]

[10]Jesus answered her, "If you knew the gift of God and who it is that is saying to you 'Give me a drink,' you would have asked him, and he would have given you living water."

[11]The woman said to him: "Sir, you have nothing to draw with, and the well is deep; whence then have you this living water? [12]Are you greater than our father Jacob who gave us the well, and drank thereof himself and his sons and his cattle?"

(Jn. 4:1–12) *(continued)*

---

a   "his disciples."—The apostles. (See Ch. 22, fn. *a*.)

b   "When the Lord learned of this he left Judea"—This is the earliest recorded hint of opposition to Jesus' teachings. Because of this opposition Jesus left Jerusalem and returned to Capernaum in Galilee.

c   "He had to pass through Samaria."—Samaria lies between Judea in the south and Galilee in the north. See map on page 5.

d   "Sychar"—See map on page 24.

e   "It was about the sixth hour."—Probably 6:00 P.M., at the end of a day of travel.

f   "For Jews have no dealings with Samaritans."—The Jews and the Samaritans had held ill feelings toward each other for more than 600 years. This enmity had its roots in three major events. It began around 700 BC when the king of Assyria (Sargon) carried away most of the Jewish residents of Samaria. (See map on page 5.) In their place he settled various other peoples including the Cushites, Sepharvites, and Hamathites. Later Ashurbanipal (the Assyrian king) settled still other peoples there. Around 500 BC, when the Jews of Judea returned from their Babylonian captivity, the rebuilding of Jerusalem was opposed by these Samaritans. The third event that antagonized the Jews took place around 300 BC. In return for helping Alexander the Great, the Samaritans were given permission to build a temple on Mt. Gerizim, which then functioned as an alternative to the Jewish temple at Jerusalem. Increasingly since the days of Alexander, the Jews had "no dealings with the Samaritans."

Jn. 4:1–3, 7 NIV
Jn. 4:11   deep; whence then have you this living (KJV) / deep; where do you get that living (RSV)
Jn. 4:12   drank thereof himself (KJV) / drank from it himself (RSV) (143:0,5/1607,12–13)

26. Going through Samaria; The Woman at the Well (continued)

13Jesus said to her, "Everyone who drinks of this water will thirst again, 14but whosoever drinks of the water that I shall give him shall never thirst. And this water shall become in him a well of water springing up to eternal life."

15The woman said, "Sir, give me this water that I may not thirst, nor come here to draw."

16Jesus said to her, "Go call your husband and come here."

17The woman answered him, "I have no husband."

Jesus said to her, "You are right in saying, 'I have no husband'; 18the man you are now living with is not your husband."

19The woman said to him: "Sir, I perceive that you are a prophet. 20Our fathers worshiped on this mountain;*g* and you would say that in Jerusalem is the place where men ought to worship."

21Jesus said to her: "Woman, the hour is coming when neither on this mountain nor in Jerusalem will you worship the Father. 22You worship that which you know not; we (the Jews) worship what we know. 23But the hour is coming, and now is, when all true worshipers will worship the Father in spirit and in truth, for such worshipers the Father seeks. 24God is spirit,*h* and they who worship him must worship him in spirit and in truth."

25The woman said to him, "I know that the Deliverer is coming (he who is called Christ);*i* when he comes, he will show us all things."

26Jesus said to her, "I who speak to you am he."*j* (Jn. 4:13–26)

---

g "Our fathers worshiped on this mountain;"—When Alexander the Great passed through Palestine he was accorded a friendly reception by the Samaritans. In return for their cooperation Alexander allowed the Samaritans to build a temple on Mount Gerizim. Here they worshiped and gave sacrifices in the manner of the temple at Jerusalem. This practice was ended during the reign of the Maccabees when the Jews destroyed the temple.

h "God is spirit"—Jesus taught that *"God is spirit"* and that *"God is love."*

i "I know that the Deliverer is coming (he who is called Christ);"—The Jewish scriptures taught the coming of one anointed by God who would bring about the kingdom of God on earth. He was also known as the "Deliverer" because he was to deliver his people from their bondage. *Christ* is the Greek translation of *Messiah*, the Hebrew word for *anointed one*. (See also Ch. 13, fn. *c*.)

j "I who speak to you am he."—This is Jesus' first public admission and affirmation that he is the promised deliverer.

Jn. 4:14   but whosoever drinks (KJV) / but whoever drinks (RSV)
Jn. 4:18   the man you are now living with is (Gspd) / he whom you now have is (RSV)
Jn. 4:21   Woman, the / Woman, believe me, the (RSV)
Jn. 4:22   worship that which you know not; we (KJV) / worship what you do not know; we (RSV) • we (the Jews) worship / we worship (RSV) • know. / know, for salvation is from the Jews. (RSV)
Jn. 4:23   when all true / when the true (RSV) • such worshipers the (NIV) / such the (RSV) • seeks. / seeks to worship him. (RSV)
Jn. 4:24   and in truth (KJV) / and truth (RSV)
Jn. 4:25   the Deliverer is (Ch. 13, fn. *c*) / the Messiah is (RSV) (143:5/1613–4)

38

27. The Samaritan Revival

27Just then his apostles came. They marveled that he was talking with a woman, but none said, "What do you wish?" or, "Why are you talking with her?"

28So the woman left her water jar, and went away into the city, and said to the people, 29"Come, see a man who told me all that I ever did. Can this be the Messiah?" 30They went out of the city and came unto him.

31Meanwhile the disciples besought him, saying, "Rabbi, eat."

32But he said unto them, "I have meat to eat that you know not of."

33So the disciples said to one another, "Has anyone brought him food?"

34Jesus said to them: "My meat is to do the will of him who sent me and to accomplish his work.*a* 35Do you not say, 'There are yet four months, and then comes the harvest'? I tell you, lift up your eyes and see how the fields are already white for the harvest. 36He who reaps receives wages and gathers fruit for eternal life; so that sower and reaper may rejoice together. 37For here the saying holds true: 'One sows and another reaps.' 38I send you to reap that for which you did not labor; others have labored, and you have entered into their labor."*b*

39Many Samaritans from that city believed in him because of the woman's testimony, "He told me all that I ever did." 40So when the Samaritans came to him, they asked him to stay with them; and he stayed there two days. 41And many more believed because of his word. 42They said to the woman, "It is no longer because of your words that we believe, for we have heard for ourselves, and we know that this is indeed the Savior of the world."

(Jn. 4:27–42)

---

a "My meat is to do the will of him who sent me and to accomplish his work."—Here is revealed Jesus' one great purpose in life and the core of his personal religion, *the doing of the Father's will*. The center of the one prayer he taught his apostles (The Lord's Prayer) was, *"Your kingdom come, your will be done."* And he faced a cruel and unjust death with the triumphant prayer that had guided his life, *"Not my will, but yours, be done."*

The work Jesus sought to accomplish in his earth life was the establishment of the kingdom of heaven on earth—the rule of God in the heart of every individual. To this end he preached the gospel of the kingdom, the good news that we are all the children of a loving heavenly Father, the sons and daughters of God. When we believe this "good news" and accept our sonship with God, his will becomes our will, and the kingdom of heaven is born in our hearts.

b "others have labored, and you have entered into their labor."—Here Jesus is referring to the work of John the Baptist.

Jn. 4:27   his apostles came. (Ch. 22, fn. *a*) / his disciples came. (RSV)
Jn. 4:29   the Messiah?" (Ch. 13, fn. *c*) / the Christ?" (RSV)
Jn. 4:30   (KJV)
Jn. 4:32   (KJV) • that you know / that ye know (KJV)
Jn. 4:34   My meat is (KJV) / My food is (RSV)
Jn. 4:35   months, and then / months, then (RSV) (143:5–6/1614–5)

28. Teachings on Prayer

[1]He was praying in a certain place, and when he ceased, one of his disciples said to him, "Lord, teach us to pray, as John taught his disciples."

[2]And he said to them, [9]"When you pray, say:

Our Father who is in heaven,
Hallowed be your name.
[10]Your kingdom come;
Your will be done
on earth as it is in heaven.
[11]Give us this day our daily bread;
[12]And forgive us our debts,
As we also have forgiven our debtors.
[13]Lead us not into temptation,
But deliver us from evil."[a]

[5]And he said to them: "Suppose one of you has a friend, and you go to him at midnight and say to him, 'Friend, lend me three loaves, [6]for a friend of mine has arrived on a journey, and I have nothing to set before him;' [7]and he answers from within, 'Trouble me not, for the door is now shut and my children and I are in bed; I cannot get up and give you anything.' [8]I tell you, though he will not get up and give him anything because he is his friend, yet because of his importunity he will rise and give him whatever he needs. [9]And, I tell you: ask and it shall be given you; seek, and you shall find; knock, and it shall be opened to you. [10]For everyone who asks receives; he who seeks finds; and to him who knocks it shall be opened."

(Lk. 11:1–2; Mt. 6:9–13; Lk. 11:5–10) *(continued)*

---

a Commentary on *The Lord's Prayer*—"Our Father who is in heaven," teaches us to recognize and approach God as "Our Father." He is our loving heavenly Father, and we may come before him as his sons and daughters on earth. "Hallowed be your name" leads us to come into his presence with reverence, humility, and a worshipful attitude. "Your kingdom come; your will be done on earth as it is in heaven," is the central petition of the prayer. The complete fulfillment of this prayer would mean the rule of God in the heart of every individual on earth, but it begins in us when our personal will becomes the doing of the Father's will. In "Give us this day our daily bread," *our bread for tomorrow* is an alternative (and perhaps better) translation of *our daily bread*. (See *Oxford Bible*, p. 1178.) "And forgive us our debts, as we also have forgiven our debtors," teaches us that the way to receive and experience God's forgiveness is to forgive others. "Lead us not into temptation," is best understood in the sense of "Save us in temptation." God leads us in the ways of *righteousness* and saves us in times of temptation.

Mt. 6:9   who is in (NRSV) / who art in (RSV) • be your name (NRSV) / be thy name (RSV)
Mt. 6:10   Your kingdom (NRSV) / Thy kingdom (RSV) • Your will (NRSV) / Thy will (RSV)
Lk. 11:5   them: "Suppose one of you has a friend, and you go / them: "Which of you who has a friend, and you will go (RSV)
Lk. 11:7   he answers from (NRSV) / he will answer from (RSV) • within, 'Trouble me not, for the (KJV) / within, 'Do not bother me; (RSV) • children and I are in (NAB) / children are with me in (RSV)
Lk. 11:9   it shall be (KJV) / it will be (RSV) • you shall find (KJV) / you will find (RSV)
Lk. 11:10 it shall be (KJV) / it will be (RSV)   (144:1–3/1618–20)

28. Teachings on Prayer (continued)

[11]"What father among you, if his son asks for bread, will give him a stone? Or if he asks for a fish, will give him a serpent? [13]If you then, who are evil, know how to give good gifts to your children, how much more shall your Father who is in heaven give good gifts to those who ask him!"

[1]And he told them a story, to the effect that they ought always to pray and not lose heart. [2]He said: "In a certain city there was a judge who neither feared God nor regarded man. [3]And there was a widow in that city who kept coming to him and saying, 'Protect me from my adversary.' [4]For a while he refused, but afterward he said to himself: 'Though I neither fear God nor regard man, [5]yet because this widow bothers me I will vindicate her or she will wear me out by her continual coming.'"

[20]"If you have faith, you will say to this mountain: 'Move from here to there,' and it will move; and nothing will be impossible to you."

[25]"And whenever you stand praying, forgive, if you have anything against anyone; so that your Father also who is in heaven may forgive you your trespasses."

[6]"When you pray, go into your room and shut the door and pray to your Father who is in secret; and your Father who sees in secret will reward you."[b]

(Lk. 11:11, 13; 18:1–5; Mt. 17:20; Mk. 11:25; Mt. 6:6)

---

b   Lessons from Jesus' teachings on prayer: Lk. 11:5–10 (preceding page) teaches us that just as persistence will win favors from our fellow man, so will persistence in prayer win favors from God—his answer to our prayers ("ask and it shall be given you"). Lk. 11:11, 13 again assures us that God does answer our prayers. He answers them in accordance with his divine wisdom and Fatherly love for us. Our relation to God is like that of a human child to his earthly father. We should pray as children to a loving heavenly Father. Lk. 18:1–5 again urges us to be persistent in prayer; we "ought always to pray and not lose heart." Mt. 17:20 emphasizes the importance of praying with faith. Faith adds power to prayer—the greater the faith, the greater the power ("nothing will be impossible to you"). In this verse "mountain" is best understood in the sense of a "mountain of difficulty." Mk. 11:25 reminds us to pray with a forgiving heart. God's forgiveness may be received only by those who first forgive others. Mt. 6:6 teaches us to pray in private and in secret—in the spirit and in the heart. Jesus rarely prayed out loud or in public, but he did spend much time alone in nature communing with God.

Lk. 11:11   fish, will / fish, instead of a fish, will (RSV)
Lk. 11:13   more shall your (KJV) / more will your (RSV) • good gifts to (KJV) / good things to (RSV)
Lk. 18:1   a story, to / a parable, to (RSV)
Lk. 18:3   Protect me from my (Phi) / Vindicate me against my (RSV)
Mt. 17:20   If / He said to them, "Because of your little faith, For truly I say to you, if (RSV) • faith, you / faith as a grain of mustard seed, you (RSV)
Mt. 6:6   When / But when (RSV) (144:2–3/1619–20)

29. Jesus Speaks of John

[2]Now when John heard in prison about the deeds of Jesus, he sent word by his disciples, [3]and said to him, "Are you he who is to come, or shall we look for another?"

[4]And Jesus answered them, "Go and tell John what you hear and see—[5]that the poor have good tidings preached to them. [6]And blessed is he who takes no offense at me."

[7]As they went away, Jesus began to speak to the crowds concerning John: "What did you go out into the wilderness to behold? A reed shaken by the wind? [8]A man clothed in soft raiment? Those who wear soft raiment are in kings' houses. [9]Why then did you go out? To see a prophet? Yes, I tell you, and more than a prophet. [10]This is he of whom it is written: 'Behold, I send my messenger before your face, who shall prepare the way before you.'[a] [11]Verily, I say to you, among those born of woman there has risen no one greater than John the Baptist; yet he who is but little in the kingdom of heaven is greater than he. [15]He who has ears to hear, let him hear."

[16]"But to what shall I compare this generation? It is like children sitting in the market places and calling to their playmate, [17]'We piped to you, and you did not dance; we wailed, and you did not mourn.' [18]For John came neither eating nor drinking, and they say he has a devil. [19]The Son of Man came eating and drinking, and they say, 'Behold, a gluttonous man and a winebibber, a friend of publicans and sinners!' But, wisdom is justified by her children."

[25]At that time Jesus declared: "The Father, Lord of heaven and earth, has hidden these things from the wise and understanding, and revealed them to babes. [28]Come to me, all you who labor and are heavy laden, and I will give you rest. [29]Take my yoke upon you, and learn from me, and you shall find rest for your souls."

(Mt. 11:2–11, 15–19, 25, 28–29)

---

a "Behold, I send my messenger before your face, who shall prepare the way before you."—(Malachi 3:1) Here Jesus affirms that he (Jesus) is the one prophesied by Malachi and that John is his forerunner.

Mt. 11:2 of Jesus, he / of the Christ, he (RSV)
Mt. 11:5 that the / that the blind receive their sight and the lame walk, lepers are cleansed and the deaf hear, and the dead are raised up and the (RSV)
Mt. 11:8 A / Why then did you go out? To see a (RSV) • Those / Behold, those (RSV)
Mt. 11:10 before your face / before thy face (RSV) • prepare the way / prepare thy way (RSV) • before you / before thee (RSV)
Mt. 11:11 Verily, I (KJV) / Truly, I (RSV) • is but little in (ASV) / is least in (RSV)
Mt. 11:18 (KJV) • he has a / He hath a (KJV)
Mt. 11:19 (KJV) • a gluttonous man and / a man gluttonous and (KJV) • justified by her / justified of her (KJV)
Mt. 11:25 The Father / I thank thee, Father (RSV) • earth, has hidden / earth, that then hast hidden (RSV)
Mt. 11:29 me, and / me; for I am gentle and lowly in heart and (RSV) (135:11/1506–7; 144:8/1626–7)

30. Death of John the Baptist

[17]Herod had seized John and bound him in prison for the sake of Herodias, his brother Philip's wife, because he had married her. [18]For John said to Herod, "It is not lawful for you to have your brother's wife." [19]And Herodias had a grudge against him, and wanted to kill him, but she could not. [20]For Herod feared John, knowing that he was a righteous and holy man, and kept him safe. When he heard him he was much perplexed and yet he heard him gladly.

[21]But an opportunity came when Herod on his birthday gave a banquet for his high officials, officers, and the leading men of Galilee. [22]For when Herodias' daughter came in and danced, she pleased Herod and his guests; and the king said to the girl, "Ask me for whatever you wish, and I will grant it [23]even to half my kingdom."

And he vowed to her, "Whatever you ask me I will give you."

[24]She went out and said to her mother, "What shall I ask?"

And she said, "The head of John the Baptist."

[25]And she hurried back at once to the king and asked, "I want you to give me at once the head of John the Baptist on a platter."

[26]And the king was exceedingly sorry, but because of his oath and his guests he did not want to break his word to her. [27]And immediately the king sent a soldier of the guards and gave orders to bring his head. He went and beheaded him in the prison, [28]and brought his head on a platter and gave it to the girl. And the girl gave it to her mother.

[29]When John's disciples heard of it, they came and took his body and laid it in a tomb.

(Mk. 6:17–29)

Mk. 6:17   Herod had seized / For Herod had sent and seized (RSV)
Mk. 6:21   his high officials, officers, and (NIV) / his courtiers and (RSV)
Mk. 6:23   even to half / even half (RSV)
Mk. 6:24   the Baptist. (KJV) / the baptizer. (RSV)
Mk. 6:25   And she hurried back at once to (Gspd) / And she came in immediately, with haste to (RSV)
Mk. 6:29   When John's disciples (NEB) / When the disciples (RSV)   (135:10,12/1508; 144:9/1627)

43

VIII. Eventful Times at Capernaum

31. The Large Catch of Fish

[31]And Jesus went down to Capernaum, a city of Galilee.[a]

[1]While the people pressed upon him to hear the word of God, he was standing by the lake of Gennesaret (Sea of Galilee). [2]And he saw two boats by the lake; but the fishermen had gone out of them and were washing their nets. [3]Getting into one of the boats, which was being used by a man named Simon, he asked him to put out a little from the land. And he sat down and taught the people from the boat.

[4]And when he had ceased speaking he said to Simon, "Put out into the deep and let down your nets for a catch."

[5]And Simon answered: "Master, we toiled all night and took nothing! But at your word I will let down the nets."

[6]And when they had done this, they enclosed a great shoal of fish; and as their nets were breaking, [7]they beckoned to their partners in the other boat to come and help them. And they came and filled both the boats, so that they began to sink. [8]But when Simon saw it, he fell down at Jesus' knees, saying: "Depart from me, for I am a sinful man, O Lord." [9]For he was astonished, and all that were with him, at the catch of fish[b] which they had taken.

[11]And when they had brought their boats to land, they left everything and followed him.

(Lk. 4:31, 5:1–9, 11)

---

a "And Jesus went down to Capernaum, a city of Galilee."—Summary of recent events (Sec. VII): Following Jesus' choosing, ordaining, and training the twelve apostles, he begins his public ministry by leaving Galilee and attending the feast of the Passover at Jerusalem. Here he meets with Nicodemus and has a memorable discussion on "the birth of the spirit." He returns to Galilee through Samaria. He meets a woman at Jacob's well and reveals to her that he is the expected deliverer. She tells the people of the town about Jesus and he is well received by the Samaritans. Jesus teaches the apostles about prayer and gives them *The Lord's Prayer.* Jesus receives a message from John, who is in prison, and sends him a return message. Jesus then speaks of John to the crowd, describing him as more than a prophet and saying that "among those born of woman there has risen no one greater than John." Soon after receiving Jesus' message, John the Baptist is beheaded by Herod. This event will mark the beginning of a more aggressive phase of Jesus' ministry. He and his apostles now journey back to Capernaum, and from this home base he launches his first open and public preaching tour of Galilee.

b "For he was astonished, and all that were with him, at the catch of fish"—This was certainly an extraordinary occurrence, but perhaps not a miracle. Jesus was a fisherman, probably an expert fisherman, and quite familiar with the Sea of Galilee. Perhaps he merely directed the fishermen to the fish's habitat at that particular time of the day and season. The Jews were miracle minded and tended to view all such unusual episodes as miraculous happenings.

Lk. 4:31   And Jesus went / And he went (RSV)
Lk. 5:1   Gennesaret (Sea of Galilee). / Gennesaret. (RSV)
Lk. 5:3   was being used by a man named Simon, he / was Simon's, he (RSV)
Lk. 5:8   Simon saw / Simon Peter saw (RSV) (145:0,1/1628–9)

32. Teaching at the Synagogue

21On the Sabbath Jesus entered the synagogue and taught. 22And they were astonished at his teaching, for he taught them as one who had authority, and not as the scribes.

23And there was in their synagogue a man with an unclean spirit;*a* 24and he cried out: "What have you to do with us, Jesus of Nazareth? Have you come to destroy us? I know who you are, the holy one of God."

25But Jesus said: "Be silent!"

26And the unclean spirit, convulsing him and crying with a loud voice, came out of him.

27And they were all amazed, so that they questioned among themselves, saying: "What is this? A new teaching! With authority he commands even the unclean spirits, and they obey him."

28And at once his fame spread everywhere throughout all the surrounding region of Galilee.

(Mk. 1:21–28)

---

a "And there was in their synagogue a man with an unclean spirit;"—The Jews tended to view epilepsy as possession by an "unclean spirit." Even the person suffering a seizure would often believe it was caused by an evil spirit. This event was portrayed as possession by an unclean spirit, but it may have been a case of a (misunderstood) epileptic seizure in which Jesus helped the man regain his composure and self-control.

Mk. 1:21 On / And they went into Capernaum; and immediately on (RSV) • Sabbath Jesus entered / Sabbath he entered (RSV)
Mk. 1:23 And there / And immediately there (RSV)
Mk. 1:25 silent!" / silent, and come out of him!" (RSV) (145:2/1629–31)

33. The Healing at Sundown

²⁹And immediately Jesus left the synagogue, and entered the house of Simon and Andrew, with James and John. ³⁰Now Simon's mother-in-law lay sick with a fever, and they told him of her. ³¹And he came and took her by the hand and lifted her up, and the fever left her; and she served them.

³²That evening, at sundown, they brought to him all who were sick.^{*a*} ³³And the whole city was gathered together about the door. ³⁴And he healed many who were sick with various diseases.

³⁵In the morning, a great while before day, he rose and went out to a lonely place, and there he prayed. ³⁶And Simon and those who were with him pursued him, ³⁷and they found him and said to him, "Everyone is searching for you."

⁴³But he said to them, "I must preach the good news of the kingdom of God to the other cities also;^{*b*} for I was sent for this purpose."^{*c*}

(Mk. 1:29–37; Lk. 4:43)

---

a   "That evening, at sundown, they brought to him all who were sick."—One day ended and the next day began at sundown. Since this was the Sabbath, the people waited until the end of the Sabbath (at sundown) to go in search of healing. This they did in accordance with Jewish law and custom.

b   "I must preach the good news of the kingdom of God to the other cities also;"—Jesus has just performed his greatest miracle to date, the supernatural healing of "all who were sick" in the city of Capernaum. Everyone is looking for him because of the great wonder he has wrought. But Jesus realizes that the crowds seek him because of his miraculous healings, not because of his spiritual ministry. He is not willing that his mission of proclaiming the gospel and establishing the kingdom of God be compromised by his healing ministry. Therefore Jesus elects to leave Capernaum at the height of his popular favor, in order to preach "the good news of the kingdom of God" in the other cities of Galilee.

This "good news of the kingdom of God" is Jesus' teaching that we are all sons and daughters of God, our loving heavenly Father. By faith in this saving truth we may enter the kingdom of heaven and gain eternal salvation. (See also Ch. 34, fn. *a*.)

c   "I was sent for this purpose." Why did Jesus come down to earth? Here is revealed the purpose of his bestowal on our world. The Father sent Jesus to "preach the good news of the kingdom of God."

Mk. 1:29   immediately Jesus left / immediately he left (RSV)
Mk. 1:30   and they / and immediately they (RSV)
Mk. 1:32   sick. / sick and possessed with demons. (RSV)
Mk. 1:34   diseases. / diseases, and cast out many demons; (RSV)
Mk. 1:35   In / And in (RSV) (145:2–5/1631–6)

IX. The First Preaching Tour of Galilee

34. Healing the Leper

²³And Jesus went about all Galilee, teaching in their synagogues and preaching the gospel of the kingdom*a* and healing every disease and every infirmity among the people. ²⁴So his fame spread throughout all Syria, and they brought him all the sick, those afflicted with various diseases and pains, demoniacs, epileptics, and paralytics, and he healed them. ²⁵And great crowds followed him from Galilee and the Decapolis and Jerusalem and Judea and from beyond the Jordan.

⁴⁰And a leper*b* came to him beseeching him, and kneeling said to him, "If you will, you can make me clean."

⁴¹Moved with compassion, he stretched out his hand and touched him, and said to him, "I will—be clean."

⁴²And immediately the leprosy left him, and he was made clean.

⁴³And he sternly charged him, and sent him away at once, ⁴⁴and said to him, "See that you say nothing to anyone; but go show yourself to the priest, and offer for your cleansing what Moses commanded for a testimony."

⁴⁵But he went out and began to talk freely about it, and to spread the news, so that Jesus could no longer openly enter the town, but was out in the country; and people came to him from every quarter.

(Mt. 4:23–25; Mk. 1:40–45)

---

a "And Jesus went about all Galilee . . . preaching the gospel of the kingdom"—In the two millennia since he lived on earth many things have been taught about Jesus and in his name, but what did Jesus actually teach? Here this question is clearly answered. Jesus taught and preached "the gospel of the kingdom."

What is "the gospel of the kingdom"? Jesus' gospel is many-sided and complete, but its central truth is the fatherhood of God, combined with the sonship and consequent brotherhood of man. This is the good news that God is our loving heavenly Father and we are all his children, sons and daughters of God; and as his children we are all brothers and sisters to one another in God's heavenly family. By faith in this gospel we may gain entrance into the Father's kingdom and attain eternal salvation.

b "leper"—lep•ro•sy n. 1: a chronic disease caused by infection with an acid-fast bacillus (*Mycobacterium leprae*) and characterized by the formation of nodules on the surface of the body and especially on the face or by the appearance of tuberculoid macules on the skin that enlarge and spread and are accompanied by loss of sensation followed sooner or later in both types by involvement of nerves with eventual paralysis, wasting of muscle, and production of deformities and mutilations. (*Webster's Unabridged*)

Mk. 1:41   with compassion, he (KJV) / with pity, he (RSV)
Mk. 1:44   a testimony. (KJV) / a proof to the people. (RSV)
Mk. 1:45   enter the town, (KJV) / enter a town, (RSV)   (146:0,4/1637,43–4)

47

35. Cana and the Nobleman Who Believed

⁴⁶Jesus came again to Cana in Galilee, where he had made the water wine. At Capernaum there was a certain nobleman whose son was ill. ⁴⁷When he heard that Jesus had come from Judea to Galilee he went and begged him to come down to Capernaum and heal his son, for he was at the point of death.

⁴⁸Jesus said to him, "Unless you see signs and wonders you will not believe."

⁴⁹The nobleman said to him, "Sir, come down before my child dies." ⁵⁰Jesus said to him, "Go; your son will live."

The man believed the word that Jesus spoke to him and went his way. ⁵¹As he was going down, his servants met him and told him that his son was living. ⁵²So he asked them the hour when he began to mend, and they said to him, "Yesterday at the seventh hour the fever left him." ⁵³The father knew that was the hour when Jesus had said to him, "Your son will live"; and he himself believed, and all his household.

(Jn. 4:46–53)

Jn. 4:46 Jesus came / So he came (RSV) • At Capernaum / And at Capernaum (RSV) • was a certain nobleman whose (KJV) / was an official whose (RSV)
Jn. 4:47 down to Capernaum and / down and (RSV)
Jn. 4:48 Jesus said / Jesus therefore said (RSV)
Jn. 4:49 The nobleman said (KJV) / The official said (RSV) (146:5/1644–5)

36. The Widow's Son at Nain

¹¹Soon afterward Jesus went to a city called Nain,ᵃ and his disciples and a great crowd went with him. ¹²As he drew near to the gate of the city, a young man who had died was being carried out. He was the only son of his mother, and she was a widow. A large crowd from the city was with her.

¹³And when the Lord saw her, he had compassion on her and said to her, "Do not weep." ¹⁴And he came and touched the bier, and the bearers stood still.

And he said, "Young man, I say to you, arise."

¹⁵And the man sat up, and began to speak. And Jesus gave him to his mother.

¹⁶Fear seized them all; and they glorified God, saying, "A great prophet has arisen among us!" and "God has visited his people!" ¹⁷And this report concerning him spread throughout all the surrounding country and the whole of Judea.

(Lk. 7:11–17)

a "Nain"—See map on page 24.

Lk. 7:12 city, a / city, behold, a (RSV) • out. He was the / out, the (RSV) • widow. A / widow; and a (RSV)
Lk. 7:15 the man / the dead man (RSV) • And Jesus gave / And he gave (RSV)
Lk. 7:17 spread throughout all the surrounding country and the whole of Judea. / spread through the whole of Judea and all the surrounding country. (RSV) (146:6/1645–6)

48

37. The Faith of the Centurion

¹After Jesus had ended all his sayings in the hearing of the people he entered Capernaum.*ᵃ*

²Now a centurion*ᵇ* had a slave who was dear to him, who was sick and at the point of death. ³When he heard of Jesus, he sent to him elders of the Jews, asking him to come and heal his slave. ⁴And when they came to Jesus, they besought him earnestly, saying, "He is worthy to have you do this for him, ⁵for he loves our nation, and he built us our synagogue."

⁶And Jesus went with them.

When he was not far from the house, the centurion sent friends to him, saying to him, "Lord, do not trouble yourself, for I am not worthy to have you come under my roof; ⁷therefore I did not presume to come to you. But say the word, and let my servant be healed. ⁸For I am a man set under authority, with soldiers under me; and I say to one, 'Go,' and he goes; and to another, 'Come,' and he comes; and to my slave, 'Do this,' and he does it."

⁹When Jesus heard this he marveled at him, and turned and said to the multitude that followed him, "I tell you, not even in Israel have I found such faith."*ᶜ*

¹⁰And when those who had been sent returned to the house, they found the slave well.

(Lk. 7:1–10)

---

a "After Jesus had ended all his sayings in the hearing of the people he entered Capernaum."—After completing their first preaching tour of Galilee, Jesus and his apostles return to their home base of Capernaum.

b "a centurion"—A captain of the Roman guard at Capernaum.

c "When Jesus heard this he marveled at him, and turned and said to the multitude that followed him, 'I tell you, not even in Israel have I found such faith.'"—Why does Jesus so exalt faith?

We are mortal and finite beings, living in a material world. With our physical senses and associated minds we may know and understand this world, but we are unable to know a world that lies above and beyond the material level. Jesus taught a spiritual world, a world that *transcends* the physical. He said, *"God is spirit,"* and centered his teachings on an inner spiritual kingdom, declaring, *"The kingdom of God is within you."* As material and finite beings, we lack the capacity to know this spiritual kingdom and its infinite God.

It is only through the exercise of faith that we are able to go beyond ourselves and recognize a higher spiritual reality. It is only through faith that we may know the truth of the loving heavenly Father and experience our sonship with him.

Faith adds *power* to our quest for God.

Faith is the price of admission to the kingdom of heaven.

Lk. 7:1   After Jesus had / After he had (RSV) (147:0–1/1647–8)

49

X. The Second Passover Visit to Jerusalem

38. Sabbath at the Pool of Bethesda

¹There was a feast of the Jews,*ᵃ* and Jesus went up to Jerusalem. ²Now there is in Jerusalem by the Sheep Gate a pool, in Hebrew called Bethesda, which has five porches. ³In these lay a multitude of invalids, blind, lame, and paralyzed, waiting for the moving of the water.*ᵇ* ⁵One man was there who had been ill for thirty-eight years.

⁶When Jesus saw him and knew that he had been lying there a long time, he said to him, "Do you want to be healed?"

⁷The sick man answered him, "Sir, I have no man to put me into the pool when the water is troubled, and while I am going in, another steps down before me."

⁸Jesus said to him, "Rise, take up your bed and walk."

⁹And at once the man was healed, and he took up his bed and walked. ¹⁵The man went away and told the Jews that it was Jesus who had healed him. ¹⁶And this is why the Jews persecuted Jesus, because he did this on the Sabbath.

²⁴Jesus said: "Truly, truly, I say to you, he who hears my word and believes has eternal life;*ᶜ* he does not come into judgment, but has passed from death to life."

(Jn. 5:1–3, 5–9, 15–16, 24)

---

a "a feast of the Jews,"—This refers to the Jewish feast of the Passover, which took place each year in April. This is the second recorded Passover following Jesus' baptism, so it probably occurred in April, AD 28, and Jesus would have been 33 years old. (See Ch. 25, fn. *a*.)

b "waiting for the moving of the water."—The pool of Bethesda was a hot spring that would bubble up at irregular intervals. It was believed that the first person to enter the pool after one of these periodic disturbances would be healed. (*Oxford Bible*, p. 1292)

c "he who hears my word and believes has eternal life;"—He who hears Jesus' gospel of the kingdom and believes the good news that he is a child of God receives the gift of eternal life.

Jn. 5:1   There / After this there (RSV)
Jn. 5:2   five porches. (KJV) / five porticos. (RSV)
Jn. 5:3   paralyzed, waiting for the moving of the water. (RSV alternate insert; Oxford Bible, p. 1292) / paralyzed. (RSV)
Jn. 5:8   your bed and (KJV) / your pallet and (RSV)
Jn. 5:9   his bed and (KJV) / his pallet and (RSV)
Jn. 5:24   believes has / believes him who sent me has (RSV) (147:3/1649–50)

50

39. The Meal with Simon the Pharisee

³⁶One of the Pharisees asked Jesus to eat with him, and he went into the Pharisee's house, and took his place at table. ³⁷A woman of the city who was a sinner, when she learned that he was at table in the Pharisee's house, brought an alabaster flask of ointment, ³⁸and standing behind him at his feet, weeping, she began to wet his feet with her tears and wiped them with the hair of her head and kissed his feet and anointed them with the ointment.

³⁹Now when the Pharisee who had invited him saw it, he said to himself, "If this man were a prophet, he would have known who and what sort of woman this is touching him, for she is a sinner."

⁴⁰And Jesus answering said to him, "Simon, I have something to say to you."

And he answered, "What is it, Teacher?"

⁴¹"A certain creditor had two debtors. The one owed five hundred denarii*a* and the other fifty. ⁴²When they could not pay, he forgave them both. Now which of them will love him more?"

⁴³Simon answered, "The one, I suppose, who was forgiven the most."

And he said to him, "You have judged rightly."

⁴⁴Then turning toward the woman he said to Simon, "Do you see this woman? I entered your house, yet you gave me no water for my feet. She has wet my feet with her tears and wiped them with her hair. ⁴⁵You gave me no kiss, but from the time I came in she has not ceased to kiss my feet. ⁴⁶You did not anoint my head with oil, but she has anointed my feet with ointment. ⁴⁷Therefore I tell you, her sins, which are many, are forgiven, and this has led her to love much; but he who is forgiven little, sometimes loves little." ⁴⁸And he said to her, "Your sins are forgiven."

⁴⁹Then those who were at table with him began to say among themselves, "Who is this, who even forgives sins?"

⁵⁰And he said to the woman, "Your faith has saved you;*b* go in peace."

(Lk. 7:36–50)

---

a "denarii"—A *denarius* was equal to a day's wage for a laborer.

b "Your faith has saved you"—It is the woman's faith that saved her from her sins and opened the way to eternal salvation. In Jesus' gospel faith is the price we pay for entrance into the Father's eternal kingdom.

Lk. 7:36 asked Jesus to / asked him to (RSV)
Lk. 7:37 A / And behold, a (RSV)
Lk. 7:43 suppose, who was forgiven the most. / suppose, to whom he forgave more. (RSV)
Lk. 7:44 feet. She / feet, but she (RSV)
Lk. 7:47 forgiven, and this has led her to love much; / forgiven, for she loved much; (RSV) • little, sometimes loves / little, loves (RSV) (147:5/1651–2)

40. Going through the Grainfields

23One Sabbath Jesus was going through the grainfields; and as they made their way his disciples began to pluck heads of grain. 24And the Pharisees said to him, "Look, why are they doing what is not lawful on the Sabbath?"*a*

25And he said to them, "Have you never read what David did when he was in need and was hungry, he and those who were with him: 26how he entered the house of God when Abiatar was high priest, and ate the bread of the Presence, which it is not lawful for any but the priests? And David also gave it to those who were with him."

27And he said to them, "The Sabbath was made for man and not man for the Sabbath. 28The Son of Man is Lord even of the Sabbath."

(Mk. 2:23–28)

---

a   "Look, why are they doing what is not lawful on the Sabbath?"—After his last visit to Jerusalem (Section X, page 50), Pharisees seem always to be following Jesus, ever seeking to entrap him and find him guilty of wrongdoing or law breaking.

Mk. 2:23   Sabbath Jesus was / Sabbath he was (RSV)
Mk. 2:26   priests? And David also / priests to eat, and also (RSV)
Mk. 2:28   The / so the (RSV) (147:6/1654–5)

XI. Back in Capernaum

41. New Wine and Old Wine Skins

[33]And the Pharisees said to him, "The disciples of John fast often and offer prayers and so do the disciples of the Pharisees, but yours eat and drink."[a]

[34]And Jesus said to them, "Can you make wedding guests fast while the bridegroom[b] is with them? [35]The days will come, when the bridegroom is taken away from them, and then they will fast in those days. [16]No one puts a piece of unshrunk cloth on an old garment, for the patch tears away from the garment and a worse tear is made. [17]Neither is new wine put into old wine skins; if it is, the skins burst and the wine is spilled, and the skins are destroyed. [38]But new wine must be put into fresh wine skins."

(Lk. 5:33–35; Mt. 9:16–17; Lk. 5:38)

---

a   "The disciples of John fast often and offer prayers and so do the disciples of the Pharisees, but yours eat and drink."—It is natural for the human child to pray to his heavenly Father, but fasting was not taught by Jesus. Fasting was a part of the old order but was not a part of the new gospel of the kingdom. Jesus compares the attempt to make his gospel fit into the Jewish tradition to the foolish practice of putting new wine into old wineskins.

b   "bridegroom"—John the Baptist referred to Jesus as a "bridegroom." (See Ch. 21, Jn. 3:29.)

Lk. 5:33   And the Pharisees said / And they said (RSV)
Mt. 9:16   No / And no (RSV) (147:7/1655–6)

42. Healing on the Sabbath

¹Jesus entered the synagogue, and a man was there who had a withered hand. ²And the Pharisees watched him to see whether he would heal him on the Sabbath, so that they might accuse him.

³And he said to the man who had the withered hand, "Come here." ⁴And he said to them, "Is it lawful on the Sabbath to do good, to save life?"

But they were silent.

⁵And he looked around at them and said to the man, "Stretch out your hand."

He stretched it out, and his hand was restored.ᵃ

⁶The Pharisees went out, and immediately held counsel with the Herodiansᵇ against him, how to destroy him.

(Mk. 3:1–6)

---

a   "his hand was restored."—Here the master performs a miracle of healing as a challenge to the meaningless restrictions that had been placed upon the observance of the Sabbath day of rest.

b   "Herodians"—A political party that sought emancipation from direct Roman rule through the restoration of the Herodian dynasty.

Mk. 3:1   Jesus entered / Again he entered (RSV)
Mk. 3:2   And the Pharisees watched (Mk. 3:6) / And they watched (RSV)
Mk. 3:4   good, to save life? / good or to do harm, to save life or to kill? (RSV)
Mk. 3:5   them and / them with anger, grieved at their hardness of heart, and (RSV) (148:7/1664–65)

43. Jesus Heals a Paralytic

[1]And when Jesus returned to Capernaum after some days, it was reported that he was at home.[a] [2]And many were gathered together, so that there was no longer room for them, not even about the door; and he was preaching to them. [3]And they came, bringing to him a paralytic carried by four men. [4]And when they could not get near him because of the crowd they removed the roof above him; and when they had made an opening, they let down the bed on which the paralytic lay.

[5]And when Jesus saw their faith, he said to the paralytic, "My son, your sins are forgiven."

[6]Now some of the scribes were sitting there, questioning in their hearts, [7]"Why does this man speak thus? It is blasphemy! Who can forgive sins but God alone?"

[8]Jesus, perceiving in his spirit that they thus questioned within themselves, said to them: "Why do you question thus in your hearts? [9]Which is easier, to say to the paralytic, 'Your sins are forgiven,' or to say, 'Rise, take up your bed and walk'? [10]But that you may know that the Son of Man has authority on earth to forgive sins, [11]I say to this afflicted man, 'Rise, take up your bed and go home.'"

[12]And he rose, and immediately took up the bed and went out before them all. They were all amazed and glorified God, saying, "We never saw anything like this!"

(Mk. 2:1–12)

---

a   "he was at home."—Perhaps the home of James and John Zebedee, who lived at Capernaum, as did Andrew and Peter.

Mk. 2.1   when Jesus returned / when he returned (RSV)
Mk. 2:2   preaching to / preaching the word to (RSV)
Mk. 2:4   the bed on (KJV) / the pallet on (RSV)
Mk. 2:8   Jesus, / And immediately, Jesus, (RSV)
Mk. 2:9   your bed and (KJV) / your pallet and (RSV)
Mk. 2:11   I say to this afflicted man, 'Rise, / "I say to you, rise, (RSV) • your bed and (KJV) / your pallet and (RSV)
Mk. 2:12   the bed and (KJV) / the pallet and (RSV) • all. They / all so that they (RSV) (148:9/1666–7)

XII. Another Preaching Tour of Galilee

44. The Women's Evangelistic Corps

[1]Soon afterward Jesus went on through cities and villages, preaching and bringing the good news of the kingdom of God.[a] And the twelve were with him, [2]and also some women[b] who had been healed: Mary, called Magdalene, [3]and Joanna, the wife of Chuza, Herod's steward, and Susanna, and many others, who provided their support out of their private means. (Lk. 8:1–3)

---

a "preaching and bringing the good news of the kingdom of God"—The good news that God is our loving and merciful heavenly Father. (See also Ch. 34, fn. *a*.)

b "and also some women"—Jesus and the apostles are embarking on another preaching tour through the cities and villages of Galilee. In this tour they are joined for the first time by a group of women evangelists. These women formed a separate corps of gospel teachers "who provided their support out of their private means."

In a time when women were not allowed on the main floor of the synagogue, being confined to the women's quarters, this was a bold and courageous move. Jesus' decision to recognize women as teachers of the gospel forever emancipated women from the prevailing belief in the spiritual inferiority of women. Jesus taught the spiritual equality of male and female and by this act gave due recognition to women's place in religious work.

Lk. 8:1 afterward Jesus went / afterward he went (RSV)
Lk. 8:2 healed: / healed of evil spirits and infirmities: (RSV) • Magdalene, / Magdalene, from whom seven demons had gone out. (RSV)
Lk. 8:3 provided their support out of their private means. (NASB) / provided for them out of their means. (RSV) (150:1/1678–9)

45. Sending Out the Twelve Two by Two

7And he called to him the twelve, and began to send them out two by two.

37He said to his disciples, "The harvest is plenteous, but the laborers are few. 38Pray therefore the Lord of the harvest to send out more laborers into his harvest."

24"The disciple is not above his master; nor the servant above his lord. 25It is enough for the disciple that he be on a level with his master, and the servant as his lord. If they have called the master of the house Beelzebub, how much more shall they call them of his household."

26"So have no fear of them. Nothing is covered that shall not be revealed, or hidden that shall not be known. 27What I tell you in the dark, utter in the light. What you hear whispered, proclaim upon the housetops. 28And do not fear those who kill the body, but cannot kill the soul."

29"Are not two sparrows sold for a penny? And not one of them will fall to the ground without your Father's will. 30Even the hairs of your head are all numbered. 31Fear not, therefore; you are of more value than a great many sparrows."

36"A man's foes will be of his own household. 37He who loves father or mother more than this gospel is not worthy of the kingdom."

6And they departed and went through the villages, preaching the gospel everywhere.[a]

(Mk. 6:7; Mt. 9:37–38, 10:24–31, 36–37; Lk. 9:6)

---

a "And they departed and went through the villages, preaching the gospel everywhere."— The core message Jesus directed his apostles to bring to the world was known as "the gospel of the kingdom." This is the good news that we are all children of God and through faith we may realize and experience this ennobling truth. (See also Ch. 34, fn. *a*.)

Mk. 6:7   two. / two and gave them authority over unclean spirits. (RSV)
Mt. 9:37   He / Then he (RSV) • is plenteous, but (KJV) / is plentiful, but (RSV) • out more laborers (LAM) / out laborers (RSV)
Mt. 10:24   (KJV)
Mt. 10:25   (KJV) • be on a level with his (Wey) / be as his (KJV)
Mt. 10:26   them. Nothing / them for nothing (RSV) • that shall not (KJV) / that will not (RSV)
Mt. 10:27   light. What / light; and what (RSV)
Mt. 10:30   Even / But even (RSV)
Mt. 10:36   A / And a (RSV) • than this gospel is / than me is (RSV) • of the kingdom. / of me. (RSV)
Lk. 9:6   gospel everywhere. / gospel and healing everywhere. (RSV) (150:4/1681–2)

46. Discourse at the Nazareth Synagogue

16And he came to Nazareth, where he had been brought up; and he went to the synagogue, as his custom was, on the Sabbath day. He stood up to read 17and there was given to him the book of the prophet Isaiah. He opened the book and found the place where it is written:

18"The Spirit of the Lord is upon me because he has anointed me*a* to preach good tidings to the poor. He has sent me to proclaim release to the captives and recovering of sight to the blind, to set at liberty those who are oppressed and 19to proclaim the acceptable year of the Lord."

20And he closed the book and gave it back to the attendant and sat down; and the eyes of all in the synagogue were fixed on him. 21And he began speaking to them by saying, "Today this scripture has been fulfilled."

22And all spoke well of him, and wondered at the gracious words which proceeded out of his mouth.

(Lk. 4:16–22)

---

a "he has anointed me"—The literal meaning of *Messiah* (Greek: *Christ*) is "the anointed one." Jesus, after quoting this scripture from Isaiah ("he has anointed me"), affirms that the scripture is fulfilled in him ("Today this scripture has been fulfilled").

Lk. 4:16   day. He / day. And he (RSV)
Lk. 4:18   Isaiah 61:1 • good tidings to (Is. 61:1) (KJV) / good news to (RSV)
Lk. 4:19   Isaiah 61:2
Lk. 4:21   began speaking to them by saying, "Today / began to say to them, "Today (RSV) • fulfilled." / fulfilled in your hearing." (RSV) (150:8/1684–6)

47. Jesus Is Rejected at Nazareth

⁵⁴After Jesus had taught them in their synagogue, they were astonished and said, "Where did this man get this wisdom and these mighty works? ⁵⁵Is not this the carpenter's son? Is not his mother called Mary? And are not his brothers James and Joseph and Simon and Judas? ⁵⁶And are not all his sisters with us? Where then did this man get all this?" ⁵⁷And they took offense at him.

²³And he said to them, "Doubtless you will quote to me this proverb, 'Physician, heal yourself,' and say to me, 'What we have heard you did at Capernaum, do here also in your own country.'"

²⁴And he said to them, "Truly, I say to you, a prophet is not without honor save in his own land."

²⁸When they heard this, all in the synagogue were filled with wrath. ²⁹And they rose up and put him out of the city, and led him to the brow of the hill on which their city was built, that they might throw him over the edge. ³⁰But passing through the midst of them he went his way.

(Mt. 13:54–57; Lk. 4:23–24, 28–30)

Mt. 13:54 After Jesus had taught them in their synagogue, they / and coming to his own country he taught them in their synagogue so that they (RSV)
Lk. 4:23 yourself,' and say to me, 'What / yourself; what (RSV)
Lk. 4:24 you, a prophet is not without honor save in his own land / you, no prophet is acceptable in his own country (RSV)
Lk. 4:29 him over the edge. (NEB) / him down headlong. (RSV)
Lk. 4:30 went his way. (KJV) / went away. (RSV) (150:9/1686–7)

XIII. Teaching Beside the Sea

48. The Parable of the Sower

[1]Jesus began to teach beside the Sea of Galilee. A very large crowd gathered about him, so that he got into a boat and sat in it on the sea; and the whole crowd was beside the sea on the land.

[2]And he taught them many things in parables,[a] and in his teaching he said to them, [3]"Listen! A sower went out to sow, [4]and as he sowed some seed fell along the path, and birds came and devoured it. [5]Other seed fell on rocky ground where it had not much soil, and immediately it sprang up since it had no depth of soil, [6]but when the sun rose, it was scorched, and since it had no root it withered away. [7]Other seed fell among thorns, and the thorns grew up and choked it and it yielded no grain. [8]And other seed fell into good soil and brought forth grain, growing up and increasing and yielding thirtyfold, and sixtyfold, and a hundredfold. [9]He who has ears to hear, let him hear."

(Mk. 4:1–8; Mt. 13:9) *(continued)*

---

a "And he taught them many things in parables"—At this time Jesus suddenly initiates a wholly new form of teaching—the parable. *The Parable of the Sower* is Jesus' first recorded parable and it is immediately followed by numerous other parables. Jesus continued to teach in parables throughout the remainder of his earth ministry and his last parable (*The Parable of the Talents*) was spoken just three days before his death.

Parables introduce spiritual truth by moving from the known (natural and material world) to the unknown (spiritual and supermaterial world). They use the analogy existing between the natural and the spiritual to teach the truths of the kingdom.

Parables encourage critical thinking and creative imagination, but they should not be approached as allegories where each individual detail holds some definite and hidden meaning. Although the individual hearer is free to assign special meaning to particular aspects of a parable, they should be thought of as simple stories that are designed to portray one essential and vital truth. For example, in *The Parable of the Sower*, even though specific interpretations are offered, the thrust of the parable is to teach that varying degrees of success may be expected by those who seek to minister the gospel of the kingdom.

Parables, as used by Jesus, possess a number of important advantages:

(1) Parables tell simple stories that are easy to understand. They use imagery and situations that are familiar. Thus they are well adapted to the minds and comprehension of the listeners.

(2) Parables appeal to a wide variety of intellects and temperaments, and leave each individual free to interpret the parable in accordance with his or her own mental and spiritual endowments.

(3) Parables arouse a minimum of self-defense and other negative attitudes that close the mind to new truth. They evade personal prejudice and make it easy to receive spiritual truth that one might otherwise have been unwilling to accept.

(4) To reject the truth contained in parables forces one into conflict with one's own honest judgment and fair decision. Parables stimulate thinking and tend to force thought to the desired conclusion.

(5) Parables enabled Jesus to teach new truth while avoiding any outward clashing with established authority and tradition. (See also Ch. 48, fn. *b*.)

Mk. 4:1   Jesus began / Again he began (RSV) • Sea of Galilee. / sea. (RSV) • A very / And a very (RSV)
Mk. 4:6   but when / and when (RSV)   (151:1/1688–9)

48. The Parable of the Sower (continued)

¹⁰Then the disciples came and asked him, "Why do you speak to them in parables?"

¹¹And he answered them, "To you it has been given to know the mysteries of the kingdom of heaven, but to them it has not been given. ¹²And we will do this so that they may indeed see but not perceive, and may indeed hear but not understand.*ᵇ* ¹²For to him who has shall more be given, and he shall have an abundance; but from him who has not, even what he has shall be taken away."*ᶜ*

¹⁴"With them indeed is fulfilled the prophecy of Isaiah which says: ¹⁵'For this people's heart has waxed gross, and their ears are dull of hearing, and their eyes they have closed lest they should perceive with their eyes and hear with their ears and understand with their heart.'"

²⁶And he said, "The kingdom of God is as if a man should scatter seed upon the ground; ²⁷and should sleep and rise night and day, and the seed should sprout and grow he knows not how. ²⁸The earth produces of itself, first the blade, then the ear, then the full grain in the ear. ²⁹And when the grain is ripe, at once he puts in the sickle, because the harvest has come."

(Mt. 13:10–11; Mk. 4:12; Mt. 13:12, 14–15; Mk. 4:26–29)

---

b "they may indeed see but not perceive, and may indeed hear but not understand."—The multitudes that now gather to hear Jesus' teachings are composed not only of genuine truth seekers, but also of others who lack spiritual discernment, as well as enemies who seek his destruction. By teaching in parables Jesus enables those who desire to know the truth to understand his meaning, while those who lack discernment or seek to use his teachings against him are only confounded. They "see but do not perceive" and "hear but do not understand."

Jesus refers to these individuals who are not seeking truth by quoting the prophet Isaiah: "For this people's heart has waxed gross, and their ears are dull of hearing, and their eyes they have closed lest they should perceive with their eyes and hear with their ears and understand with their heart."

c "For to him who has shall more be given, and he shall have an abundance; but from him who has not, even what he has shall be taken away."—Those who love the truth and seek entrance into the kingdom will gain new truth from parables because they will be able to understand the parables' meaning, while those who do not follow in the way of truth are only more confused and confounded by parables—"even what (understanding) he has shall be taken away."

Mt. 13:10   and asked him, / and said to him, (RSV)
Mt. 13:11   the mysteries of (KJV) / the secrets of (RSV) • of heaven, but (KJV) / of God, but (RSV)
Mk. 4:12   And we will do this so / so (RSV)
Mt. 13:12   has shall more (KJV) / has will more (RSV) • he shall have (KJV) / he will have (RSV) • has shall be (KJV) / has will be (RSV)
Mt. 13:14   says: / says: 'You shall indeed hear but never understand and you shall indeed see but never perceive. (RSV)
Mt. 13:15   Isaiah 6:9–10 • has waxed gross, and (KJV) / has grown dull, and (RSV) • are dull of (KJV) / are heavy of (RSV) • heart.'" / heart, and turn for me to heal them.'" (RSV)
Mk. 4:29   And when / But when (RSV) (151:1,3/1689,93)

61

49. More Parables Beside the Sea[a]

24Another parable he put before them, saying, "The kingdom of heaven may be compared to a man who sowed good seed in his field; 25but while men were sleeping, his enemy came and sowed weeds among the wheat, and went away. 26So when the plants came up and bore grain, then the weeds appeared also. 27And the servants of the householder came and said to him: 'Sir, did you not sow good seed in your field? How then has it weeds?' 28He said to them, 'An enemy has done this.' The servants said to him, 'Then do you want us to go and gather them?' 29But he said, 'No, lest in gathering the weeds you root up the wheat along with them. 30Let them both grow together until the harvest; and at harvest time I will say to the reapers, 'Gather the weeds first and bind them in bundles to be burned, but gather the wheat into my barn.'"

31Another parable he put before them, saying, "The kingdom of heaven is like a grain of mustard seed which a man took and sowed in his field. 32It is the smallest of all seeds, but when it has grown it is the greatest of shrubs and becomes a tree so that the birds of the air come and make nests in its branches."

33He told them another parable. "The kingdom of heaven is like leaven which a woman took and hid in three measures of flour, till it was all leavened."

(Mt. 13:24–33) *(continued)*

---

a "More Parables Beside the Sea"—Jesus teaches eight parables beside the Sea of Galilee. They may be identified and listed as follows:
(1) *The Parable of the Sower*
(2) *The Parable of the Seed*
(3) *The Parable of the Weeds*
(4) *The Grain of Mustard Seed*
(5) *The Parable of the Leaven*
(6) *The Treasure Hidden in a Field*
(7) *The Pearl of Great Price*
(8) *The Parable of the Net*

(151:4/1693–4)

49. More Parables Beside the Sea (continued)

[44]"The kingdom of heaven is like[b] a treasure hidden in a field, which a man found and covered up. Then in his joy he goes and sells all that he has and buys that field."

[45]"Again, the kingdom of heaven is like a merchant in search of fine pearls, [46]who, on finding one pearl of great price, went forth and sold all that he had and bought it."

[47]"Again, the kingdom of heaven is like a net which was thrown into the sea and gathered fish of every kind. [48]When it was full, men drew it ashore and sat down and sorted the good into vessels but threw away the bad."

[33]With many such parables he spoke the word to them as they were able to hear it. [34]He did not speak to them without a parable; but privately to his own disciples he explained everything.[c]

(Mt. 13:44–48; Mk. 4:33–34)

---

b   "The kingdom of heaven is like"—The central focus of Jesus' teaching mission on earth was the kingdom of heaven. The fundamental importance and centrality of the kingdom idea is clearly shown in Jesus' parables. Many begin with words such as these: "The kingdom of heaven is like . . . "

This heavenly kingdom that Jesus taught is the rule of God in the heart of the individual believer. Jesus' parables help us understand various aspects of this inner spiritual kingdom. For example: *The Sower* describes the mixed reception of the kingdom in those who hear it proclaimed; *The Parable of the Seed*, *The Grain of Mustard Seed*, and *The Parable of the Leaven* picture the growth and development of the kingdom; *The Treasure Hidden in a Field* and *The Pearl of Great Price* emphasize the great value of the kingdom; and *The Parable of the Weeds* and *The Parable of the Net* refer to the inevitable judgment and separation of good and evil that characterizes the kingdom.

c   "He did not speak to them without a parable; but privately to his own disciples he explained everything."—Jesus continued to teach openly to his apostles and devoted believers, but from this time forward, when speaking to large crowds and those who opposed him, he taught mainly in parables.

Mt. 13:45 great price, went (KJV) / great value, went (RSV) (151:4/1693–4)

63

50. The Visit to Gerasa

¹⁸Now when Jesus saw great crowds around him, he gave orders to go over to the other side.*ᵃ* ²³And when he got into the boat his apostles followed him. ³⁷And a great storm of wind arose,*ᵇ* and the waves beat into the boat, so that the boat was already filling. ³⁸Jesus was in the stern, asleep on the cushion. They woke him and said to him, "Teacher, do you not care if we perish?"

³⁹And he awoke and said, "Peace, be still."

And the wind ceased, and there was a great calm.

⁴⁰He said to them, "Why are you afraid? Have you no faith?"

⁴¹And they were filled with awe, and said to one another, "Who then is this, that even the wind and sea obey him?"

(Mt. 8:18, 23; Mk. 4:37–41)

---

a   "go over to the other side"—Go to the other side of the Sea of Galilee (go from Capernaum to the eastern shore). (See map on page 69.) Jesus is seeking rest from the crowds; he is so fatigued that even a violent windstorm does not awaken him.

b   "a great storm of wind arose"—Violent and sudden windstorms are characteristic of the Sea of Galilee. These gales come on quickly and sometimes go away just as suddenly.

Mt. 8:23   his apostles followed (Ch. 22, fn. *a*) / his disciples followed (RSV)
Mk. 4:38   Jesus / But he (RSV) • cushion. They / cushion and they (RSV)
Mk. 4:39   and said, "Peace / and rebuked the wind and said to the sea, "Peace (RSV)   (151:5/1694–5)

51. The Gerasa Lunatic

[1]They came to the other side of the sea, to the country of the Gerasenes.[a] [2]And when he had come out of the boat, there met him a man [3]who lived among the tombs; and no one could bind him anymore, even with a chain. [4]He had often been bound with fetters and chains, but the chains he wrenched apart, and the fetters he broke in pieces; and no one had the strength to subdue him. [5]Night and day among the tombs and on the mountains he was always crying out, and bruising himself with stones. [6]And when he saw Jesus from afar, he ran and worshiped him; [7]and crying out with a loud voice, he said, "What have you to do with me, Jesus? I beseech you, do not torment me."

[11]Now a great herd of swine was feeding there on the hillside; [13]and the herd rushed down over the steep bank[b] into the sea, and were drowned in the sea. [14]The herdsmen fled, and told it in the city and in the country. And the people came to see what it was that had happened. [15]And they came to Jesus, and saw the man sitting there, clothed and in his right mind, and they were afraid. [16]And those who had seen it told what had happened to the man and to the swine. [17]And they began to beg Jesus to depart from their neighborhood.[c] [18]As he was getting into the boat, the man begged him that he might be with him.

[19]But he refused, and said to him, "Go home to your friends, and tell them how much the Lord has done for you, and how he has had mercy on you."

[20]And the man went away and began to proclaim in the Decapolis[d] how much Jesus had done for him; and all men marveled.

(Mk. 5:1–7, 11, 13–20)

---

a "the country of the Gerasenes"—Also referred to as the country of the Gaderenes. (Mt. 8:28) Gerasa (Kheresa) is identified with ruins now called Kerza. It is about five miles from where the Jordan enters the Sea of Galilee. (See map on page 69.)

b "the steep bank"—Most of the eastern shore slopes up gently to the highlands beyond, but just south of Geresa is the only place where steep hills come close to the water such that swine could have rushed over a steep bank. (*Haley's Bible Handbook*, p. 467)

c "And they began to beg Jesus to depart from their neighborhood."—The herdsmen and those who witnessed the event all believed that Jesus had cast a legion of demons out of the troubled man, and that the demons had then entered a herd of swine and caused them to rush over the cliff to their death. This made them afraid, perhaps of losing more of their swine.

d "Decapolis"—The area east of the Jordan that contained a number of Greek cities. (See map on page 24.)

Mk. 5:2   him a / him out of the tombs a (RSV) • man who / man with an unclean spirit, who (RSV)
Mt. 5:7   Jesus? I / Jesus, Son of the Most High God? I (RSV) • I beseech you, do / I adjure you, by God, do (RSV)
Mt. 5:13   herd rushed / herd numbering about 2,000 rushed (RSV)
Mk. 5:15   the man sitting / the demoniac sitting (RSV) • mind, and / mind, the man who had had the legion; and (RSV)
Mk. 5:16   the man and / the demoniac and (RSV)
Mk. 5:18   man begged / man who had been possessed with demons begged (RSV) (151:6/1695–7)

XIV. Events Preceding the Crisis at Capernaum

52. On the Way to Jairus' House

²¹And when Jesus had crossed again in the boat to the other side (from Gerasa back to Capernaum), a great crowd gathered about him; and he was beside the sea. ²²Then came one of the rulers of the synagogue, Jairus by name; and seeing him, he fell at his feet, ²³and besought him, saying, "My little daughter is at the point of death. Come and lay your hands on her, so that she may be made well, and live." ²⁴And he went with him.

And a great crowd followed and thronged about him. ²⁵There was a woman who had a flow of blood for twelve years, ²⁶and who had suffered much under many physicians. She had spent all that she had, and was no better but rather grew worse. ²⁷She had heard the reports about Jesus, and came up behind him in the crowd and touched his garment. ²⁸For she said, "If I touch even the hem of his garment, I shall be made whole." ²⁹And immediately the hemorrhage ceased; and she felt in her body that she was healed of her disease.

³⁰And Jesus, perceiving in himself that power had gone forth from him, immediately turned about in the crowd, and said, "Who touched my garments?"

³¹And his disciples said to him, "You see the crowd pressing around you, and yet you say, 'Who touched me?'"

³²And he looked around to see who had done it. ³³But the woman, knowing what had been done to her, came in fear and trembling and fell down before him, and told him the whole truth. ³⁴And he said to her, "Daughter, your faith has made you whole;ᵃ go in peace."

(Mk. 5:21–34)

---

a "your faith has made you whole"—This incident is a very clear example of the healing power of living faith. It required only the contact of the woman's *faith* with the person of Jesus and a miraculous healing was effected. Jesus was not even aware of the healing, nor did he consciously will it; creative power went out from him in response to the woman's faith. Jesus uses this incident to emphasize that *faith* had wrought the cure; he did not want others to think that her superstition in associating the cure with the touching of his garment had been effective. He announces to the woman and the great crowd that thronged about him, *"your faith has made you whole."*

Mk. 5:21   side (from Geresa back to Capernaum), a (See Ch. 51) / side, a (RSV)
Mk. 5:25   There / And there (RSV)
Mk. 5:26   physicians. She / physicians and she (KJV)
Mk. 5:28   even the hem of his garment, I / even his garments, I (RSV) • made whole (KJV) / made well (RSV)
Mk. 5:34   you whole; (KJV) / you well; (RSV) • peace." / peace, and be healed of your disease." (RSV) (152:0/1698)

53. Awakening Jairus' Daughter

35While he was still speaking, there came from the ruler's house some who said, "Your daughter is dead. Why trouble the teacher any further?"

36But ignoring what they said, Jesus said to the ruler of the synagogue, "Fear not, only believe." 37And he allowed no one to follow him except Peter and James and John the brother of James. 38When they came to the house of the ruler of the synagogue, he saw a tumult, people weeping and wailing loudly. 39And when he had entered, he said to them, "Why do you make a tumult and weep? The child is not dead but sleeping."*a*

40And they laughed at him. But he put them all outside, and took the child's father and mother and those who were with him, and went in where the child was. 41Taking her by the hand he said to her, "Talitha cumi"; which means, "Little girl, I say to you, arise."

42And immediately the girl got up and walked (she was twelve years of age) and they were overcome with amazement. 43And he strictly charged them that no one should know this and told them to give her something to eat. (Mk. 5:35–43)

---

a "The child is not dead but sleeping."—Although the crowd of mourners at Jairus' house thought the girl had died, Jesus here specifically states that the girl is not dead, but only sleeping. Perhaps she had slipped into a coma following a serious illness and Jesus brought her out of it.

Mk. 5:36   synagogue, "Fear not, only (ASV) / synagogue, "Do not fear, only (RSV)
Mk. 5:42   were overcome / were immediately overcome (RSV) (152:1/1699)

54. Feeding the Five Thousand

31Jesus said to the apostles, "Let us go away by ourselves to a lonely place and rest a while." For many were coming and going, and they had no leisure even to eat. 32And they went away in the boat to a lonely place*a* by themselves. 33Now many saw them going, and they ran there on foot from all the towns, and got there ahead of them. 34When Jesus went ashore he saw a great throng, and he had compassion on them, because they were like sheep without a shepherd; and he began to teach them many things. 35And when it grew late, his disciples came to him and said, "This is a lonely place, and the hour is now late; 36send them away, to go into the country and villages around about and buy themselves something to eat."

37But he answered them, "You give them something to eat."

And they said to him, "Shall we go and buy two hundred denarii worth of bread, and give it to them to eat?"

38And he said to them, "How many loaves have you? Go and see."

And when they had found out, they said, "Five loaves, and two fish."

39Then he commanded them all to sit down by companies upon the green grass. 40So they sat down in groups, by hundreds and by fifties. 41And taking the five loaves and the two fish he looked up to heaven, and blessed them, and broke the loaves, and gave them to the disciples to set before the people; and he divided the two fish among them all. 42And they all ate and were satisfied. 43And they took up twelve baskets full of fragments, and of the fish. 44And those who ate the loaves and the fish were five thousand.

(Mk. 6:31–44)

---

a "And they went away in the boat to a lonely place"—John, in discussing this event states only that they went "to the other side of the Sea of Galilee." (Jn. 6:1) Since Jesus' early ministry centers around Capernaum and they "went away in the boat," they probably left from Capernaum. They returned to Capernaum after the feeding of the 5,000. (Ch. 56, Jn. 6:23–26)

Where did they go? The most likely location is the area of Bethsaida-Julias. There was a public park at Magidan, just south of Bethsaida-Julias, on the other side of the Sea of Galilee and less than five miles away by boat. (See map on page 24.)

Mk. 6:31   Jesus said to the apostles, "Let us go away by ourselves to / And he said to them, "Come away by yourselves to (RSV)
Mk. 6:33   going, and / going, and knew them, and (RSV)
Mk. 6:34   When Jesus went / As he went (RSV)
Mk. 6:38   Five loaves, and / Five, and (RSV)
Mk. 6:43   (KJV) • the fish (RSV) / the fishes (KJV)
Mk. 6:44   loaves and the fish were / loaves were (RSV) (152:2/1700–2)

55. The Attempt to Make Jesus King

[14]When the people saw the sign which he had done,[a] they said, "This is indeed the prophet who is to come into the world!"[b]

[15]Perceiving then that they were about to come and take him by force to make him king, Jesus withdrew again to the mountain by himself.

[16]When evening came, his apostles went down to the sea, [17]got into a boat, and started across the sea to Capernaum. It was now dark, and Jesus had not yet come to them. [18]The sea rose because a strong wind was blowing. [48]And they made headway painfully, for the wind was against them. [53]And when they had crossed over, they came to land at Gennesaret, and moored to the shore.

(Jn. 6:14–18; Mk. 6:48, 53)

---

a "saw the sign which he had done"—The feeding of the five thousand. (See Ch. 54.)

b "the prophet who is to come into the world"—The ancient prophets predicted a Messiah who would usher in an era of wondrous plenty, e.g., "And I will set over them one shepherd, my servant David, and he shall feed them. And I will send down the showers in their season; they shall be showers of blessing." (Ez. 34:23, 26) Jesus had fed the five thousand, and they believed this fulfilled the prophecy and meant Jesus should be their king. (See also Ch. 13, fn. *c*.)

Jn. 6:16   his apostles went (Ch. 22, fn. *a*) / his disciples went (RSV)
Mk. 6:48   And they made headway / And he saw that they were making headway (RSV) (152:3–4/1702–3)

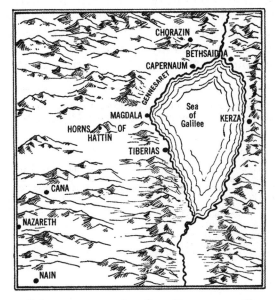

"they came to land at Gennesaret"

XV. The Crisis at Capernaum

56. Sermon on the Bread of Life

²³Boats from Tiberias came near the place where they ate the bread after the Lord had given thanks.ᵃ ²⁴When the people saw that Jesus was not there, nor his disciples, they themselves got into the boats and went to Capernaum, seeking Jesus.

²⁶Jesus said to them, "You seek me because you ate your fill of the loaves. ²⁷Labor not for the food which perishes, but for the spiritual food which endures to eternal life, which the Son of Man shall give you."

²⁸Then they said to him, "What must we do, to be doing the works of God?"

²⁹Jesus answered them, "This is the work of God, that you believe him whom He has sent."

³⁰So they said to him, "Then what sign do you do, that we may see, and believe you? What work do you perform? ³¹Our fathers ate the manna in the wilderness, as it is written, 'He gave them bread from heaven to eat.'"

³²Jesus then said to them, "I say to you, it was not Moses who gave you the bread from heaven; my Father gives you the true bread from heaven. ³³The bread of God is that which comes down from heaven and gives life to the men of the world."

³⁴They said to him, "Lord give us this bread."

³⁵Jesus said to them, "I am the bread of life, he who comes to me shall not hunger, and he who believes me shall not thirst. ³⁶You have seen me and yet do not believe. ³⁷All that the Father gives me shall come to me, and him who comes to me I will not cast out."

(Jn. 6:23–24, 26–37) *(continued)*

---

a   "the place where they ate the bread after the Lord had given thanks."—This refers to the feeding of the five thousand, which probably occurred at Magidan Park south of Bethsaida-Julias. (See map on page 24.)

Jn. 6:23   Boats / However, boats (RSV)
Jn. 6:24   When / So when (RSV)
Jn. 6:26   Jesus said to them / Jesus answered them (RSV) • them, "You / them, "Truly, truly, I say to you, you (RSV) • me because / me not because (RSV) • you ate / you saw the signs but because you ate (RSV)
Jn. 6:27   Labor not for (KJV) / Do not labor for (RSV) • the spiritual food / the food (RSV) • Man shall give (KJV) / Man will give (RSV)
Jn. 6:29   believe him / believe in him (RSV)
Jn. 6:32   them, "I / them, "Truly, truly, I (RSV)
Jn. 6:34   bread." / bread always." (RSV)
Jn. 6:35   believes me / believes in me (RSV)
Jn. 6:36   You / But I said to you that you (RSV)
Jn. 6:37   me shall come (KJV) / me will come (RSV)   (153:2/1710–1)

56. Sermon on the Bread of Life (continued)

[38]"For I have come down from heaven, not to do my own will, but the will of him who sent me.[b] [39]And this is the will of him who sent me, that I should lose nothing of all that he has given me. [40]And this is the will of my Father, that everyone who sees the Son and believes him should have eternal life."

[41]The Jews then murmured at him, because he said, "I am the bread which came down from heaven." [42]And they said, "Is not this Jesus, the son of Joseph, whose father and mother we know? How does he now say, 'I have come down from heaven'?"

[43]Jesus answered them, "Do not murmur among yourselves. [45]It is written in the prophets, 'And they shall all be taught by God.' Everyone who has heard and learned from the Father comes to me. [46]Not that anyone has seen the Father except him who is from God; he has seen the Father. [47]Truly, truly, I say to you, he who believes has eternal life."

[48]"I am the bread of life. [49]Your fathers ate the manna in the wilderness, and they died. [50]This is the bread which comes down from heaven, that a man may eat of it and never die. [51]I am this living bread, and if any man eats of this bread, he shall live for ever."[c]

[59]This he said in the synagogue, as he taught at Capernaum.[d]

[60]Many of his disciples, when they heard this, said, "This is a hard saying, who can understand it?"

(Jn. 6:38–43, 45–51, 59–60)

---

b   "For I have come down from heaven, not to do my own will, but the will of him who sent me."—Jesus' life on earth was devoted to one great purpose—*doing the Father's will.* His life of faith submission to God's will is our ideal example; it inspires us to ever seek to know and do the Father's will.

c   "I am this living bread and if any man eats of this bread, he shall live for ever."—Jesus *is* the Word of God; his life in the flesh and the word he spoke *is* the bread of life.

d   "as he taught at Capernaum"—This sermon in the synagogue marks the turning point in Jesus' relations with the Jerusalem religious leaders. Before this time there had existed an increasingly uneasy peace. After this sermon, in which Jesus proclaimed himself to be the "bread of life," there existed open hostility between the established religious leaders and Jesus.

Jn. 6:39   me. / me, but raise it up at the last day (RSV)
Jn. 6:40   And this (KJV) / For this (RSV) • believes him / believes in him (RSV)
Jn. 6:45   Isaiah 54:13
Jn. 6:51   am this living / am the living (RSV) • bread, and if / bread which came down from heaven; if • any man eats (KJV) / any one eats (RSV) • he shall live (KJV) / he will live (RSV)
Jn. 6:69   heard this, said / heard it, said (RSV) • can understand it? / can listen to it? (RSV) (153:2–3/1711–2)

57. After the Sermon

¹The Pharisees along with the scribes who had come from Jerusalem ²noticed that some of his disciples ate with hands defiled, that is, unwashed. ³(For the Pharisees, and all the Jews, do not eat unless they wash their hands, observing the tradition of the elders; ⁴and when they come from the market place, they do not eat unless they purify themselves; and there are many other traditions which they observe, including the washing of cups and pots and vessels of bronze.) ⁵And the Pharisees and the scribes asked him, "Why do your disciples not live according to the tradition of the elders, but eat with hands defiled?"

³He answered them, "And why do you transgress the commandment of God for the sake of your tradition? ⁴For God commanded, 'Honor your father and your mother.' ⁵But you say, 'If anyone tells his father or his mother, What you would have gained from me is given to God, he need not honor his father.'ᵃ ⁶So, for the sake of your tradition, you have made void the word of God. ⁸You leave the commandment of God, and hold fast the tradition of men. And many such like things you do."

(Mk. 7:1–5; Mt. 15:3–6; Mk. 7:8) *(continued)*

---

a   "need not honor his father"—That is, the children would say that the part of their wealth they would normally have given to their parents had been given to God instead. This enabled them to not share their wealth with their parents in need—thereby they disobeyed the commandment to "honor your father and your mother."

The Jerusalem religious leaders accused Jesus of transgressing the tradition of the elders; he answered them by pointing out that they put their own teachings and traditions above God's commandments.

Mk. 7:1   The / Now when the (RSV) • Pharisees along with the / Pharisees gathered together to him with some of the (RSV)
Mk. 7:2   noticed that (NEB) / they saw that (RSV)
Mk. 7:4   observe, including the / observe, the (RSV)
Mt. 15:4   mother.' / mother,' and, 'he who speaks evil of father or mother let him surely die.' (RSV)
Mk. 7:8   men. And many such like things you do. (KJV) / men. (RSV) (153:3/1712)

57. After the Sermon (continued)

10And he called the people to him and said: "Hear and understand: 11It is not what goes into the mouth that defiles a man, but what comes out of the mouth."

12Then the apostles came and said to him, "Do you know that the Pharisees were offended when they heard this saying?"

13He answered, "Every plant which my heavenly Father has not planted will be rooted up. 14Let them alone. They are blind guides. And if the blind lead the blind, both shall fall into the pit."

15But Peter said to him, "Explain the parable to us."

16And he said, "Are you also still without understanding? 17Do you not see that whatever goes into the mouth passes into the stomach, and so passes on? 18But what comes out of the mouth proceeds from the heart, and this defiles a man. 19For out of the heart come evil thoughts, murder, adultery, theft, false witness, and slander. 20These are what defile a man; but to eat with unwashed hands does not defile a man."

(Mt. 15:10–20)

Mt. 15:11 It is not / not (RSV) • mouth that defiles / mouth, this defiles (RSV)
Mt. 15:12 the apostles came (Ch. 22, fn. *a*) / the disciples came (RSV)
Mt. 15:14 if the blind lead the blind, both (KJV) / if a blind man leads a blind man, both (RSV) • both shall fall (KJV) / both will fall (RSV) • into the pit (KJV) / into a pit (RSV)
Mt. 15:19 adultery, theft / adultery, fornication, theft (RSV)   (153:3/1712–3)

58. Open Conflict with the Scribes and Pharisees

²²Then a blind and dumb demonic was brought to him, and he healed him, so that the dumb man spoke and saw. ²³And all the people were amazed and said, "Can this be the son of David?"*ᵃ* ²⁴But when the Pharisees heard it they said, "It is only by Beelzebub, the prince of demons, that this man casts out demons."

²⁵Knowing their thoughts, he said to them, "Every kingdom divided against itself is laid waste, and no city or house divided against itself will stand. ²⁶And if Satan casts out Satan, he is divided against himself; how then shall his kingdom stand? ²⁹Or how can one enter a strong man's house and plunder his goods, unless he first binds the strong man? ²⁷And if I cast out demons by Beelzebub, by whom do your sons cast them out? Therefore they shall be your judges. ²⁸But if it is by the spirit of God that I cast out demons, then the kingdom of God has come upon you. ³⁰He who is not with me is against me, and he who does not gather with me scatters.

³¹Therefore I tell you, every sin and blasphemy shall be forgiven men, but the blasphemy against the Spirit shall not be forgiven."

³³"You must either make the tree good and its fruit good, else will the tree become corrupt and its fruit corrupt. The tree is known by its fruit.*ᵇ* ³⁴You brood of vipers! how can you bring forth good, when you have already chosen evil? For out of the abundance of the heart the mouth speaks. ³⁵The good man out of his good treasure brings forth good, and the evil man out of his evil treasure brings forth evil."

³⁸Then some of the scribes and Pharisees said to him, "Teacher, we wish to see a sign from you."

³⁹But he answered them, "An evil and faithless generation seeks for a sign; but no sign shall be given to it except the sign of the prophet Jonah. ⁴⁰For as Jonah was three days and three nights in the belly of the whale, so will the Son of Man be three days and three nights in the heart of the earth."

(Mt. 12:22–26, 29, 27–28, 30–31, 33–35, 38–40)

---

a   "the son of David"—The "son of David" was a commonly accepted title for the promised Messiah. (See also Ch. 13, fn. *c*.)

b   "The tree is known by its fruit."—Paul, in his letter to the Galatians, lists some of the fruit of the spirit as "love, joy, peace, patience, kindness, goodness, faithfulness, gentleness, [and] self-control." (Gal. 5:22)

Mt. 12:26 then shall his (KJV) / then will his (RSV)
Mt. 12:31 blasphemy shall be (KJV) / blasphemy will be (RSV) • spirit shall not (KJV) / spirit will not (RSV)
Mt. 12:33 you must either (Phi) / Either (RSV) • good, else will the tree become corrupt and its fruit corrupt / good; or make the tree bad and its fruit bad. (RSV) • The / For the (RSV)
Mt. 12:34 you bring forth good / speak good (RSV) • you have already chosen evil / you are evil (RSV)
Mt. 12:39 and faithless generation (Gspd) / and adulterous generation (RSV) (153:4/1713–4)

59. Later Words with the Apostles

61But Jesus, knowing in himself that his apostles murmured, said to them, "Do you take offense at this? 62Then what if you were to see the Son of Man ascending where he was before?"

63"It is the spirit that quickens, the flesh is of no avail; the words that I have spoken to you are spirit and life. 64But there are some of you that do not believe." (For Jesus knew from the first who those were that did not believe, and who it was that would betray him.)

66After this*a* many of his disciples drew back and no longer went about with him.

67Jesus said to the twelve, "Do you also wish to go away?"

68Simon Peter answered him, "Lord, you have taught us the words of eternal life; 69and we have believed, and have come to know, that you are the Holy One of God."

(Jn. 6:61–64, 66–69)

---

a "After this"—After Jesus refused the crowd's effort to make him king and the Jerusalem religious leaders openly opposed and denounced him, many of his followers turned away, and Jesus no longer enjoyed popular favor.

Jn. 6:61   his apostles murmured, (Ch. 22, fn. *a*) / his disciples murmured, (RSV) • murmured, said / murmured at it, said (RSV)
Jn. 6:63   that quickens, the (KJV) / that gives life, the (RSV)
Jn. 6:64   knew from the first who / knew who (RSV)
Jn. 6:68   Lord, you / Lord, to whom shall we go? You (RSV) • have taught us the / have the (RSV) (153:5/1715–6)

60. Last Words at Capernaum

7Now Herod the tetrarch heard of all that was done, and he was perplexed. It was said by some that John had been raised from the dead, 8by some that Elijah had appeared, and by others that one of the old prophets had risen. 9Herod said, "John I beheaded; but who is this about whom I hear such things?"

46While Jesus was speaking to the people, behold, his mother and his brothers stood outside, asking to speak to him. 48But he replied to the man who told him, "Who is my mother, and who are my brothers?" 49And stretching out his hand toward his disciples, he said, "Here are my mother and my brothers! 50For whoever does the will of my Father in heaven is my brother, and sister, and mother."[a]

27As he said this a woman in the crowd raised her voice and said to him, "Blessed is the womb that bore you, and the breasts that you sucked!"

28But he said, "Blessed rather are those who hear the word of God and keep it!"[b]

(Lk. 9:7–9; Mt. 12:46, 48–50; Lk. 11:27–28)

---

a   "whoever does the will of my Father in heaven is my brother, and sister, and mother."—Here again is revealed the core of Jesus' personal religion, the doing of the Father's will. All those who do the Father's will are part of Jesus' spiritual family, members of the divine brotherhood of the kingdom of heaven.

b   "Blessed rather are those who hear the word of God and keep it"—Jesus' teachings are the word of God. Our part is to *learn* the teachings of Jesus ("hear the word of God") and then to *live* the teachings ("keep it").

Lk. 9:7   perplexed. It / perplexed because it (RSV)
Mt. 12:46   While Jesus was speaking to / While he was still speaking to (RSV) (154:0,6/1717,21–22)

XVI. The Retreat from Galilee

61. At Tyre and Sidon

²¹And Jesus went away from there (Capernaum) and withdrew to the district of Tyre and Sidon. ²⁴And he entered a house and would not have anyone know it; yet he could not be hid.

²²And behold a Canaanite woman from that region came out and cried, "Have mercy on me; my daughter is severely possessed by a demon."

²⁸Then Jesus answered her, "O woman, great is your faith! Be it done for you as you desire."

And her daughter was healed instantly.

(Mt. 15:21; Mk. 7:24; Mt. 15:22, 28)

Mt. 15:21 there (Capernaum) and / there and (RSV)
Mt. 15:22 me; my / me, O Lord, Son of David; my (RSV) (156:0–1/1734–5)

62. At Magadan

³⁹Jesus went to the region of Magadan.ᵃ ¹And the Pharisees and Sadducees came, and to test him they asked him to show them a sign from heaven.

²He answered them, "When it is evening, you say it will be fair weather, for the sky is red; ³in the morning it will be foul weather, for the sky is red and threatening. You know how to discern the face of the sky, but you cannot discern the signs of the times. ⁴An evil generation seeks for a sign, but no sign shall be given." So he left them and departed.

⁶And Jesus said to his disciples, "Take heed and beware of the leaven of the Pharisees and Sadducees."

(Mt. 15:39; 16:1–4, 6)

---

a   "Magadan"—a public park just south of Bethsaida-Julius. (See map on page 24.)

Mt. 15:39 Jesus went / And sending away the crowds, he got into the boat and went (RSV)
Mt. 16:3 in / And in (RSV) • be foul weather, for (KJV) / be stormy today, for (RSV) • discern the face of (KJV) / interpret the appearance of (RSV) • cannot discern the (KJV) / cannot interpret the (RSV)
Mt. 16:4 evil generation / evil and adulterous generation (RSV) • given." / given to it except the sign of Jonah." (RSV) (157:2/1744–5)

63. At Caesarea Philippi; Peter's Confession

¹³Now when Jesus came into the district of Caesarea Philippi,*ᵃ* he asked his apostles, "Who do men say that the Son of Man is?"

¹⁴And they said, "Some say John the Baptist, others say Elijah, and others Jeremiah, or one of the prophets."

¹⁵He said to them, "But who do you say that I am?"

¹⁶Simon Peter replied, "You are the Messiah, the Son of the living God."*ᵇ*

¹⁷And Jesus said, "Flesh and blood has not revealed this to you, but my Father who is in heaven. ¹⁸And I tell you, on this rock I will build my church,*ᶜ* and the powers of death shall not prevail against it. ¹⁹And I will give you the keys of the kingdom."

²⁴Then Jesus told his disciples, "If any man would come after me, let him deny himself and take up his cross and follow me."*ᵈ*

(Mt. 16:13–19, 24)

---

a "Caesarea Philippi"—The capital of the tetrarch Philip's domain. (See map on page 24.)

b "You are the Messiah, the Son of the living God."—Here, for the first time, the apostles (with Peter as their spokesman) affirm their belief that Jesus is not only the Messiah (the Christ, the anointed one)—but also the *divine* Son of God.

c "on this rock I will build my church"—What is this *rock*? It is the apostle's confession, through the insight of the Father's spirit ("Flesh and blood has not revealed this to you, but my Father who is in heaven"), that Jesus is the *Son of God*. Jesus declares that on this rock of recognized spiritual reality (You are "the Son of the living God"), he will build his church—the spiritual brotherhood of the kingdom of heaven.

d "take up his cross and follow me."—Assume the obligations of sonship with God.

Mt. 16:13 his apostles, "Who (Ch. 22, fn. *a*) / his disciples, "Who (RSV)
Mt. 16:16 are the Messiah, the (Ch. 13, fn. *c*) / are Christ, the (RSV)
Mt. 16:17 Jesus said, "Flesh / Jesus answered him, "Blessed are you Simon Bar-Jona! For flesh (RSV)
Mt. 16:18 you, on / you, you are Peter, and on (RSV)
Mt. 16:19 kingdom." / kingdom of heaven, and whatever you bind on earth shall be bound in heaven, and whatever you loose on earth shall be loosed in heaven." (RSV) (157:3/1745–6)

PART 3
THE SON OF GOD

XVII. The Mount of Transfiguration

64. The Transfiguration

[1]And after six days[a] Jesus took with him Peter, James, and John, and led them up a high mountain[b] apart by themselves. [2]And he was transfigured before them. His face shone like the sun, and his garments became white as light. [3]And behold there appeared to them Moses and Elijah, talking with him.

[5]And Peter said to Jesus, "Master, it is well that we are here; let us make three booths, one for you and one for Moses and one for Elijah." [6]For he did not know what to say, for they were exceedingly afraid.

[7]And a cloud overshadowed them, and a voice came out of the cloud, "This is my beloved Son; give heed to him."

[8]And suddenly looking around they no longer saw anyone with them but Jesus only.

(Mt. 17:1–3; Mk. 9:5–8)

---

a "after six days"—Six days after Peter's confession of the apostles' belief that Jesus is the Son of God.

b "led them up a high mountain"—Jesus and the apostles have retreated to the domains of Herod Philip, north of Galilee. They have recently been at Caesarea Philippi. Mt. Hermon is about 10 miles northeast of Caesarea Philippi and is the only "high mountain" in these parts. The apostles probably camped at the foot of Mt. Hermon while Jesus and the three ascended the mountain. (See map on page 24.)

Mt. 17:1   Peter, James / Peter and James (RSV) • John and / John his brother and (RSV) • apart by themselves. / apart. (RSV)
Mt. 17:2   them. His / them and his (RSV)
Mk. 9:7   give heed to (NASB alt. trans.) / listen to (RSV) (158:0–1/1752–4)

65. Coming Down the Mountain

[9]And as they were coming down the mountain, he charged them to tell no one what they had seen, until the Son of Man should have risen from the dead.[a] [10]So they kept the matter to themselves, questioning what the rising from the dead meant.

[11]And they asked him, "Why do the scribes say that first Elijah must come?"[b]

[12]And Jesus replied, "Elijah does come first to prepare the way for the Son of Man, who must suffer many things and be rejected. [13]But I tell you that Elijah has come,[c] and they did to him whatever they pleased."

(Mk. 9:9–13)

---

a   "until the Son of Man should have risen from the dead."—This is Jesus' first mention of the fact that he will die and rise from the dead. It must have shocked the apostles exceedingly.

b   "Why do the scribes say that first Elijah must come?"—The scribes and rabbis had collected many prophecies scattered throughout the Jewish Scriptures that described a coming Messiah who would deliver them from their bondage and inaugurate a new age of righteousness. Furthermore, they believed that this "anointed one" would be preceded by one who would come to prepare the way for this Messiah. In this regard they looked to the prophecy of Malachi who said, "Behold, I shall send you Elijah the prophet before the coming of the great and dreadful day of the Lord." (Mal. 4:5)

c   "I tell you that Elijah has come"—Peter and the apostles have recently confessed their belief that Jesus is the Messiah, the Son of God. (Ch. 63) Here Jesus identifies John the Baptist as his forerunner, the Elijah of Malachi's prophecy. (See fn. *b* above.)

Mk. 9:9   And as / As soon as (RSV)
Mk. 9:12   to prepare the way for / to restore all things for • for the Son / and how it is written of the Son (RSV) • Man, who must suffer / man, that he should suffer (RSV) • be rejected. (Mof) / be treated with contempt. (RSV)
Mk. 9:13   pleased. / pleased as it is written of him. (RSV) (158:2/1754)

81

66. Jesus Heals the Epileptic Boy

¹⁴And when they came to the disciples, they saw a great crowd about them, and scribes arguing with them. ¹⁵And immediately all the crowd, when they saw him, were greatly amazed, and ran up to him and greeted him.

¹⁶And he asked them, "What are you discussing with them?"

¹⁷And one of the crowd answered him, "Teacher, I brought my son to you, for he has an evil spirit; ¹⁸and whenever it seizes him, it dashes him down, and he foams and grinds his teeth and becomes rigid;ᵃ and I asked your disciples to cast it out, and they were not able."

¹⁹And he answered them, "O faithless generation, how long am I to be with you? How long shall I bear with you? Bring him to me."

²⁰And they brought the boy to him; and he fell on the ground and rolled about, foaming at the mouth.

²¹And Jesus asked his father, "How long has he been like this?"

And he said, "From childhood. ²²And it has often cast him into the fire and into the water, to destroy him; but if you can do anything, have pity on us and help us."

²³Jesus said to him, "All things are possible to him who believes."

²⁴Immediately the father of the child cried out and said, "I believe. Help my unbelief!"ᵇ

²⁵And Jesus rebuked the unclean spirit, saying to it, "I command you, come out of him, and never enter him again."

²⁶And after crying out and convulsing him terribly, it came out, and the boy was like a corpse; so that most of them said, "He is dead."

²⁷But Jesus took him by the hand and lifted him up, and he arose.

(Mk. 9:14–27)

---

a   "he has an evil spirit; and whenever it seizes him, it dashes him down, and he foams and grinds his teeth and becomes rigid"—On the surface this appears to be a case of simple epilepsy. As the *Oxford Bible* notes, "the symptoms point to an epileptic seizure." (*Oxford Bible*, p. 1226) However, a little later in the passage Jesus clearly casts out a demon. Perhaps this was a case of both epilepsy and demon possession.

b   "I believe. Help my unbelief!"—This statement of commingled faith and doubt presents an accurate and revealing picture of the human condition. We have faith but we must also reckon with our doubts. There is but one great struggle the believer must face, and that is to "fight the good fight of faith" over doubt.

Mk. 9:17 has an evil spirit; (Rieu) / has a dumb spirit; (RSV)
Mk. 9:19 long shall I bear (ASV) / long am I to bear (RSV)
Mk. 9:20 and / when the spirit saw him immediately it convulsed the boy and (RSV)
Mk. 9:21 he been like this? (Gspd) / he had this? (RSV)
Mk. 9:23 Jesus / And Jesus (RSV) • him, "All / him, "If you can! All (RSV)
Mk. 9:25 And Jesus rebuked / And when Jesus saw that a crowd came running together, he rebuked (RSV) • it, "I / it, "You dumb and deaf spirit, I (RSV) (158:4–5/1755–8)

67. Peter Protests Jesus' Death

[31]And he began to teach them that the Son of Man must suffer many things, and be rejected by the elders, the chief priests and the scribes, and be killed, and after three days rise again. [32]And he said this plainly.

And Peter took him, and began to rebuke him.[a] [33]But turning and looking at his apostles, he rebuked Peter, and said, "Get behind me, Satan! You are not on the side of God, but of men. [23]You are a stumbling block to me."

[34]And he said to them, "If any man would come after me, let him disregard himself, and take up his responsibilities, and follow me. [35]For whoever would save his life [selfishly], shall lose it, but whoever loses his life for my sake and the gospel's, shall save it. [36]What does it profit a man, to gain the whole world and lose his own soul? [37]What shall a man give in exchange for [eternal] life? [38]For whoever is not ashamed of me and of my words in this sinful generation, of him will the Son of Man also not be ashamed, when he comes in the glory of his Father with the holy angels."

(Mk. 8:31–33; Mt. 16:23; Mk. 8:34–38)

---

a   "and began to rebuke him."—This would indeed be an announcement hard for the apostles to accept. They have recently confessed that Jesus is the Son of God; now he tells them that he is to suffer and die at the hands of men.

This would also mean that the apostles will be left alone in the world without their beloved leader and Master. But perhaps uppermost in their minds is the inherent contradiction of this fact with their long cherished Jewish idea of a Messiah who would sit upon the throne at Jerusalem ruling the nations.

Mk. 8:31   elders, the / elders and the (RSV)
Mk. 8:33   and looking at his / and seeing his (RSV) • his apostles, he (Ch. 22, fn. *a*) / his disciples, he (RSV) • Satan! You / Satan! For you (RSV)
Mk. 8:34   he said / he called to him the multitude with his disciples and said (RSV) • him disregard himself / him deny himself (RSV) • his responsibilities, and / his cross and (RSV)
Mk. 8:35   life [selfishly], shall lose (KJV) / life will lose (RSV) • it, but whoever / it; and whoever (RSV) • gospel's, shall save (KJV) / gospel's will save (RSV)
Mk. 8:36   What / For what (RSV) • and lose his own soul? (KJV) / and forfeit his life? (RSV)
Mk. 8:37   What / For what (RSV) • What shall a (KJV) / what would a (RSV) • in exchange for (KJV) / in return for (RSV) • for [eternal] life? / for his life? (RSV)
Mk. 8:38   is not ashamed / is ashamed (RSV) • this sinful / this adulterous and sinful (RSV) • also not be / also be (RSV) (158:7/1759–60)

68. Back in Capernaum

[30]They went on from there[a] and passed through Galilee. And he would not have anyone know it. [33]And they came to Capernaum; and when he was in the house[b] he asked them, "What were you discussing on the way?"

[34]But they were silent; for on the way they had discussed with one another who was the greatest (in the kingdom).

[35]And he sat down and called the twelve; and he said to them, "If anyone would be first, he must be servant of all."

[36]And he took a child, and put him in the midst of them; and taking him in his arms he said to them: [3]"Truly I say to you, unless you turn and become like children, you will make little progress in the kingdom of heaven. [4]Whoever humbles himself like this child, the same is greatest in the kingdom of heaven. [37]Whoever receives one such child receives me. And whoever receives me receives not only me but him who sent me. [6]But whosoever causes one of these little ones to stumble, it would be better for him to have a great millstone fastened round his neck and to be drowned in the depths of the sea. [8]And if your hand or your eye causes you to stumble, sacrifice them; it is better to enter life minus these than to be shut out of the kingdom. [10]See that you do not despise these little ones, for their angels do always behold the faces of the heavenly hosts."

(Mk. 9:30, 33–36; Mt. 18:3–4; Mk. 9:37; Mt. 18:6, 8, 10)

---

a   "went on from there"—That is, they went on from the vicinity of Mt. Hermon back to Galilee. (See map on page 24.)

b   "in the house"—Perhaps the house of Andrew and Peter, who lived at Capernaum.

Mk. 9:34   greatest (in the kingdom). / greatest. (RSV)
Mk. 9:35   be servant / be last of all and servant (RSV)
Mt. 18:3   will make little progress in the / will never enter the (RSV)
Mt. 18:4   child, the same is greatest (KJV) / child, he is the greatest (RSV)
Mk. 9:37   child receives / child in my name receives (RSV) • not only me (Phi) / not me (RSV)
Mt. 18:6   ones to / ones who believe in me to (RSV)
Mt. 18:8   your eye causes (Mt. 18:9) / your foot causes (RSV) • to stumble, sacrifice them; / to sin, pluck it out and throw it away; (RSV) • life minus these than / life maimed or lame than (RSV) • than to be shut out of the kingdom. / than with two hands or two feet to be thrown into the eternal fire. (RSV)
Mt. 18:10   for their / for I tell you that in heaven their (RSV) • of the heavenly hosts / of my Father who is in heaven (RSV) (158:7–8/1759,61)

XVIII. Teaching on Forgiveness

69. The Sermon on Forgiveness

¹²"If a man has a hundred sheep, and one of them goes astray, does he not leave the ninety-nine on the mountains and go in search of the one that went astray? ¹³And if he finds it, he rejoices over it more than over the ninety-nine that never went astray. ¹⁴Even so, it is not the will of my Father who is in heaven that one of these little ones should perish."

¹⁵"If your brother sins against you, go and tell him his fault,ᵃ between you and him alone. If he listens to you, you have won your brother. ¹⁶But if he will not hear you, take one or two others along with you that every word may be confirmed by the evidence of two or three witnesses. ¹⁷If he refuses to listen to them, tell it to the congregation, and if he refuses to listen even to the congregation, let him be to you as a heathen and a tax collector. ¹⁸Whatever you bind on earth shall be bound in heaven, and whatever you loose on earth shall be loosed in heaven.ᵇ ¹⁹Where two of you agree on earth about anything they ask, it shall be done for them by my Father in heaven.ᶜ ²⁰For where two or three are gathered in my name, there am I in the midst of them."

(Mt. 18:12–20) *(continued)*

---

a   "tell him his fault"—Jesus' way is to speak with tact, tolerance, and patience.

b   "Whatever you bind on earth shall be bound in heaven, and whatever you loose on earth shall be loosed in heaven."—Whatever is decided upon and decreed by the brotherhood of believers on earth will be recognized in heaven.

c   "Where two of you agree on earth about anything they ask, it shall be done for them by my Father in heaven."—(if it is not inconsistent with the Father's will).

Mt. 18:12   "If / "What do you think? If (RSV)
Mt. 18:13   it, he / it, truly, I say to you, he (RSV)
Mt. 18:14   Even so, (KJV) / So, (RSV)
Mt. 18:15   have won your (Wms) / have gained your (RSV)
Mt. 18:16   he will not hear you, take (KJV) / he does not listen, take (RSV)
Mt. 18:17   the congregation, and (Gspd) / the church; and (RSV)
Mt. 18:18   Whatever / Truly, I say to you, whatever (RSV)
Mt. 18:19   Where two / Again I say to you, if two (RSV) • it shall be (KJV) / it will be (RSV)
Mt. 18:20   there am I in (KJV) / there I am in (RSV) (159:1/1762–3)

69. The Sermon on Forgiveness (continued)

²¹Then Peter came up and said to him, "Lord, how often shall my brother sin against me, and I forgive him? As many as seven times?"

²²Jesus said to him, "Not seven times, but seventy-seven times.ᵈ ²³Therefore the kingdom may be likened toᵉ a king who wished to settle accounts with his servants. ²⁴When he began the reckoning, one was brought to him who owed him ten thousand talents.ᶠ ²⁵And as he could not pay, his lord ordered him to be sold, with his wife and children and all that he had, and payment to be made. ²⁶So the servant fell on his knees, imploring him, 'Lord, have patience with me, and I will pay you everything.' ²⁷And out of compassion for him the lord of that servant released him and forgave him the debt."

²⁸"But that same servant, as he went out, came upon one of his fellow servants who owed him a hundred denarii,ᵍ and seizing him by the throat he said, 'Pay what you owe.' ²⁹So his fellow servant fell down and besought him, 'Have patience with me, and I will pay you.' ³⁰He refused and went and put him in prison till he should pay the debt. ³¹When his fellow servants saw what had taken place, they were greatly distressed, and they went and reported to their lord all that had taken place. ³²Then his lord summoned him and said to him: 'You wicked servant! I forgave you all the debt because you besought me; ³³and should not you have mercy on your fellow servant as I had mercy on you?' ³⁴And in anger his lord delivered him to the jailers, till he should pay all his debt."

(Mt. 18:21–34)

---

d   "Not seven times, but seventy-seven times."—Seventy-seven is an alternate translation of this verse, which is often translated "seventy times seven." (*Oxford Bible*, p. 1195) In Genesis 4:24 Lamech expresses his enthusiasm over the metal weapons of his son, "If Cain is avenged seven times, truly Lamech is avenged seventy-seven times." Perhaps Jesus is here using this statement of revenge by Lamech to teach his lesson on forgiveness.

e   "Therefore the kingdom may be likened to"—This *Parable of the Unforgiving Servant* reminds us of Jesus' prayer, "forgive us our debts, as we forgive our debtors." (Ch. 28, Mt. 6:12) Both convey the same idea: God forgives us (as the king forgave his servant), but to receive that forgiveness we must also forgive others. We expect mercy and forgiveness from our heavenly Father, therefore we should also show forgiveness and mercy to our fellow man.

f   "ten thousand talents"—A talent was more than fifteen years' wages of a laborer. (*Oxford Bible*, p. 1195) Ten thousand talents in silver content would amount to almost $10,000,000 and would be much more in buying power. (*Master Study Bible*, p. 1009)

g   "a hundred denarii"—The denarius was equivalent to one day's wage.

Mt. 18:22 "Not seven (Phi) / "I do not say to you seven (RSV) • but seventy-seven times. (RSV alt. trans.) / but seventy times seven. (RSV)
Mt. 18:23 be likened to (KJV) / be compared to (RSV)
Mt. 18:27 of compassion for (KJV) / of pity for (RSV) (159:1/1763–4)

86

70. The Strange Preacher

[38]John said to him, "Teacher, we saw a man casting out demons in your name, and we forbade him, because he was not following us."

[39]But Jesus said, "Forbid him not; for no one who does a mighty work in my name will be able soon after to speak evil of me. [40]For he that is not against us is for us. [41]For truly I say to you, whoever gives you a cup of water to drink will by no means lose his reward."[a]

(Mk. 9:38–41)

---

a   "will by no means lose his reward."—That is, such a service of love will be rewarded in heaven.

Mk. 9:39   Forbid him not; (KJV) / Do not forbid him; (RSV)
Mk. 9:41   drink will / drink because you bear the name of Christ, will (RSV)   (159:2/1794)

XIX. Jesus Attends the Feast of Tabernacles

71. Proclaiming the Gospel in Jerusalem

¹Jesus would not go about in Judea, because the Jews sought to kill him. ²Now the Jews' feast of Tabernacles was at hand.*ᵃ* ³Some said to him, "Leave here and go to Judea, that your disciples may see the works you are doing. ⁴For no man works in secret if he seeks to be known openly. If you do these things, show yourself to the world." ⁵For even his brothers did not believe in him. (Jn. 7:1–5)

---

a "Now the Jews' feast of Tabernacles was at hand."—This was the celebration of the final harvest and came in the cool autumn months (September–October). Thus it was much better attended than either the Passover at the end of winter or Pentecost (the "feast of Weeks") at the beginning of summer. The fact that this feast was attended by Jews from all over the known world made it an ideal occasion for Jesus' first public proclamation of the gospel in Jerusalem. This particular feast probably occurred in September–October, AD 29, and Jesus would have been around 35 years old.

The feast of Tabernacles was held in commemoration of the time the Hebrews lived in the wilderness before they entered Canaan. As part of this celebration, families built small huts or booths using palm and willow branches and other greenery. For many Jews the feast of Tabernacles included a pilgrimage to Jerusalem. The feast was appointed by Moses in Leviticus: "On the fifteenth day of the seventh month [according to the ecclesiastical calendar], when you have gathered in the produce of the land, you shall keep the feast of the Lord seven days. And you shall take on the first day the fruit of goodly trees, branches of palm trees, and boughs of leafy trees, and willows of the brook. You shall dwell in booths for seven days; all that are native in Israel shall dwell in booths, that your generations may know that I made the people of Israel dwell in booths when I brought them out of the land of Egypt. Thus Moses declared to the people of Israel the appointed feasts of the Lord." (Lev. 23:39, 40, 42–44)

Jn. 7:1   Jesus would / he would (RSV)
Jn. 7:3   Some said / So his brothers said (RSV) (162:1/1788–90)

72. On the Way to the Feast

⁵¹When the days drew near for him to be received up, he set his face to go to Jerusalem.ᵃ ⁵²And he sent messengers ahead of him, who went and entered a village of Samaritans, to make ready for him; ⁵³but the people would not receive him.

⁵⁴And when his disciples James and John saw it, they said, "Lord, do you want us to bid fire come down from heaven and consume them?"

⁵⁵But he turned and rebuked them and said, "You know not what manner of spirit you are of."ᵇ

⁵⁶And they went on to another village.

(Lk. 9:51–56)

---

a   "he set his face to go to Jerusalem."—Even though his followers had urged him to make himself known in Jerusalem, they certainly must have been taken aback when Jesus boldly chose to attend this feast, since the Jewish religious leaders at Jerusalem now sought to have him arrested and killed. (See Ch. 71.)

b   "You know not what manner of spirit you are of."—James and John are manifesting a vengeful attitude, and Jesus rebukes them for it.

Lk. 9:53   him. / him because his face was set toward Jerusalem. (RSV)
Lk. 9:55   KJV • spirit you are (RSV) / spirit ye are (KJV) (162:0/1788)

73. The First Talk in the Temple

²The feast of Tabernacles[a] was at hand. ¹¹The Jews were looking for Jesus at the feast, and saying, "Where is he?" ¹²And there was much muttering about him among the people. While some said, "He is a good man," others said, "No, he is leading the people astray." ¹³Yet for fear of the Jews[b] no one spoke openly of him.

¹⁴About the middle of the feast Jesus went up into the temple and taught. ¹⁵The Jews marveled at it, saying, "How is it that this man has learning, when he has never studied?"[c]

¹⁶So Jesus answered them, "My teaching is not mine, but his who sent me. ¹⁷If any man's will is to do his will, he shall know whether the teaching is from God or whether I am speaking on my own authority. ¹⁸He who speaks on his own authority seeks his own glory, but I seek the glory of him who sent me. ¹⁹Did not Moses give you the law? Yet you do not keep the law. Why do you seek to kill me?"

²⁰The people answered, "You have a demon! Who is seeking to kill you?"

²¹Jesus answered them, ²²"You circumcise a man upon the Sabbath ²³in accordance with the law of Moses, but you are angry with me because on the Sabbath I made a man's whole body well. ²⁴Do not judge by appearances, but judge with right judgment."

²⁵Some of the people of Jerusalem said, ²⁷"We know where this man comes from; but when the Messiah appears no one will know where he comes from."

(Jn. 7:2, 11–25, 27) *(continued)*

---

a   "the feast of Tabernacles"—See Ch. 71, fn. *a*, for a discussion of the feast of the Tabernacles.

b   "the Jews"—"The Jews" here refers especially to the Jewish Sanhedrin, the Supreme Court and ruling body of the Jewish nation. It was they who sought to apprehend Jesus, bring him to trial before their court, and condemn him to death. (See also Ch. 13, fn. *b*.)

c   "has never studied"—(at the schools of the rabbis in Jerusalem).

Jn. 7:2   The feast / the Jews' feast (RSV)
Jn. 7:18   but I seek the glory of him who sent me. / but he who seeks the glory of him who sent him is true, and in him there is no falsehood. (RSV)
Jn. 7:19   Yet you do not keep / Yet none of you keep (RSV)
Jn. 7:21   them, / them, "I did one deed and you all marvel at it. (RSV)
Jn. 7:22   You / Moses gave you circumcision (not that it is from Moses, but from the fathers), and you (RSV)
Jn. 7:23   in accordance with the law of Moses, but you are angry / If on the sabbath a man receives circumcision so that the law of Moses may not be broken, are you angry (RSV)
Jn. 7:25   Jerusalem said / Jerusalem therefore said (RSV) • said, / said, "Is not this the man whom they seek to kill? (RSV)
Jn. 7:27   We / Yet we (RSV) • but when / and when (RSV) • the Messiah appears (Ch. 13, fn. *c*) / the Christ appears (RSV) (162:1–2/1788–91)

73. The First Talk in the Temple (continued)

28So Jesus proclaimed as he taught in the temple, "You know me and you know where I come from? But I have not come for myself; and he who sent me is true. 29I know him, for I come from him and he sent me."

30So they sought to arrest him; but no one laid hands on him, because his hour had not yet come. 31Yet many of the people believed in him; they said, "When the Messiah appears, will he do more signs than this man has done?"

32The Pharisees heard the crowd thus muttering about him, and the chief priests and Pharisees sent officers to arrest him.

33Jesus then said, "I shall be with you a little longer, and then I go to him who sent me. 34And then you will seek me, but you will not find me; for where I am you cannot come."

35The Jews said to one another, "Where does this man intend to go that we shall not find him? Does he intend to go among the Greeks? 36What does he mean by saying, 'You will seek me and you will not find me,' and, 'Where I am you cannot come'?"

45The officers then went back to the chief priests and Pharisees, who said to them, "Why did you not bring him?"

46The officers answered, "No man ever spoke like this man!"

47The Pharisees answered them, "Are you also led astray? 48Have any of the authorities or the Pharisees believed in him? 49But this people who know not the law are accursed."

50And one of them said, 51"Does our law judge a man without first giving him a hearing and learning what he does?"

52They replied, "Are you from Galilee too? Search and you will see that no prophet is to rise from Galilee." (Jn. 7:28–36, 45–52)

Jn. 7:28   come for myself; (KJV) / come of my own accord; (RSV) • and he / he (RSV) • true. / true and him you do not know. (RSV)
Jn. 7:31   the Messiah appears, (Ch. 13, fn. *c*) / the Christ appears, (RSV)
Jn. 7:34   And then you / you (RSV) • me, but you / me, and you (RSV) • for where / where (RSV)
Jn. 7:35   to go among / to go to the dispersion among (RSV) • Greeks? / Greeks and teach the Greeks? (RSV)
Jn. 7:47   you also led (KJV) / you led (RSV) • astray? / astray, you also? (RSV)
Jn. 7:48   or the / or of the (RSV)
Jn. 7:49   (KJV) • who know not / who knoweth not (KJV)
Jn. 7:50   And one of them said, / Nicodemus, who had gone to him before, and who was one of them said (RSV) • said, "Does / said to them, "Does (RSV) (162:2/1791–92)

74. The Woman Caught in Adultery

²Early in the morning he came again to the temple; all the people came to him, and he sat down and taught them. ³The Jews brought a woman who had been caught in adultery, and placing her in the midst ⁴they said to him, "Teacher, this woman has been caught in the act of adultery. ⁵Now in the law Moses commanded us to stone such a woman. What do you say about her?" ⁶This they said to test him, that they might have some charge to bring against him.ᵃ

Jesus bent down and wrote with his finger on the ground. ⁸And once more he bent down and wrote with his finger on the ground. ⁹But when they read it, they went away, one by one, beginning with the eldest, and Jesus was left alone with the woman standing before him. ¹⁰Jesus looked up and said to her, "Woman, where are your accusers? Has no one condemned you?"

¹¹She said, "No one, Lord." And Jesus said, "Neither do I condemn you, go your way."

(Jn. 8:2–6, 8–11)

---

a   "This they said to test him, that they might have some charge to bring against him."—The Jewish leaders may have reasoned thus: If Jesus opposed stoning her, he could be accused of setting himself above Moses and the Jewish law; if he approved the stoning, he could be brought before the Roman authorities, who denied the Jews the right to execute the death sentence without their approval; and if he refused to answer, they could accuse him of cowardice.

Jn. 8:3   The Jews brought / The scribes and Pharisees brought (RSV)
Jn. 8:5   such a woman. / such. (RSV)
Jn. 8:9   they read it, / they heard it, (RSV)
Jn. 8:10   are your accusers? (Ber) / are they? (RSV)
Jn. 8:11   go your way." (ASV) / go, and do not sin again." (RSV)   (162:3/1792–3)

75. "I Am the Light of the World"

[12]Again Jesus spoke to them, saying, "I am the light of the world. He who follows me shall not walk in darkness but shall have the light of life."

[13]The Pharisees then said to him, "You are bearing witness to yourself; your testimony is not true."

[14]Jesus answered, "Even if I do bear witness to myself, my testimony is true, for I know whence I came and whither I go. You know not whence I come or whither I go. [15]You judge according to the flesh. I judge no man. [16]Yet even if I do judge, my judgment is true, for it is not I alone that judge, but I and he who sent me. [17]In your law it is written that the testimony of two men is true—[18]I bear witness to myself, and the Father who sent me bears witness to me."

[19]They said to him, "Where is your Father?"

Jesus answered, "You know neither me nor my Father; if you knew me, you would know my Father also."

[20]These words he spoke as he taught in the temple; but no one arrested him.

[21]Again he said to them, "I go away, and you will seek me [and not find me], for where I am going you cannot come. [23]You are from beneath; I am from above. You are of this world; I am not of this world. [24]You shall die in your sins unless you believe that I am he.[a] [26]I have much to tell you. But he who sent me is true, and I declare to the world what I have heard from him. [28]When the Son of Man is lifted up, then you will know that I am he, and that I do nothing of myself but speak thus as the Father taught me. [29]And he who sent me is with me; he has not left me alone, for I always do what is pleasing to him."

[30]As he spoke thus, many believed.

(Jn. 8:12–21, 23–24, 26, 28–30)

---

a   "I am he."—"I am the light of the world." (Jn. 8:12)

Jn. 8:12   me shall not (KJV) / me will not (RSV) • but shall have (KJV) / but will have (RSV)
Jn. 8:14   I came and (KJV) / I have come and (RSV) • I go. (KJV) / I am going. (RSV) • You know not whence / But you do not know whence (RSV) • I go. (KJV) / I am going. (RSV)
Jn. 8:15   no man. (KJV) / no one. (RSV)
Jn. 8:19   him, "Where / him therefore, "Where (RSV)
Jn. 8:20   spoke as / spoke in the treasury, as (RSV) • him. / him because his hour had not yet come. (RSV)
Jn. 8:21   me [and not find me], for where / me and die in your sin; where (RSV)
Jn. 8:23   You / He said to them you (RSV) • from beneath; (KJV) / from below; (RSV)
Jn. 8:24   You / I told you that you (RSV) • You shall die (KJV) / you would die (RSV)
Jn. 8:26   to tell you. / to say about you (RSV) • you. / you and much to judge. (RSV)
Jn. 8:28   When / So Jesus said, "When (RSV) • When the Son of Man is lifted up, then / "When you have lifted up the Son of Man, then (RSV) • nothing of myself but (KJV) / nothing on my own authority but (RSV)
Jn. 8:30   believed. / believed in him. (RSV) (162:5/1794–5)

93

76. Teachings on Spiritual Freedom

31Jesus then said to the Jews who had believed in him, "If you continue in my word, you are truly my disciples. 32You shall know the truth, and the truth shall make you free."

33They answered him, "We are descendants of Abraham, and have never been in bondage to anyone; how is it that you say, 'You will be made free'?"

34Jesus answered them, "Verily, verily, I say to you, everyone who commits sin is a slave to sin. 35The slave does not continue in his master's house forever; but the son continues forever [in his father's house]. 36If the Son therefore shall make you free, you shall be free indeed."

37"I know that you are descendants of Abraham, yet you seek to kill me because my word finds no place in your hearts. 38I speak of what I have seen with my Father, and you do what you have heard from your father."

39They answered him, "Abraham is our father."

Jesus said to them, "If you were Abraham's children, you would do the works of Abraham.*a* 40But now you seek to kill me, a man who has told you the truth which I heard from God. This is not what Abraham did. 42If God were your Father, you would love me, for I proceeded and came forth from God; I came not of my own accord, but he sent me. 43Why do you not understand what I say? It is because you cannot bear to hear my word.

(Jn. 8:31–40, 42–43) *(continued)*

---

a "If you were Abraham's children, you would do the works of Abraham."—Jesus uses the word child (plural children) in two distinct ways. *Webster's Unabridged* defines these two meanings as: (1) "a son or daughter; a male or female descendant," and (2) "one who in character or practice shows strong signs of the relationship to or the influence of another (as a disciple of a teacher)." It is in this second sense that Jesus uses the word children here. In this sense, to be a child of Abraham means to follow in the ways of Abraham.

Thus, Jesus affirms that the Jews are children of Abraham in the first sense ("I know that you are descendants of Abraham"—Jn. 8:37), while pointing out that they are not children of Abraham in the sense of being followers of his teachings and practices. "But now you seek to kill me, a man who has told you the truth which I heard from God. This is not what Abraham did." (Jn. 8:40)

We may be children of God in both senses. In the first sense (being a descendant), we are already children of God—he is our Creator Father. In the second sense (being a follower), we may become true children of God by believing that he is our Father and choosing to do his will. ("It is *my* will that *your* will be done.")

Jn. 8:32   You / and you (RSV) • You shall know (KJV) / you will know (RSV) • truth shall make (KJV) / truth will make (RSV)
Jn. 8:34   them, "Verily, verily, I (KJV) / "Truly, truly, I (RSV)
Jn. 8:35   in his master's house (Wey) / in the house (RSV) • but the (KJV) / the (RSV) • forever [in his father's house]. / forever. (RSV)
Jn. 8:36   (KJV) • free, you shall (RSV) / free, ye shall (KJV)
Jn. 8:37   in your hearts. (Rieu) / in you. (RSV)
Jn. 8:39   do the works of Abraham. (KJV) / do what Abraham did. (RSV)
Jn. 8:42   If / Jesus said to them, "If (RSV) (162:7/1796–7)

94

76. Teachings on Spiritual Freedom (continued)

[44]You are of your father the devil, and your will is to do your father's desires.[b] He has nothing to do with the truth, because there is no truth in him. [45]But because I tell the truth you do not believe me."

[46]"Which of you convicts me of sin? If I proclaim the truth, why do you not believe? [47]He who is of God hears the words of God; the reason why you do not hear them is that you are not of God."

[48]The Jews answered him, "Are we not right in saying that you have a demon?"

[49]Jesus answered, "I have not a demon; but I honor my Father, and you dishonor me. [50]I seek not my own glory; there is one who seeks it and he will be the judge. [51]Verily, verily, I say to you, if anyone keeps my word, he will never see death."

[52]The Jews said to him, "Now we know that you have a devil.

Abraham died, as did the prophets. And you say, 'If anyone keeps my word, he will never taste death.' [53]Are you greater than our father Abraham, who died? And the prophets are dead! Who do you claim to be?"

[54]Jesus answered, "If I glorify myself, my glory is as nothing. It is my Father who glorifies me, the very one of whom you say that he is your God. [55]But you have not known him. I know him. [56]Your father Abraham rejoiced to see my days, and [by faith] he saw it and was glad."

[57]The Jews then said to him, "You are not yet fifty years old, and have you seen Abraham?"

[58]Jesus said to them, "Verily, verily, I say to you, before Abraham was, I am."

[59]So they took up stones to cast at him; but Jesus hid himself, and went out of the temple.

(Jn. 8:44–59)

---

b "You are of your father the devil, and your will is to do your father's desires."—Here Jesus makes clear the spiritual meaning of fatherhood and sonship—the "child" is the one whose will is to do what his father desires. (See also Ch. 76, fn. *a*.) The unbelieving Jews who seek Jesus' destruction have chosen the ways of evil (and the devil) rather than the will and way of God. Thus, they are children of the devil.

Jn. 8:44 He has / He was a murderer from the beginning, and has (RSV)
Jn. 8:46 I proclaim the / I tell the (RSV) • believe? / believe me? (RSV)
Jn. 8:48 you have / you are a Samaritan and have (RSV)
Jn. 8:50 I seek not my (KJV) / I do not seek my (RSV)
Jn. 8:51 Verily, verily, I (KJV) / Truly, truly, I (RSV)
Jn. 8:52 a devil. (KJV) / a demon. (RSV)
Jn. 8:53 prophets are dead! (KJV) / prophets died! (RSV)
Jn. 8:54 me, the very one of (Phi) / me, of (RSV)
Jn. 8:56 (KJV) • and [by faith] he / and he (KJV)
Jn. 8:58 Verily, verily, I (KJV) / Truly, truly, I (RSV)
Jn. 8:59 to cast at (KJV) / to throw at (RSV) (162:7/1796–7)

77. Martha and Mary[a]

[38]Jesus entered a village and a woman named Martha received him into her house. [39]And she had a sister called Mary, who sat at the Lord's feet and listened to his teaching. [40]But Martha was distracted with much serving; and she went to him and said, "Lord, do you not care that my sister has left me to serve alone? Tell her then to help me." [41]But the Lord answered her, "Martha, Martha, you are anxious and troubled about many things. [42]Only one thing is needful. Mary has chosen the good portion, which shall not be taken away from her." (Lk. 10:38–42)

---

a "Martha and Mary"—Martha and Mary were the sisters of Lazarus and lived at Bethany, a small village about two miles from Jerusalem. All three were very close to Jesus and he later raised Lazarus from the dead. (See Chs. 98, 102, and 103.)

Lk. 10:38 Jesus entered / Now as they went on their way, he entered (RSV) (162:8/1797–8)

XX. Ordination of the Seventy

78. The Ordination Address

¹The Lord appointed seventy others, and sent them on ahead of him, two by two, into every town and place where he himself was about to come.

²And he said to them, "The harvest is indeed plentiful, but the laborers are few; pray therefore the Lord of the harvest to send out laborers into his harvest. ³I send you forth as lambs among wolves. ⁴Carry neither purse nor bag.*ᵃ* And salute no one on the road. ⁵Whatever house you enter, first say: 'Peace be to this house.' ⁶If there is anyone there who loves peace, your peace shall rest upon him; but if not it shall return to you.*ᵇ* ⁷And remain in the same house, eating and drinking what they provide, for the laborer is worthy of his hire. Do not go from house to house. ⁹Minister to the sick. ¹⁰But whenever you enter a town and they do not receive you, say, even as you leave, ¹¹'Nevertheless, know this, that the kingdom of God has come near you.' ¹⁶He who hears you hears me. And he who rejects you*ᶜ* rejects me. And he who rejects me rejects him who sent me."   (Lk. 10:1–7, 9–11, 16)

---

a   "Carry neither purse nor bag."—Carry neither money nor extra clothing.

b   "your peace shall rest upon him; but if not it shall return to you."—You shall stay there or depart for another house.

c   "he who rejects you"—He who rejects your gospel message.

Lk. 10:1   The / After this the (RSV)
Lk. 10:2   is indeed plentiful, / is plentiful, (RSV)
Lk. 10:3   I / behold I (RSV) • you forth as (KJV) / you out as (RSV) • lambs among wolves. (KJV) / lambs in the midst of wolves. (RSV)
Lk. 10:4   Carry neither purse (KJV) / Carry no purse (RSV) • purse nor bag. (KJV) / purse, no bag, no sandals; (RSV)
Lk. 10:6   If there is anyone there who loves peace, your (Gspd) / And if a son of peace is there, your (RSV)
Lk. 10:7   laborer is worthy of his hire. (KJV) / laborer deserves his wages. (RSV)
Lk. 10:9   Minister to the / Heal the (RSV) • sick. / sick in it and say to them, 'The kingdom of God has come near to you.' (RSV)
Lk. 10:10   you, say, even as you leave, / you, go into its streets and say, (RSV)
Lk. 10:11   near you. (KJV) / near. (RSV) (163:1/1800–1)

79. The Requirements of Ordination

57As they were going along the road, a man said to Jesus, "I will follow you wherever you go."

58And Jesus said to him, "Foxes have holes, and birds of the air have nests; but the Son of Man has nowhere to lay his head."

59But he said, "Lord, let me first go and bury my father."

60But Jesus said to him, "Leave the dead to bury their dead;*a* but as for you, go and proclaim the kingdom of God."*b*

61Another said, "I will follow you, Lord, but let me first say farewell to those at my home."

62Jesus said to him, "No man, having put his hand to the plow, if he turns back, is fit for the kingdom of God."*c*

16And behold, one came up to him, saying, "Teacher, what good deed must I do, to have eternal life?"

19And Jesus said: "You know the commandments: do not kill, do not commit adultery, do not steal, do not bear false witness, do not defraud, and honor your father and mother."

20The young man said to him, "All these things I have observed, what do I still lack?"

21Jesus said to him, "If you wish to go the whole way,*d* go, sell what you possess and give to the poor; come and follow me, and you shall have treasure in heaven."

22When the young man heard this he went away sorrowful, for he had great possessions.

(Lk. 9:57–62; Mt. 19:16; Mk. 10:19; Mt. 19:20–22)

---

a   "Leave the dead to bury their dead"—As an ordained minister of the gospel, go forth proclaiming the kingdom of God and leave others to attend to the affairs of this world (bury the dead).

b   "go and proclaim the kingdom of God."—Here again is revealed Jesus' central concept— *the kingdom of God*. He came to establish this kingdom on earth and ordained his followers to proclaim this kingdom to the world.

    What is Jesus' kingdom? It is the will of God dominant and transcendent in the heart of the believer. We may enter this kingdom by believing Jesus' gospel that we are all children of God and choosing to abide by our Father's will.

c   "fit for the kingdom of God."—Fit to be an ordained messenger of the kingdom.

d   "If you wish to go the whole way"—If you wish to be not merely a disciple, but an ordained minister of the kingdom.

Lk. 9:57   to Jesus, "I / to him, "I (RSV)
Lk. 9:60   their dead. / their own dead. (RSV)
Lk. 9:62   No man, having put his (KJV) / No one who puts his (RSV) • plow, if he turns back / plow, and turns back (RSV)
Mk. 10:19   defraud, and honor / defraud, honor (RSV)
Mt. 19:21   you wish to go the whole way, go, (NEB) / you would be perfect, go, (RSV) • poor; come and follow me, and you shall have treasure in heaven." / poor, and you will have treasure in heaven; and come follow me." (RSV) (163:2/1801–3)

80. The Discussion Concerning Wealth

23And Jesus said to his disciples, "It is hard for those who have riches to enter into the kingdom of heaven. 24It is easier for a camel to go through the eye of a needle than for a [self-satisfied] rich man to enter the kingdom of God."*a*

25When the disciples heard this they were greatly astonished, saying, "Who then can be saved?"

26But Jesus looked at them and said to them, "With men this is impossible, but with God all things are possible."

27Then Peter said in reply, "Lo, we have left everything and followed you, what then shall we have?"

29And he said to them, "Truly, I say to you, there is no man who has left house or wife or brothers or parents or children for the sake of the kingdom of God 30who shall not receive manifold more in this world, and in the world to come life everlasting. 30But many that are first shall be last, and the last shall be first."

(Mt. 19:23–27; Lk. 18:29–30; Mt. 19:30) *(continued)*

---

a "It is easier for a camel to go through the eye of a needle than for a [self-satisfied] rich man to enter the kingdom of God."—Here Jesus makes his point by modifying the Jewish saying: "It is easier for a camel to go through the eye of a needle than for the heathen to inherit eternal life."

Mt. 19:23 It is hard (ASV) / Truly I say to you, it will be hard (RSV)
Mt. 19:24 It / Again I tell you, it (RSV) • a [self-satisfied] rich / a rich (RSV)
Lk. 18:30 who shall not (KJV) / who will not (RSV) • this world, and / this time, and (RSV) • the world to come life everlasting. (KJV) / the age to come eternal life. (RSV)
Mt. 19:30 first shall be (KJV) / first will be (RSV) • last shall be first." (KJV) / last first." (RSV) (163:3/1803–4)

80. The Discussion Concerning Wealth (continued)

[1]"The kingdom of heaven is like a householder who went out early in the morning to hire laborers for his vineyard.[b] [2]After agreeing with the laborers for a denarius[c] a day, he sent them into his vineyard. [3]And going out about the third hour he saw others standing idle in the market place; [4]and he said, 'You go in the vineyard too, and whatever is right I will give you.' So they went. [5]Going out again about the sixth hour and the ninth hour, he did the same. [6]And about the eleventh hour he went out and found others standing; and he said to them, 'Why do you stand here idle all day?' [7]They said to him, 'Because no one has hired us.' He said to them, 'You go into the vineyard too.' [8]And when evening came, the owner of the vineyard said to his steward, 'Call the laborers and pay them their wages, beginning with the last, up to the first.' [9]And when those hired about the eleventh hour came, each of them received a denarius. [10]Now when the first came, they thought they would receive more; but each of them also received a denarius. [11]And on receiving it they grumbled at the householder, [12]saying, 'These last worked only one hour, and you have made them equal to us who have borne the burden of the day and the scorching heat.'

[13]But he replied to one of them, 'Friend, I do you no wrong. Did you not agree with me for a denarius? [14]Take what belongs to you, and go; I choose to give this last as I give to you. [15]Is it not lawful to do what I choose with what belongs to me? Or do you begrudge my generosity?'"

(Mt. 20:1–15)

---

b "The kingdom of heaven is like a householder who went out early in the morning to hire laborers for his vineyard."—This parable, *The Laborers in the Vineyard*, is an example of Jesus' preceding statement, "many that are first shall be last, and the last shall be first." (Ch. 80, Mt. 19:30) The laborers whom the householder hired first were the last to be paid, while those who were hired last were the first to be paid.

All the laborers were paid the same wage. This parable teaches us that our reward for serving God is the same whether we come to this service early or late in life. All are granted entrance into the kingdom of heaven, life eternal.

c "a denarius"—The standard wage for a day's labor.

Mt. 20:1   The / For the (RSV)
Mt. 20:15   Is it not lawful to (KJV) / Am I not allowed to (RSV)   (163:3/1804)

81. The Return of the Seventy

[17]The seventy returned with joy, saying, "Lord, even the demons are subject to us in your name!"

[18]And he said to them, "I beheld Satan fall like lightning from heaven. [20]Nevertheless do not rejoice in this, that the spirits are subject to you; but rather rejoice that your names are written in heaven."

[21]In that same hour he rejoiced in the Holy Spirit and said, "I thank you, my Father, Lord of heaven and earth, that you have hidden these things[a] from the wise and men of understanding and revealed them to the children of the kingdom. Yea, Father, so it was well pleasing before you. [22]Everything has been put into my hands and no one knows who the Son is except you, or who you are except the Son, and anyone to whom the Son chooses to reveal you."

[23]Then turning to the disciples he said privately, "Blessed are the eyes which see what you see. [24]For I tell you that many prophets and kings[b] desired to see what you now see, and did not see it, and to hear what you hear, and did not hear it."

[13]"But woe to you Chorazin, Bethsaida, and Capernaum![c] If the mighty works done in you had been done in Tyre and Sidon, they would have repented long ago in sackcloth and ashes. [14]It shall indeed be more tolerable for Tyre and Sidon at the judgment than for you."

(Lk. 10:17–18, 20–24, 13–14)

---

a   "these things"—the gospel of the kingdom.

b   "prophets and kings"—great men of past ages.

c   "Chorazin, Bethsaida, and Capernaum."—Probably the cities that did not well receive the gospel message of the seventy.

Lk. 10:18 I beheld Satan (KJV) / I saw Satan (RSV)
Lk. 10:20 but rather rejoice / but rejoice (RSV)
Lk. 10:21 thank you, my Father, / thank thee, Father, (RSV) • that you have hidden / that thou hast hidden (RSV) • to the children of the kingdom. / to babes. (RSV) • before you. / before thee. (RSV)
Lk. 10:22 Everything has been put into my hands and (Phi) / All things have been delivered to me by my Father; and (RSV) • except you, or / except the Father, or (RSV) • who you are except / who the Father is except (RSV) • reveal you." / reveal him." (RSV)
Lk. 10:13 But woe to / Woe to (RSV) • Chorazin, Bethsaida, / Chorazin! Woe to you, Bethsaida! (RSV) • Bethsaida, and Capernaum! If (Lk. 10:15) / Bethsaida! For if (RSV) • ago in / ago sitting in (RSV)
Lk. 10:14 (KJV) • It / But it (KJV) • shall indeed be / shall be (RSV) (163:6/1806–8)

XXI. At the Feast of Dedication

82. Parable of the Good Samaritan

25And behold, a lawyer stood up to put Jesus to the test, saying "Teacher, what shall I do to inherit eternal life?"

26Jesus said to him, "What is written in the law? How do you read [the scriptures]?"

27And he answered, "You shall love the Lord your God with all your heart, and with all your soul, and with all your strength, and with all your mind, and your neighbor as yourself."[a]

28And Jesus said to him, "You have answered right; do this, and you will live."

(Lk. 10:25–28) *(continued)*

---

a   "You shall love the Lord your God with all your heart, and with all your soul, and with all your strength, and with all your mind, and your neighbor as yourself."—The first part of this admonition is taken from Deuteronomy 6:4–5: "Hear, O Israel: the Lord our God is one Lord; and you shall love the Lord your God with all your heart, and with all your soul, and with all your might." The second part comes from Leviticus 19:18: "You shall not take vengeance or bear any grudge against the sons of your people, but you shall love your neighbor as yourself." The lawyer answered well in that he summarized the highest teachings of the Jewish religion, which were also the teachings of Jesus.

Love is the rule of living in the kingdom—supreme devotion to God and loving your neighbor as yourself.

Lk. 10:25 put Jesus to / put him to (RSV)
Lk. 10:26 Jesus said / He said (RSV) • read [the scriptures]?" / read?" (RSV)
Lk. 10:28 And Jesus said / And he said (RSV) (164:1/1809)

²⁹But the lawyer, desiring to justify himself, said to Jesus, "And who is my neighbor?"^b

³⁰Jesus replied, "A certain man was going down from Jerusalem to Jericho, and he fell into the hands of robbers, who stripped him and beat him, and departed, leaving him half dead. ³¹Now by chance a certain priest was going down that road; and when he saw him he passed by on the other side. ³²So likewise a Levite, when he came to the place and saw him, passed by on the other side. ³³But a Samaritan, as he journeyed, came to where he was; and when he saw him, he had compassion, ³⁴and went to him and bound up his wounds, pouring on oil and wine; and then he set him on his own beast and brought him to an inn, and took care of him. ³⁵And on the morrow he took out two denarii and gave them to the innkeeper, saying, 'Take care of him; and whatever more you spend, I will repay you when I come back.' ³⁶Which of these three, do you think, proved to be a neighbor to the man who fell among the robbers?"

³⁷He answered, "He who showed mercy on him."

And Jesus said to him, "Go and do likewise."   (Lk. 10:29–37)

---

b   "But the lawyer, desiring to justify himself, said to Jesus, 'And who is my neighbor?' "— The lawyer in asking this question knew that Jewish law defined one's neighbors as other Jews, "the children of one's people." ("You shall not take vengeance or bear any grudge against the sons of your people, but you shall love your neighbor as yourself."—Leviticus 19:18) He also knew that if Jesus taught that non-Jews were one's neighbors he would be placing himself in conflict with Jewish law. Jesus answers this attempt to ensnare him with one of his greatest parables, *The Good Samaritan*.

Whatever the lawyer's motives, the question is a good one. Since Jesus has just affirmed the great commandment to "love your neighbor as yourself," the question "Who is my neighbor?" is really equivalent to the question, "Who should we love as we love ourselves?" For many, one's neighbors consist only of those who live in their immediate neighborhood. For others it is those of one's town or region, race or nationality. Jesus in *The Parable of the Good Samaritan* expands the neighbor concept to include the whole world—even our enemies.

Lk. 10:29 But the lawyer, desiring / But he, desiring (RSV)
Lk. 10:30 "A certain man (KJV) / "A man (RSV) • fell into the hands of robbers, (Rieu) / fell among robbers, (RSV)
Lk. 10:31 a certain priest (KJV) / a priest (RSV)
Lk. 10:35 And on the morrow he (KJV) / And the next day he (RSV)
Lk. 10:36 proved to be a neighbor (NASB) / proved neighbor (RSV)
Lk. 10:37 He answered, "He / He said, "He (RSV) • answered, "He who (KJV) / answered, "The one who (RSV)
           (164:1/1809–10)

83. Healing the Man Born Blind

[1]As Jesus passed by, he saw a man who had been blind from birth. [2]And his disciples asked him, "Master, who sinned, this man or his parents, that he was born blind?"[a]

[3]Jesus answered, "It was not that this man sinned, or his parents, but that the works of God might be made manifest in him. [4]We must do the works of him who sent me while it is day; for the night comes when no one can work. [5]As long as I am in the world, I am the light of the world."

[6]As he said this, he spat on the ground and made clay with the spittle and applied the clay to the man's eyes, [7]saying to him: "Go, wash in the pool of Siloam."

So he went and washed and came back seeing. [8]The neighbors and those who had seen him before as a beggar, said, "Is not this the man who used to sit and beg?"

[9]Some said, "It is he"; others said, "No, but he is like him."

He said, "I am he."

[10]They said to him, "Then how were your eyes opened?"

[11]He answered, "A man called Jesus made clay and anointed my eyes, and said to me, 'Go to Siloam and wash'; so I went and washed and received my sight."

[12]They said to him, "Where is he?"

He said, "I do not know."

(Jn. 9:1–12)

---

a   "Master, who sinned, this man or his parents, that he was born blind?"—The Jews tended to believe that such cases of blindness at birth were the result of the sins of the parents.

Jn. 9:1   As Jesus passed / As he passed (RSV) • man who had been blind from birth (Rieu) / man blind from his birth (KJV)
Jn. 9:2   him, "Master, who ("Rabbi" translated "Master") / him, "Rabbi, who (RSV)
Jn. 9:4   must do the / must work the (RSV) • for the night / night (RSV)
Jn. 9:6   clay with the spittle (TCNT) / clay of spittle (RSV) • and applied the clay to the (NASB) / and anointed the (RSV) • eyes, / eyes with the clay, (RSV)
Jn. 9:7   Siloam." / Siloam" (which means sent). (RSV)
Jn. 9:9   am he." (KJV) / am the man." (RSV)
Jn. 9:11   A man (KJV) / The man (RSV)   (164:3/1811–3)

84. Before the Sanhedrin

[13]They brought to the Pharisees [Sanhedrin][a] the man who had formerly been blind. [14]Now it was a Sabbath day when Jesus made the clay and opened his eyes.[b] [15]The Pharisees again asked him how he had received his sight. And he said to them, "He put clay on my eyes, and I washed, and I now see."

[16]Some of the Pharisees said, "This man cannot be from God, for he does not observe the Sabbath." But others said, "How can a man who is a sinner do such signs?" And there was a division among them.

[17]So they again said to the blind man, "What do you say about him, since he has opened your eyes?"

He said, "He is a prophet."

[18]The Jews did not believe that he had been blind and had received his sight until they called the parents of the man who had received his sight. [19]They asked them, "Is this your son who you say was born blind? How then does he now see?"

[20]His parents answered, "We know that this is our son, and he was born blind, [21]but how he now sees we do not know, nor do we know who opened his eyes. Ask him; he is of age; he will speak for himself." [22]His parents said this because they feared the Jews, for the Jews [Sanhedrin] had already agreed that if anyone should confess him to be the Messiah, he was to be put out of the synagogue. [23]Therefore his parents said, "He is of age, ask him."

[24]So for the second time they called the man who had been blind, and said to him, "Give God the praise; we know that this man is a sinner."

[25]He answered, "Whether he is a sinner, I know not; but one thing I do know, that whereas I was blind, now I see."

(Jn. 9:13–25) *(continued)*

---

a   "the Pharisees [Sanhedrin]"—The Sanhedrin was the high ruling body of the Jews. It was composed of Pharisees (scribes and rabbis) and Sadducees (priests and certain wealthy Jews) and was presided over by the High Priest. Since the Sanhedrin was the Jewish supreme court, it was they who would have conducted such an investigation into Sabbath breaking (healing the blind man on the Sabbath).

b   "Now it was a Sabbath day when Jesus made the clay and opened his eyes."—Perhaps it was Jesus' plan to bring his life and teachings more forcefully to the attention of the rulers of the Jews by this act of healing on the Sabbath day.

Jn. 9:13   Pharisees [Sanhedrin] the (See fn. *a* above.) / Pharisees the (RSV)
Jn. 9:15   I now see (Mof) / I see (RSV)
Jn. 9:16   man cannot be from (TCNT) / man is not from (RSV) • not observe the (Phi) / not keep the (RSV)
Jn. 9:19   They asked / and asked (RSV)
Jn. 9:22   Jews [Sanhedrin] had (See fn. *a* above.) / Jews had (RSV) • be the Messiah, he (Ch. 13, fn. *c*) / be Christ, he (RSV)
Jn. 9:25   I know not (KJV) / I do not know (RSV) • but one (Bas) / one (RSV) • I do know (Wms) / I know (RSV) • that whereas I (KJV) / that though I (RSV) (164:4/1813–5)

26They said to him, "What did he do to you? How did he open your eyes?"

27He answered them, "I have told you already, and you would not listen. Why do you want to hear it again? Do you too want to become his disciples?"

28And they reviled him, saying, "You are his disciple, but we are disciples of Moses. 29We know that God has spoken to Moses, but as for this man, we do not know where he comes from."

30The man answered, "Why, this is a marvel! You do not know where he comes from, and yet he opened my eyes. 31We know that God does not listen to sinners, but if anyone is a worshiper of God and does his will, God listens to him. 32Never since the world began has it been heard that anyone opened the eyes of a man born blind. 33If this man were not of God, he could have done nothing."

34They answered him, "You were born in sin, and would you teach us?" And they cast him out of the synagogue.

35Jesus heard that they had cast him out, and having found him he said, "Do you believe in the Son of God?"

36He answered, "Tell me who he is that I may believe in him."

37Jesus said to him, "You have seen him, and it is he who now speaks to you."

38He said, "Lord, I believe," and he worshiped him.

(Jn. 9:26–38)

Jn. 9:34   in sin, (KJV) / in utter sin, (RSV) • out of the synagogue. (Wms) / out. (RSV)
Jn. 9:35   of God?" (RSV alt. trans.) / Man?" (RSV)
Jn. 9:36   Tell me who he is that (NEB) / And who is he, sir, that (RSV)
Jn. 9:37   who now speaks (Ber) / who speaks (RSV) (164:4/1814–5)

85. Teaching at Solomon's Porch

22It was the feast of the dedication[a] at Jerusalem; 23it was winter, and Jesus was walking in the temple, in the portico of Solomon. 24So the Jews gathered round him and said to him, "How long will you keep us in suspense? If you are the Messiah, tell us plainly." 25Jesus answered them, "I told you, and you do not believe. The works that I do in my Father's name bear witness to me. 26But you do not believe, because you do not belong to my flock. 27My sheep hear my voice, and I know them, and they follow me. 28And I give eternal life; and they shall never perish, and no one shall snatch them out of my hand. 29My Father, who has given them to me, is greater than all, and no one is able to snatch them out of the Father's hand. 30The Father and I are one."

31The Jews took up stones again to stone him.

32Jesus answered them, "I have shown you many good works from the Father; for which of these do you stone me?"

33The Jews answered him, "For no good work would we stone you but for blasphemy,[b] because you, being a man, make yourself God."

34Jesus answered them, 36"You say of him whom the Father sent into the world, 'You are blaspheming,' because I said, 'I am the Son of God.' 37If I do not the works of my Father, believe me not, 38but if I do the works of God, even though you do not believe me, believe the works. The Father is in me and I am in the Father."

39Again they tried to arrest him, but he escaped from their hands.

40He went away again beyond the Jordan [Perea] to the place where John had first baptized, and there he remained.

(Jn. 10:22–34, 36–40)

---

a   "It was the feast of the dedication"—The feast of the dedication occurred during December and January. This visit of Jesus would have occurred around January AD 30, and Jesus would have been about 35 years old.

b   "blasphemy"—blas•phe•my n. [from the Greek blasphemein, to speak evil of] 1: irreverence toward God: (1) indignity offered to God in speaking, writing, or signs (2) the act of claiming the attributes or prerogatives of deity. (Webster's Unabridged)

Jn. 10:24   the Messiah, tell (Ch. 13, fn. c) / the Christ, tell (RSV)
Jn. 10:25   name bear / name, they bear (RSV)
Jn. 10:26   my flock. (TCNT) / my sheep. (RSV)
Jn. 10:30   The Father and I are one." / I and the Father are one." (RSV)
Jn. 10:33   For no good work would we (TCNT) / It is not for a good work that we (RSV)
Jn. 10:34   them, / them, "Is it not written in your law, 'I said, you are Gods'? (RSV)
Jn. 10:36   You / Do you (RSV) • Father sent / Father consecrated and sent (RSV)
Jn. 10:37   KJV
Jn. 10:38   do the works of God, even (Jn. 10:37) / do them, even (KJV) • works. The / works, that you may know and understand that the (RSV)
Jn. 10:40   again beyond the (KJV) / again across the (RSV) • Jordan [Perea] to / Jordan to (RSV) (164:5/1815–6)

XXII. The Last Preaching Mission Begins

86. "I Am the Good Shepherd"

⁴¹And many came to him;ᵃ and they said, "John did no sign, but everything that John said about this man was true."

⁴¹Jesus said to them,ᵇ "If you were blind, you would have no sin; but since you claim that you can see, your sin remains."

¹"Every shepherd who does not enter the sheepfold by the door, but climbs in by another way, is a thief and a robber; ²but he who enters by the door is the shepherd of the sheep. ³To him the gatekeeper opens; the sheep hear his voice, and he calls his own sheep by name and leads them out. ⁴When he has brought out all his own, he goes before them, and the sheep follow him, for they know his voice. ⁵A stranger they will not follow, but they will flee from him, for they know not the voice of strangers."

⁶This parableᶜ Jesus used with them, but they did not understand what he was saying to them.

(Jn. 10:41; 9:41; 10:1–6) *(continued)*

---

a "And many came to him"—Jesus and the apostles have hastened away from the jurisdiction of the Jewish authorities after the feast of dedication. (See Ch. 85, Jn. 10:40.) They have journeyed north and west across the Jordan River to the province of Perea. (See map on page 16.) And in this province of Perea, Jesus now begins his last preaching tour before his arrest and crucifixion.

b "Jesus said to them"—Apparently a number of Jesus' enemies (the Jerusalem religious teachers and leaders) have followed him and make up a part of the crowd gathered about him. It is to them that he declares, "If you were blind, you would have no sin; but since you claim that you can see, your sin remains." (Jn. 9:41)

c "This parable"—In this parable of *The Good Shepherd* Jesus contrasts himself, the true shepherd, with a false shepherd ("a thief and a robber"). These false shepherds (the Pharisees and Jerusalem religious leaders) are a part of Jesus' audience, and in the parable Jesus depicts them as "strangers" whom the sheep (those who hunger for truth and thirst for righteousness) will not follow.

Jn. 9:41   no sin; (KJV) / no guilt; (RSV) • but since you claim (Ber) / but now that you say, (RSV) • that you can
            see (Rieu) / 'we see,' (RSV) • your sin remains." (KJV) / your guilt remains." (RSV)
Jn. 10:1   Every shepherd who / Truly, truly, I say to you, he who (RSV) • way, is / way, that man is (RSV)
Jn. 10:5   they know not the (KJV) / they do not know the (RSV)
Jn. 10:6   This parable Jesus (KJV) / This figure Jesus (RSV) (165:1–2/1817–8)

86. "I Am the Good Shepherd" (continued)

7So Jesus again said to them, "I am the door to the [Father's] sheepfold. 8All who seek to enter without me are thieves and robbers; and the sheep will not heed them. 9I am the door. If anyone enters by me, he will be saved, and will go in and find pasture. 10The thief comes only to steal and kill and destroy; I have come that you may have life, and have it more abundantly. 11I am the good shepherd. The good shepherd lays down his life for the sheep. 12He who is a hireling and not a shepherd, whose own the sheep are not, sees the wolf coming and leaves the sheep and flees, and the wolf snatches them and scatters them. 13He flees because he is a hireling and cares nothing for the sheep. 14I am the good shepherd; I know my own and my own know me, 15as the Father knows me and I the Father; and I lay down my life for the sheep. 16And I have other sheep, that are not of this fold. I must bring them also, and they will heed my voice. So there shall be one flock, one shepherd. 17For this reason the Father loves me, because I lay down my life safeguarding the sheep. But if I lay down my life I will take it up again. 18No one takes it from me, but I lay it down of my own accord. I have power to lay it down, and I have power to take it again; this charge I have received from my Father."

19There was again a division among the Jews because of these words. 20Many of them said, "He has a demon, and he is mad; why listen to him?" Others said, "These are not the sayings of one who has a demon. Can a devil open the eyes of the blind?" 42And many believed in him there.

(Jn. 10:7–20, 42)

Jn. 10:7   them, "I / them, "Truly, truly, I say to you, I (RSV) • door to the / door of the (RSV) • the [Father's] sheepfold. (Knox) / the sheep. (RSV)
Jn. 10:8   who seek to enter without me / who came before me (RSV) • and the sheep will not heed them. / but the sheep did not heed them. (RSV)
Jn. 10:9   in and / in and out and (RSV)
Jn. 10:10   I have come that / I came that (RSV) • that you may / that they may (RSV) • it more abundantly. (KJV) / it abundantly. (RSV)
Jn. 10:17   life safeguarding the sheep. But if I lay down my life I will take it up again. / life that I may take it up again. (RSV) (165:2/1818–9)

87. Trust and Spiritual Preparedness

[1]In the meantime, when so many thousands of the multitude had gathered together that they trod upon one another, he began to say to his disciples first, "Beware of the leaven of the Pharisees, which is hypocrisy.[a] [2]Nothing is covered up that shall not be revealed, or hidden that will not be known."

[3]"Therefore, whatever you have said in the dark shall be heard in the light, and whatever you have whispered in private rooms shall be proclaimed upon the housetops.[b] [4]I tell you, my friends, do not fear those who kill the body, and after that have no more that they can do."

[6]"Are not five sparrows sold for two pennies? And not one of them is forgotten before God. [7]Why, even the hairs of your head are all numbered. Fear not; you are of more value than many sparrows."

[8]"And I tell you everyone who acknowledges me before men the Son of Man also will acknowledge before the angels of God; [9]but he who denies me before men will be denied before the angels of God."

[10]"And everyone who speaks a word against the Son of Man will be forgiven; but he who blasphemes against God will not be forgiven."[c]

[11]"And when they bring you before the synagogues and before the rulers and the authorities, be not anxious how or what you are to answer or what you are to say; [12]for the spirit will teach you in that very hour what you ought to say."

(Lk. 12:1–4, 6–12)

---

a "hypocrisy"—hy•poc•ri•sy *n.* [from the Greek *hypokrisis*, act of playing a part on a stage, outward show] 1: the act or practice of pretending to be what one is not or to have principles or beliefs that one does not have; esp: the false assumption of an appearance of virtue or religion. (*Webster's Unabridged*)

b "Therefore, whatever you have said in the dark shall be heard in the light, and whatever you have whispered in private rooms shall be proclaimed upon the housetops."—Here Jesus is referring especially to his Jerusalem enemies who are secretly planning his destruction. And indeed, after his crucifixion, the closed deliberations of the Sanhedrin plotting his death were subsequently brought to light.

c "And everyone who speaks a word against the Son of Man will be forgiven; but he who blasphemes against God will not be forgiven."—A nonbeliever in Jesus might unknowingly blaspheme the Son of Man; but those who knowingly speak evil of God and ascribe his doings to the forces of evil will hardly repent of their sins. Thus they will have no capacity or opportunity to receive forgiveness.

Lk. 12:2 that shall not (KJV) / that will not (RSV)
Lk. 12:10 against God will / against the Holy Spirit will (RSV)
Lk. 12:12 the spirit will / the Holy Spirit will (RSV) (165:3/1819–20)

88. Teaching about Wealth and Material Possessions

[13]One of the multitude said to him, "Teacher, bid my brother divide the inheritance with me."

[14]But he said to him, "Man, who made me a judge or divider over you?"

[15]And he said to them, "Take heed, and beware of all covetousness;[a] for a man's life does not consist in the abundance of his possessions."

[16]And he told them a parable, saying, "The land of a rich man brought forth plentifully; [17]and he thought to himself, 'What shall I do, for I have nowhere to store my crops?' [18]And he said: 'This I will do; I will pull down my barns, and build larger ones, and there I will store all my grain and my goods. [19]And I will say to my soul, Soul, you have ample goods laid up for many years; take your ease; eat, drink, be merry.' [20]But God said to him, 'Foolish man! This night your soul is required of you; and the things you have prepared, whose will they be?' [21]So is he who lays up treasure for himself, and is not rich toward God."

(Lk. 12:13–21)

---

a "covetousness"—cov•et•ous *adj.* [from the French *coveitié*, covetousness, desire] a: marked by craving and deep desire to own wealth or possessions (it's on your account that he's been so particular about money of late, he was never *covetous* before—G.B. Shaw) b: having a craving for possession (a man *covetous* of honors) c: marked by inordinate, culpable, or envious desire for another's possessions (throwing *covetous* eyes out of their forests on the fields and vineyards of their neighbors—J.A. Froude) (*Webster's Unabridged*)

Lk. 12:20 him, 'Foolish man! This / him, 'Fool! This (RSV) (165:4/1821–22)

89. Talk to the Apostles on Wealth

[22]And Jesus said to his apostles,[a] "Do not be anxious about your life, what you shall eat or drink, nor about your body, what you shall put on. [23]Life is more than food, and the body more than clothing. [24]Consider the ravens; they neither sow nor reap, they have neither storehouse nor barn, and yet God feeds them. Of how much more value are you than the birds! [25]And which of you by being anxious can add a cubit to his stature or a day to his life? [26]If then you are not able to do as small a thing as that, why are you anxious about the rest?"

[27]"Consider the lilies, how they grow; they toil not, neither do they spin; yet I say to you, even Solomon in all his glory was not arrayed like one of these. [28]If God so clothes the grass of the field, which is alive today and tomorrow is thrown into the fire, how much more shall he clothe you. O you of little faith! [29]And do not seek what you are to eat and what you are to drink, nor be of anxious mind. [30]For all the nations of the world seek these things; and your Father knows that you need them. [31]Instead, seek his kingdom, and these things shall be yours as well."

[32]"Fear not, little flock, for it is your Father's good pleasure to give you the kingdom. [33]Provide yourselves with purses that wax not old, where no thief approaches and no moth destroys. [34]For where your treasure is, there will your heart be also."

(Lk. 12:22–34)

---

a "Jesus said to his apostles"—This teaching, given to his chosen apostles who had forsaken all to follow him, must be somewhat different from his instruction given to the disciples and the multitude. Those disciples and followers are responsible for the support of their families and should contribute to the sustenance of those who have dedicated themselves fully to the work of the kingdom.

Lk. 12:22 his apostles, "Do (Ch. 22, fn. *a*) / his disciples, "Therefore, I tell you do (RSV)
Lk. 12:23 Life (Gspd) / For life (RSV)
Lk. 12:25 cubit to his stature (RSV alt. trans.) or a day to his life? / cubit to his span of life? (RSV)
Lk. 12:27 they toil not, neither do they spin / they neither toil nor spin (RSV) • I say to you (KJV) / I tell you (RSV)
Lk. 12:28 If (KJV) / But if (RSV) • grass of the field, which is alive today / grass which is alive in the field today (RSV) • the fire, how / the oven, how (RSV) • more shall he / more will he (RSV) • O you of / O men of (RSV)
Lk. 12:33 that wax not old, (KJV) / that do not grow old, (RSV) • old, where / old, with the treasure in the heavens that do not fail, where (RSV) (165:5/1823–4)

90. Watchfulness and Faithfulness

35"Let your loins be girded and your lamps burning. 36And be like men who are waiting for their master to come home from the marriage feast, so that they may open to him at once when he comes and knocks. 37Blessed are those servants whom the master finds awake when he comes. Then he will have them sit at table, and he will come and serve them."

39"You understand that if the householder had known at what hour the thief was coming, he would not have left his house to be broken into. 40You also must be ready; for the Son of Man is departing at an unexpected hour."

41Peter said, "Lord, are you telling this parable for us,*a* or for all?"

42And the Lord said, 43"Blessed is that servant whom his master when he comes will find doing his duties. 44Truly, I say to you, he will set him over all his possessions."

45"But if that servant says to himself, 'My master is delayed in coming,' and begins to mistreat his fellow servants and to eat and drink and be drunken, 46the master of that servant will come on a day when he does not expect him and at an hour he does not know, and will punish him; and will put him with the unfaithful. 48Everyone to whom much has been given, of him will much be required."

49"Fiery trials are drawing near. 50I have a baptism to be baptized with, and how I am on watch until it is accomplished! 51Do you think that I have come to give peace on earth? No, I tell you, but rather division.*b* 52For henceforth in one house there will be five divided, three against two and two against three."

(Lk. 12:35–37, 39–46, 48–52)

---

a "for us"—(the apostles). At this time Jesus is very popular and attracts large crowds and many followers. But he knows that soon great trials will be upon them. He is warning the apostles to be watchful and ready, "Let your loins be girded and your lamps burning."

b "Do you think that I have come to give peace on earth? No, I tell you, but rather division."— Jesus is the Prince of Peace; but his coming to earth did not bring peace—not at first, at least. Although the individual believer will find great peace in his heart, the world will not know Jesus' peace until all are willing to accept his teaching of the kingdom of heaven. Until then there will be inevitable division between believers and nonbelievers.

Lk. 12:37 Then he will have / truly, I say to you, he will gird himself and have (RSV)
Lk. 12:39 You understand that / But know this that (RSV)
Lk. 12:40 is departing at / is coming at (RSV)
Lk. 12:42 said, / said, "Who is the faithful and wise steward, whom the master will set over his household, to give them their portion of food at the proper time? (RSV)
Lk. 12:43 find doing / find so doing. (RSV) • doing his duties. (Rieu) / doing. (RSV)
Lk. 12:45 to mistreat his fellow servants and / to beat the menservants and maidservants and (RSV) • and be drunken (KJV) / and get drunk (RSV)
Lk. 12:49 "Fiery trials are drawing near. / "I came to cast fire upon the earth; (RSV)
Lk. 12:50 am on watch until / am constrained until (RSV) (165:5–6/1824)

XXIII. The Last Preaching Mission

91. Dining with the Pharisees

³⁷A Pharisee asked him to dine with him; so he went in and sat at table. ³⁸The Pharisee was astonished to see that he did not first wash before dinner. ³⁹And the Lord said, "Now you Pharisees cleanse the outside of the cup and of the dish, but inside you are full of extortion and wickedness."

⁴⁵One of the lawyers[a] answered him, "Teacher, in saying this you reproach us also."

⁴⁶And he said, "Woe upon you lawyers also! for you load men with burdens grievous to bear, and you yourselves will not lift one finger to help them. ⁴⁷Woe upon you! for you build the tombs for the prophets whom your fathers killed. ⁴⁸So you are witnesses and consent to the deeds of your fathers; for you now plan to kill the prophet who comes in this day doing what the prophets did in their day. ⁵⁰The blood of all the prophets, shed from the foundation of the world, ⁵¹may be required of this generation. ⁵²Woe upon you lawyers! for you have taken away the key of knowledge; you did not enter yourselves, and you hindered those who were entering."

⁵³As he went away from there, the scribes and the Pharisees began to press him hard, and to provoke him to speak of many things, ⁵⁴lying in wait for him, to catch him at something he might say.[b]

(Lk. 11:37–39, 45–48, 50–54)

---

a "One of the lawyers"—Evidently Jesus was invited to a meal given by a Pharisee, whose guests included a number of lawyers and Pharisees. These Pharisees, who strictly followed the practice of ceremonial washing, were shocked when Jesus did not engage in this Pharisaic practice.

b "lying in wait for him, to catch him at something he might say."—to be used to bring him to trial and judgment before the Sanhedrin in Jerusalem.

Lk. 11:37 A / While he was speaking a (RSV)
Lk. 11:39 said, "Now / said to him, "Now (RSV)
Lk. 11:46 Woe upon you (KJV) / Woe to you (RSV) • burdens grievous to (KJV) / burdens hard to (RSV) • yourselves will not lift one finger to help them. (NIV) / yourselves do not touch the burdens with one of your fingers. (RSV)
Lk. 11:47 Woe upon you! (KJV) / Woe to you! (RSV)
Lk. 11:48 for you now plan to kill the prophet who comes in this day doing what the prophets did in their day. / for they killed them, and you build their tombs. (RSV)
Lk. 11:50 The / that the (RSV)
Lk. 11:51 may be (NIV) / will be (RSV)
Lk. 11:52 Woe upon you (KJV) / Woe to you (RSV)
Lk. 11:54 catch him at / catch at (RSV) (166:1/1825–7)

92. Healing the Ten Lepers

[12]And as he entered a village, he was met by ten lepers,[a] who stood at a distance [13]and lifted up their voices and said, "Jesus, Master, have mercy on us."

[14]When he saw them he said to them, "Go and show yourselves to the priests."[b]

And as they went they were cleansed. [15]Then one of them, when he saw that he was healed, turned back, praising God with a loud voice; [16]and he fell on his face at Jesus' feet, giving him thanks. Now he was a Samaritan.

[17]Then said Jesus, "Were not ten cleansed? Where then are the nine? [18]Was no one found to return and give praise to God except this foreigner?"

[19]And he said to him, "Arise and go your way; your faith has made you whole."

(Lk. 17:12–19)

---

a "ten lepers"—See Ch. 34, fn. *b*, for a definition of leprosy.

b "Go and show yourselves to the priests."—This was required by the law of Moses: "The Lord said to Moses, 'This shall be the law of the leper for the day of his cleansing. He shall be brought to the priest; and the priest shall go out of the camp, and the priest shall make an examination.'" (Leviticus 14:1–3)

Lk. 17:19 you whole." (KJV) / you well." (RSV) (166:2/1827–8)

93. Will Few or Many Be Saved?

²²He went on his way through towns and villages, teaching and journeying toward Jerusalem.ᵃ ²³And some one said to him, "Lord, will those who are saved be few or many?"

¹³And Jesus said to them, "Enter by the narrow gate;ᵇ for the gate is wide and the way is easy, that leads to destruction, and those who enter by it are many. ¹⁴Straight is the gate and narrow is the way, that leads to life, and those who find it are few."

²⁵"When once the householder has risen up and shut the door, you will begin to stand outside and to knock at the door, saying, 'Lord, open to us.' He will answer you, 'I do not know where you come from.' ²⁶Then you will begin to say, 'We ate and drank in your presence, and you taught in our streets.' ²⁷But he will say, 'I tell you, I do not know where you come from; depart from me, all you workers of iniquity!'ᶜ ²⁸There you will weep and gnash your teeth, when you see Abraham and Isaac and Jacob and all the prophets in the kingdom of God and you yourselves thrust out. ²⁹And men will come from east and west, and from north and south, and sit at table in the kingdom of God. ³⁰And behold, some who are last will be first, and some who are first will be last."

(Lk. 13:22–23; Mt. 7:13–14; Lk. 13:25–30)

---

a "He went on his way through towns and villages, teaching and journeying toward Jerusalem."—Jesus crossed over into Perea when the authorities sought to arrest him at the feast of the dedication. (See Ch. 85.) Since he is moving toward Jerusalem he probably began this last preaching mission in northern Perea and gradually moved south. (See map on page 16.)

b "And Jesus said to them, 'Enter by the narrow gate'"—Here Jesus teaches that, although the way leading to life is "straight and narrow" and the way to destruction is "broad and wide," still, salvation is first a matter of *personal choice*. Thus, whether few or many are saved is ever dependent upon how many *choose* to "enter by the narrow gate" and fight the good fight of faith.

c "iniquity"—in•iq•ui•ty *n*. [from the Latin *iniquus*, uneven, unjust] 1: absence of or deviation from just dealing: gross injustice: WICKEDNESS (the *iniquity* of bribery). (*Webster's Unabridged*)
   We may distinguish three levels of failure to achieve the doing of God's will. Evil is an unconscious or unintended breach of the Father's will; sin is a conscious and deliberate violation of God's will; and iniquity is a willful, repeated, and persistent transgression of the divine will. Evil is the measure of our imperfection in obeying God's will; sin is the measure of our unwillingness to be spiritually guided; and iniquity is the measure of our continued rejection of the Father's way of salvation.

Lk. 13:23 few or many? / few? (RSV)
Mt. 7:13   And Jesus said to them, "Enter (Lk. 13:24) / "Enter (RSV)
Mt. 7:14   Straight is the gate and narrow is the way, that (KJV) / For the gate is narrow and the way is hard, that (RSV)
Lk. 13:30 some who are last will / some are last who will (RSV) • some who are first will / some are first who will (RSV) (166:3/1828–9)

94. Teaching about Accidents and Natural Law

¹There were some present at that time who told him of the Galileans whose blood Pilate had mingled with their sacrifices. ²And he answered them, "Do you think that these Galileans were worse sinners than all the other Galileans, because they suffered thus? ⁴Or those eighteen upon whom the tower in Siloam fell and killed them, do you think that they were worse offenders than all the others who dwelt in Jerusalem?"ᵃ

⁶And he told this parable: "A man had a fig tree planted in his vineyard; and he came seeking fruit on it and found none. ⁷And he said to the vinedresser, 'Lo, these three years I have come seeking fruit on this fig tree, and I find none. Cut it down; why should it use up the ground?' ⁸And he answered him, 'Let it alone, sir, this year also, till I dig about it and put on manure. ⁹And if it bears fruit next year well and good; but if not you can cut it down.'"

(Lk. 13:1–2, 4, 6–9)

ᵃ "do you think that they were worse offenders than all the others who dwelt in Jerusalem?"— The Jews tended to believe that prosperity was the sign of God's favor, while adversity and poverty were the result of his disapproval. The associated idea that accidents (such as the tower of Siloam falling on eighteen men) were the result of spiritual forces punishing sinners is here questioned by Jesus. He then proceeds to tell a parable, *The Parable of the Fig Tree*, that demonstrates and teaches that the events of the physical world are governed by natural laws, and only those who comply with those laws (dig about the tree and put on manure) may hope to reap the benefits (a bountiful yield).

Lk. 13:1   that time / that very time (RSV) (166:4/1830–1)

XXIV. Before the Resurrection of Lazarus

95. Sabbath Meal with the Pharisees

¹One Sabbath when he went to dine at the house of a ruler who belonged to the Pharisees, they were watching him. ²And behold, there was a man before him who had dropsy.ᵃ ³And Jesus spoke to the lawyers and Pharisees, saying, "Is it lawful to heal on the Sabbath, or not?"

⁴But they were silent.

Then he took him and healed him, and let him go. ⁵And he said to them, "Which of you, having an ox that has fallen into a well, will not immediately pull him out on a Sabbath day?"

⁶And they could not reply to this.

⁷Now he told a parableᵇ to those who were invited, when he noticed how they chose the places of honor, saying to them, ⁸"When you are invited by anyone to a marriage feast, do not sit down in a place of honor, lest a more eminent man than you be invited by him, ⁹and he who invited you both will come and say to you, 'Give place to this man,' and then you will begin with shame to take the lowest place. ¹⁰But when you are invited, go and sit in the lowest place, so that when your host comes he may say to you, 'Friend, go up higher'; then you will be honored in the presence of all who sit at table with you. ¹¹Every one who exalts himself shall be humbled, and he who humbles himself shall be exalted."

¹²"When you give a dinner or a banquet, do not always invite your friends or your brothers or your kinsmen or rich neighbors, lest they also invite you in return, and you be repaid. ¹³But when you give a feast, sometimes invite the poor, the maimed, the lame, the blind, ¹⁴and you will be blessed, because they cannot repay you."

(Lk. 14:1–14)

---

a   "dropsy"—A condition in which parts of the body such as the face, arms, and legs become swollen as the result of an abnormal accumulation of fluid.

b   "he told a parable"—*The Lowest Seat at the Feast.*

Lk. 14:5   having an / having a son or an (RSV)
Lk. 14:7   he noticed how (Wey) / he marked how (RSV)
Lk. 14:11   Every / For every (RSV) • himself shall be (KJV) / himself will be (RSV) • himself shall be (KJV) / himself will be (RSV)
Lk. 14:12   "When / He said also to the man who invited him, "When (RSV) • not always invite / not invite (RSV)
Lk. 14:13   feast, sometimes invite / feast, invite (RSV)   (167:1/1833–4)

96. Parable of the Great Banquet

15When one of those who sat at table with Jesus heard this, he said, "Blessed is he who shall eat bread in the kingdom of God!"

16But Jesus said to him, "A man once gave a great banquet, and invited many; 17and at the time for the banquet he sent his servant to say to those who had been invited, 'Come, for all is now ready.' 18But they all alike began to make excuses. The first said to him, 'I have bought a field, and I must go out and see it; I pray you, have me excused.' 19And another said, 'I have bought five yoke of oxen, and I go to examine them; I pray you, have me excused.' 20And another said, 'I have married a wife, and therefore I cannot come.' 21So the servant came and reported this to his master. Then the householder in anger said to his servant, 'Go out quickly to the streets and lanes of the city, and bring in the poor and maimed and blind and lame.' 22And the servant said, 'Sir, what you commanded has been done, and still there is room.' 23And the master said to the servant, 'Go out to the highways and hedges and compel people to come in, that my house may be filled. 24For I tell you, none of those men who were invited shall taste my banquet.'" (Lk. 14:15–24)

Lk. 14:15   with Jesus heard / with him heard (RSV) • he said, "Blessed / he said to him, "Blessed (RSV)
Lk. 14:16   But Jesus said / But he said (RSV) (167:2/1835)

97. The Woman with the Spirit of Infirmity

[10]Now he was teaching in one of the synagogues on the Sabbath. [11]And there was a woman who had had a spirit of infirmity for eighteen years; she was bent over and could not fully straighten herself. [12]And when Jesus saw her, he called her and said to her, "Woman, you are freed from your infirmity." [13]And he laid his hands upon her, and immediately she was made straight, and she praised God.

[14]But the ruler of the synagogue, indignant because Jesus had healed on the Sabbath, said to the people, "There are six days on which work ought to be done; come on those days and be healed, but not on the Sabbath day."

[15]Then the Lord answered him, "You hypocrites! Does not each of you on the Sabbath untie his ox or his ass from the manger, and lead it away to water it? [16]And ought not this woman, a daughter of Abraham who has been bound down by evil for eighteen years, be loosed from this bond on the Sabbath day?"

[17]And as he said this, all his adversaries were put to shame; and all the people rejoiced at all the glorious things that were done by him.

(Lk. 13:10–17)

Lk. 13:14   healed, but not / healed, and not (RSV)
Lk. 13:16   Abraham who has been bound down by evil for / Abraham whom Satan bound for (RSV) (167:3/1835–6)

98. News of Lazarus' Illness

¹Now a certain man was ill, Lazarus of Bethany, the village of Mary and her sister Martha. ²It was Mary who anointed the Lord with ointment*a* and wiped his feet with her hair, whose brother Lazarus was ill. ³So the sisters sent to him saying, "Lord, he whom you love is ill."

⁴But when Jesus heard it he said, "This illness is not unto death, it is for the glory of God, so that the Son of God may be glorified by means of it."

⁵Now Jesus loved Martha and her sister and Lazarus. ⁶When he heard that he was ill, he stayed two days longer in the place where he was. ⁷Then after this he said to the disciples, "Let us go into Judea again."

⁸The disciples said to him, "Rabbi, the Jews were but now seeking to stone you,*b* and are you going there again?"

⁹Jesus answered, "Are there not twelve hours in the day? If anyone walks in the day, he does not stumble, because he sees the light of this world. ¹⁰But if anyone walks in the night, he stumbles, because the light is not in him."

¹¹Thus he spoke, and then he said to them, "Our friend Lazarus has fallen asleep, but I go to awake him out of sleep."

¹²The disciples said to him, "Lord, if he has fallen asleep, he will recover."

¹³Now Jesus had spoken of his death, but they thought that he meant taking rest in sleep. ¹⁴Then Jesus told them plainly, "Lazarus is dead; ¹⁵and for your sake I am glad that I was not there, so that you may believe. But let us go to him."

¹⁶Thomas, called the Twin, said to his fellow disciples, "Let us also go, that we may die with him."

(Jn. 11:1–16)

---

a   "It was Mary who anointed the Lord with ointment"—See Ch. 114.

b   "the Jews were but now seeking to stone you"—This refers to Jesus' recent visit to Jerusalem during the feast of Dedication. (See Ch. 85, Jn. 10:31.)

(167:4/1836–8)

99. Parable of the Pharisee and the Publican

[9]He also told this parable to some who trusted in themselves that they were righteous and despised others: [10]"Two men went up into the temple to pray, one a Pharisee and the other a publican. [11]The Pharisee stood and prayed thus with himself, 'God, I thank thee that I am not like other men, extortioners, unjust, adulterers, or even like this tax collector. [12]I fast twice a week; I give tithes of all that I get.' [13]But the publican, standing afar off, would not even lift up his eyes to heaven, but beat his breast, saying, 'God, be merciful to me a sinner!' [14]I tell you this man went down to his house justified rather than the other; for everyone who exalts himself shall be humbled, but he who humbles himself shall be exalted."

(Lk. 18:9–14)

Lk. 18:10   a publican. (KJV) / a tax collector. (RSV)
Lk. 18:13   the publican, standing (KJV) / the tax collector, standing (RSV)
Lk. 18:14   himself shall be (KJV) / himself will be (RSV) • himself shall be (KJV) / himself will be (RSV) (167:5/1838)

100. Teaching on Marriage and Divorce

¹Now when Jesus entered the region of Judea beyond the Jordan[a] ²large crowds followed him.

³And Pharisees came up to him and tested him by asking, "Is it lawful to divorce one's wife for any cause?"

⁴He answered, "Have you not read that he who made them from the beginning made them male and female?" ⁵And he said, "For this reason a man shall leave his father and mother and be joined to his wife, and the two shall become as one."

⁷They said to him, "Why then did Moses command one to give a certificate of divorce, and to put her away?"

⁸"Moses allowed you to divorce your wives, but in the beginning it was not so."   (Mt. 19:1–5, 7–8)

---

a "the region of Judea beyond the Jordan"—The province of Perea. (See map on page 16.)

Mt. 19:1   Jesus entered / Jesus had finished these sayings, he went away from Galilee and entered (RSV)
Mt. 19:2   large / and large (RSV) • him. / him, and he healed them there. (RSV)
Mt. 19:5   And he said / and said (RSV) • become as one." / become one flesh." (RSV)
Mt. 19:8   Moses / For your hardness of heart, Moses (RSV) • but in the / but from the (RSV) (167:5/1838–9)

---

101. Jesus Blesses the Little Children

¹³And they were bringing children to him, that he might touch them; and the disciples rebuked them. ¹⁴But when Jesus saw it he was indignant, and said to them, "Suffer the little children to come unto me, and forbid them not; for of such is the kingdom of heaven. ¹⁵Truly, I say to you, whoever does not receive the kingdom of God like a child shall not enter it."[a]

¹⁶And he took them in his arms and blessed them, laying his hands upon them.

(Mk. 10:13–16)

---

a "Suffer the little children to come unto me, and forbid them not; for of such is the kingdom of heaven. Truly, I say to you, whoever does not receive the kingdom of God like a child shall not enter it."—Here Jesus teaches us to seek entrance into the kingdom of heaven with the faith and trusting dependence of a little child. And although this faith is *childlike*, resembling the trust of a child in his earthly father, it is in no sense *childish*.

Mk. 10:14 (KJV) • was indignant, and (RSV) / was much displeased, and (KJV) • of heaven. / of God. (KJV) (167:6/1839–40)

123

XXV. The Resurrection of Lazarus

102. Arrival at Bethany

[17]Now when Jesus came, he found that Lazarus had already been in the tomb four days. [18]Bethany was near Jerusalem, about two miles off, [19]and many of the Jews had come to Martha and Mary to console them concerning their brother. [20]When Martha heard that Jesus was coming, she went and met him, while Mary sat in the house. [21]Martha said to Jesus, "Lord, if you had been here, my brother would not have died. [22]And even now I know that whatever you ask from God, God will give you." [23]Jesus said to her, "Your brother will rise again."

[24]Martha said to him, "I know that he will rise again in the resurrection at the last day."

[25]Jesus said to her, "I am the resurrection and the life; he who believes in me, though he die, yet shall he live, [26]and whoever lives and believes in me shall never die. Do you believe this?"

[27]She said to him, "Yes, Lord; I believe that you are the Deliverer, the Son of God, he who is coming into the world."

[28]When she had said this, she went and called her sister Mary, saying quietly, "The Teacher is here and is calling for you." [29]And when she heard it, she rose quickly and went to him. [30]Now Jesus had not yet come to the village, but was still in the place where Martha had met him. [31]When the Jews who were with her in the house, consoling her, saw Mary rise quickly and go out, they followed her, supposing that she was going to the tomb to weep there.

[32]Then Mary, when she came where Jesus was and saw him, fell at his feet, saying to him, "Lord, if you had been here, my brother would not have died."

(Jn. 11:17–32)

Jn. 11:27   the Deliverer, the (Ch. 13, fn. *c*) / the Christ, the (RSV)   (168:0/1842–3)

103. The Resurrection of Lazarus

[33]When Jesus saw her weeping, and the Jews who came with her also weeping, he was deeply moved in spirit and troubled; [34]and he said, "Where have you laid him?"

They said to him, "Lord, come and see."

[35]Jesus wept.

[36]So the Jews said, "See how he loved him!" [37]But some of them said, "Could not he who opened the eyes of the blind man have kept this man from dying?"

[38]Then Jesus, deeply moved again, came to the tomb; it was a cave, and a stone lay upon it. [39]Jesus said, "Take away the stone."

Martha, the sister of the dead man, said to him, "Lord, by this time there will be an odor, for he has been dead four days."

[40]Jesus said to her, "Did I not tell you that if you would believe you would see the glory of God?" [41]So they took away the stone.

And Jesus lifted up his eyes, and said, "Father, I thank you that you have heard me. [42]I know that you hear me always, but I have said this on account of the people standing by, that they may believe that you did send me." [43]When he had said this, he cried with a loud voice, "Lazarus, come forth!"

[44]The dead man came out, his hands and feet bound with bandages, and his face wrapped with a cloth.

Jesus said to them, "Unbind him, and let him go."

[45]Many of the Jews therefore, who had come with Mary and had seen what he did, believed in him. [46]But some of them went to the Pharisees and told them what Jesus had done. (Jn. 11:33–46)

Jn. 11:41   thank you that you have heard (NIV) / thank thee that thou hast heard (RSV)
Jn. 11:42   I know that you hear me / I know that thou hearest me (RSV) • that you did send / that thou didst send (RSV)
Jn. 11:43   come forth!" (KJV) / come out." (RSV)   (168:1–2/1843–7)

104. The Sanhedrin Decides that Jesus Must Die

47So the chief priests and the Pharisees gathered the council,[a] and said, "What are we to do? For this man performs many signs. 48If we let him go on thus, everyone will believe in him, and the Romans will come and destroy both our holy place and our nation."[b]

49But one of them, Caiaphas, who was high priest that year, said to them, "You know nothing at all; 50you do not understand that it is expedient for you that one man should die for the people, and that the whole nation should not perish." 51He did not say this of his own accord, but being high priest that year he prophesied that Jesus should die for the nation, 52and not for the nation only, but to gather into one the children of God who are scattered abroad. 53So from that day on they took counsel how to put him to death.[c]

54Jesus therefore no longer went about openly among the Jews, but went from there to the country near the wilderness, and there he stayed with his disciples.[d]

(Jn. 11:47–54)

---

a   "the chief priests and the Pharisees gathered the council"—The Sanhedrin, the Jewish supreme court and ruling body, met to decide what to do about Jesus.

b   "If we let him go on thus, everyone will believe in him, and the Romans will come and destroy both our holy place and our nation."—The Sanhedrin knew that many of Jesus' followers regarded him as the Messiah, Israel's deliverer. They were afraid that this would lead to serious problems with the Roman authorities.

c   "So from that day on they took counsel how to put him to death."—For a long time the Sanhedrin (the Jewish high court) had sought to apprehend Jesus and bring charges against him. Now they go even further; they decree his death in advance of anything resembling a trial.

d   "Jesus therefore no longer went about openly among the Jews, but went from there to the country near the wilderness, and there he stayed with his disciples."—Probably he returned to the regions of Perea and the Decapolis, the provinces lying across the Jordan River from Judea. This area was outside the reach of the Jewish Sanhedrin.

Jn. 11:54   wilderness, and / wilderness, to a town called Ephraim; and (RSV) (168:3/1847)

XXVI. Teaching in Parables

105. Those Who Are Lost

[1]Now the tax collectors and sinners were all drawing near to Jesus. [2]And the Pharisees and the scribes murmured, saying, "This man receives sinners and eats with them."[a]

[3]So he told them this parable: [4]"What man of you, having a hundred sheep, if he has lost one of them, does not leave the ninety-nine in the wilderness, and go after the one which is lost, until he finds it? [5]And when he has found it, he lays it on his shoulders, rejoicing. [6]And when he comes home, he calls together his friends and his neighbors, saying to them, 'Rejoice with me, for I have found my sheep which was lost.' [7]Just so, I tell you, there will be more joy in heaven over one sinner who repents than over ninety-nine righteous persons who need no repentance.'

[8]"Or what woman, having ten silver coins, if she loses one coin, does not light a lamp and sweep the house and seek diligently until she finds it? [9]And when she has found it, she calls together her friends and neighbors, saying, 'Rejoice with me, for I have found the coin which I had lost.' [10]Just so, I tell you, there is joy before the angels of God over one sinner who repents."(Lk. 15:1–10) *(continued)*

---

a   "And the Pharisees and the scribes murmured, saying, 'This man receives sinners and eats with them.'"—Jesus answers this criticism by the Pharisees that he associates with sinners by telling three parables. They teach us God's attitude toward sinners, toward those who are lost in sin.

In *The Lost Sheep* the shepherd leaves his flock to go in search of a lost sheep; he rejoices greatly when the sheep is found. This parable teaches that God (and his Son) actually go in search of those who are lost. The fact that we are lost only increases God's interest. Another time Jesus said, "For the Son of Man came to seek and save the lost." (See Ch. 111, Lk. 19:10.) We know that we must search for God, but *The Lost Sheep* reveals that God also searches for us, especially when we are lost.

Like *The Lost Sheep*, *The Lost Coin* also teaches that God searches for those who are lost and rejoices when they are found; it emphasizes the diligence and thoroughness with which God conducts this search.

In *The Lost Sheep* the shepherd goes in search for the sheep that *unintentionally* went astray; *The Lost Son* (following page) depicts God's attitude toward a son who willfully and intentionally departs from his father's will and becomes lost in sin. It teaches that even when a son chooses the path of sin, the loving heavenly Father is ever willing to accept his son back into his family. This story, which so beautifully pictures the human condition and the Father's loving acceptance of an erring child, is perhaps Jesus' greatest parable.

(169:0–1/1850–1)

127

105. Those Who Are Lost (continued)

[11]And Jesus said, "There was a man who had two sons; [12]and the younger of them said to his father, 'Father, give me the share of property that falls to me.' And he divided his living between them."

[13]"Not many days later, the younger son gathered all he had and took his journey into the country, and there he squandered his property in loose living. [14]And when he had spent everything, a great famine arose in that country, and he began to be in want. [15]So he went and joined himself to one of the citizens of that country, who sent him into his fields to feed swine. [16]And he would gladly have fed on the pods that the swine ate; and no one gave him anything. [17]But when he came to himself he said, 'How many of my father's hired servants have bread enough to spare, but I perish here with hunger! [18]I will arise and go to my father, and I will say to him, "Father, I have sinned against heaven and before you; [19]I am no longer worthy to be called your son; treat me as one of your hired servants."' [20]And he arose and came to his father. But while he was yet at a distance, his father saw him and had compassion, and ran and embraced him and kissed him. [21]And the son said to him, 'Father, I have sinned against heaven and before you; I am no longer worthy to be called your son.' [22]But the father said to his servants, 'Bring quickly the best robe, and put it on him; and put a ring on his hand, and shoes on his feet; [23]and bring the fatted calf and kill it, and let us eat and make merry; [24]for this my son was dead, and is alive again; he was lost, and is found.' And they began to make merry."

[25]"Now his elder son was in the field; and as he came and drew near to the house, he heard music and dancing. [26]And he called one of the servants and asked what this meant. [27]And he said to him, 'Your brother has come, and your father has killed the fatted calf, because he has received him safe and sound.' [28]But he was angry and refused to go in. His father came out and entreated him, [29]but he answered his father, 'Lo, these many years I have served you, and I never disobeyed your command; yet you never gave me a kid, that I might make merry with my friends. [30]But when this son of yours came, who has devoured your living with harlots, you killed for him the fatted calf!'"

[31]"And he said to him, 'Son, you are always with me, and all that is mine is yours. [32]It was fitting to make merry and be glad, for this your brother was dead, and is alive; he was lost, and is found.'"

(Lk. 15:11–32)

(169:1/1851–3)

106. The Shrewd Steward

[1]And Jesus also said to the disciples, "There was a rich man who had a steward, and charges were brought to him that this man was wasting his goods. [2]And he called him and said to him, 'What is this that I hear about you? Turn in the account of your stewardship, for you can no longer be steward.'"

[3]"And the steward said to himself, 'What shall I do, since my master is taking the stewardship away from me? I am not strong enough to dig, and I am ashamed to beg. [4]I have decided what to do, so that people may receive me into their houses when I am put out of the stewardship.' [5]So, summoning his master's debtors one by one, he said to the first, 'How much do you owe my master?' [6]He said, 'A hundred measures of oil.' And he said to him 'Take your bill, and sit down quickly and write fifty.' [7]Then he said to another, 'And how much do you owe?' He said, 'A hundred measures of wheat.' He said to him, 'Take your bill, and write eighty.' [8]Even his master commended the dishonest steward for his shrewdness."[a]

"The sons of this world are more shrewd in dealing with their own generation than the sons of light.[b] [9]And I tell you, make friends for yourselves with righteousness like those who make friends with unrighteous mammon,[c] so that when it fails they may receive you into the eternal habitations."

[10]"He who is faithful in a very little is faithful also in much; and he who is dishonest in a very little is dishonest also in much. [11]If then you have not been faithful in handling worldly wealth, who will entrust to you the true riches? [12]And if you have not been faithful in that which is another's, who will give you that which is your own?"

[13]"No man can serve two masters; for either he will hate the one and love the other, or he will be devoted to the one and despise the other. You cannot serve God and mammon."

[14]The Pharisees, who were lovers of money, heard all this, and they scoffed at him.

(Lk. 16:1–14)

---

a "shrewdness"—shrewd•ness *n*. the quality or state of being shrewd, as a: sagacity in practical affairs (the political shrewdness that characterized his later career—Carol L. Thompson) b: keenness of discernment : ACUMEN (the tradition of rural shrewdness—Malcolm Cowley). (*Webster's Unabridged*)

b "The sons of this world are more shrewd in dealing with their own generation than the sons of light."—The sons of this world sometimes show more wisdom in their preparation for the future than do the children of the kingdom.

c "mammon"—Semitic word for money or riches.

Lk. 16:8　Even his master / The master (RSV) • The / for the (RSV)
Lk. 16:9　yourselves with righteousness like those who make friends with unrighteous / yourselves by means of unrighteous (RSV)
Lk. 16:11　in handling worldly wealth, who (TEV) / in the unrighteous mammon, who (RSV)
Lk. 16:13　No man can / No servant can (RSV) (169:2/1853–4)

XXVII. Going up to Jerusalem

107. The Desire for Preference

²⁰Being asked when the kingdom of God was coming, he answered them, "The kingdom of God is not coming with signs to be observed; ²¹nor will they say, 'Lo, here it is!' or 'There!' for behold, the kingdom of God is within you."^{*a*}

²⁰The mother of the sons of Zebedee came up to Jesus, with her sons, and kneeling before him she asked him for something.

²¹And he said to her, "What do you want?"

She said to him, "Command that these two sons of mine may sit, one at your right hand and one at your left, in your kingdom."^{*b*}

²²But Jesus answered, "You do not know what you are asking. Are you able to drink the cup that I am to drink?"

They said to him, "We are able."

²³He said to them, "You will drink my cup, but to sit at my right hand and at my left is not mine to grant, but it is for those for whom it has been prepared by my Father."

²⁴And when the ten heard it, they were indignant at the two brothers.

²⁵But Jesus called them to him and said, "You know that the rulers of the Gentiles lord it over them, and their great men exercise authority over them. ²⁶It shall not be so among you; but whoever would be great among you must be your servant, ²⁷and whoever would be first among you must be your minister;^{*c*} ²⁸even as the Son of Man came not to be served but to serve, and to give his life in the service of many."

(Lk. 17:20–21; Mt. 20:20–28)

---

a   "the kingdom of God is within you."—Jesus' kingdom is an inner spiritual kingdom—the rule of God in the heart of the believer. This is one of Jesus' greatest pronouncements.

b   "She said to him, 'Command that these two sons of mine may sit, one at your right hand and one at your left, in your kingdom.'"—John's mother (and the apostles) think that Jesus is going up to Jerusalem to receive his kingdom. They believe the kingdom is about to be realized on a worldwide scale and that Jesus will rule over the nations from his capital at Jerusalem.

Although Jesus' followers were destined for great disappointment when this did not happen, the concept of a future world kingdom under God's rule, a divine world government, is a valid one and was taught by Jesus. It refers to a future phase of Jesus' inner kingdom that follows the growth and expansion of his brotherhood of the kingdom on our world.

Thus, Jesus taught two concepts of the kingdom on earth; he taught the kingdom as:

(1) A present reality—existing now within the heart of the believer. Personal spiritual fellowship with God the Father. The inner submission of our will to God's will. The kingdom of God within.

(2) A future hope—when the kingdom would be realized in fullness. The Messiah rules over the nations of the world. The kingdom as an outward and worldwide phenomenon. (See also Ch. 166, fn. *b*.)   *(continued next page)*

Lk. 17:20   asked when / asked by the Pharisees when (RSV)
Lk. 17:21   is within you." (KJV) / is in the midst of you." (RSV)
Mt. 20:20   The / Then the (RSV) • to Jesus, with / to him, with (RSV)
Mt. 20:27   your minister; / your slave; (RSV)
Mt. 20:28   life in the service of many. / life as a ransom for many. (RSV) (171:0/1867–8)

130

108. On Counting the Cost

25Now great multitudes accompanied him; and Jesus turned and said to them, 26"If anyone comes to me and is not willing to forsake his own father and mother and wife and children and brothers and sisters, yes, and even his own life, he cannot be my disciple. 27Whoever does not bear his own cross and come after me, cannot be my disciple. 28For which of you, desiring to build a tower, does not first sit down and count the cost, whether he has enough to complete it? 29Otherwise, when he has laid a foundation, and is not able to finish, all who see it begin to mock him, 30saying, 'This man began to build and was not able to finish.' 31Or what king, going to encounter another king in war, will not sit down first and take counsel whether he is able with ten thousand to meet him who comes against him with twenty thousand? 32And if not, while the other is yet a great way off, he sends an embassy and asks terms of peace. 33So therefore, whoever of you does not renounce all that he has cannot be my disciple."

34"Salt is good; but if the salt has lost its savor, wherewith shall it be seasoned? 35It is fit neither for the land nor for the dunghill; men throw it away. He who has ears to hear, let him hear."

(Lk. 14:25–35)

(continued from previous page)

c   "You know that the rulers of the Gentiles lord it over them, and their great men exercise authority over them. It shall not be so among you; but whoever would be great among you must be your servant, and whoever would be first among you must be your minister."—Here Jesus distinguishes two basic ways of living: the ways of the world and the ways of the kingdom. Those who choose and live the way of the kingdom will seek more to serve others than to rule over them.

Lk. 14:25 and Jesus turned / and he turned (RSV)
Lk. 14:26 and is not willing to forsake his / and does not hate his (RSV) (171:2/1869–70)

109. Jesus Predicts His Death

³²And they were on the road, going up to Jerusalem, and Jesus was walking ahead of them; and they were amazed,ᵃ and those who followed were afraid.

And taking the twelve again, he began to tell them what was to happen to him, ³³saying, "Behold, we are going up to Jerusalem; and the Son of Man will be delivered to the chief priests and the scribes, and they will condemn him to death, and deliver him to the Gentiles; ³⁴and they will mock him, and spit upon him, and scourge him, and kill him; and after three days he will rise."

³⁴But they understood none of these things; this saying was hid from them, and they did not grasp what was said.ᵇ

(Mk.10:32–34; Lk. 18:34)

ᵃ "they were amazed"—This refers to the apostles' reaction to Jesus going up to Jerusalem in the face of the Sanhedrin's condemnation of death.

ᵇ "they did not grasp what was said."—The apostles, like all the Jewish believers, expected Jesus to establish a temporal kingdom on earth with its headquarters at Jerusalem. Thus, they could not comprehend Jesus' announcement that he would die at the hands of the chief priests and scribes.

(171:4/1871–2)

110. The Healing of Bartimaeus

³⁵As Jesus drew near to Jericho, a blind man named Bartimaeus was sitting by the roadside begging; ³⁶and hearing a multitude going by, he inquired what this meant. ³⁷They told him, "Jesus of Nazareth is passing by."

³⁸And he cried, "Jesus, Son of David, have mercy on me!" ³⁹And those who were in front rebuked him, telling him to be silent; but he cried out all the more, "Son of David, have mercy on me!"

⁴⁰And Jesus stopped, and commanded him to be brought to him; and when he came near, he asked him, ⁴¹"What do you want me to do for you?"

He said, "Lord, let me receive my sight."

⁴²And Jesus said to him, "Receive your sight; your faith has made you whole."

⁴³And immediately he received his sight and followed him, glorifying God; and all the people, when they saw it, gave praise to God.

(Lk. 18:35–43)

Lk. 18:35 As Jesus drew / As he drew (RSV) • man named Bartimaeus was (Mk. 10:46) / man was (RSV)
Lk. 18:42 you whole. / you well. (RSV) (171:5/1873)

132

111. Staying at the House of Zaccheus

¹He entered Jericho and was passing through. ²And there was a man named Zaccheus; he was a chief tax collector, and rich. ³And he sought to see who Jesus was, but could not, on account of the crowd, because he was small of stature. ⁴So he ran on ahead and climbed up into a sycamore tree to see him, for he was to pass that way.

⁵And when Jesus came to the place, he looked up and said to him, "Zaccheus, make haste and come down; for I must stay at your house today."

⁶So he made haste and came down, and received him joyfully.

⁷And when they saw it they all murmured, "He has gone in to be the guest of a man who is a sinner."

⁸And Zaccheus stood and said to the Lord, "Behold, Lord, the half of my goods I give to the poor; and if I have defrauded anyone of anything, I restore it fourfold."

⁹And Jesus said to him "Today salvation has come to this house,ᵃ and you have become indeed a son of Abraham.ᵇ ¹⁰For the Son of Man came to seek and to save the lost."   (Lk. 19:1–10)

---

a   "Today salvation has come to this house"—Jesus taught a gospel of eternal salvation, eternal survival. How do we gain this salvation?

In Jesus' gospel God is our Father and we are all his children, brothers and sisters to one another in God's heavenly family. Our part is to believe this gospel, accept the truth that we are sons and daughters of God, and by faith realize our sonship with God. (I am a son of God. / I am a daughter of God.) And as his children our part is to choose and do our Father's will. (Your will be done. / It is my will that your will be done. / Not my will, but yours, be done.)

When we wholeheartedly choose to do our Father's will, we are transformed; with every choice and decision to follow in God's way we are identified less and less with our passing material body and more and more with our inner soul and God's indwelling spirit presence.

When our body dies our soul survives through its identification and union with God's inner spirit. This is a salvation that has been gained through faith and the submission of our personal will to God's higher spiritual will.

b   "you have become indeed a son of Abraham."—You have become a true follower of the way of Abraham, the way of God. (See Ch. 76, fn. *a*.)

Lk. 19:2   named Zaccheus; (Mon) / named Zacchaeus; (RSV)
Lk. 19:5   him, "Zaccheus, make (Mon) / him, "Zacchaeus, make (RSV)
Lk. 19:8   And Zaccheus stood (Mon) / And Zacchaeus stood (RSV)
Lk. 19:9   house, and you have become indeed a / house, since he also is a (RSV) (171:6/1873–4)

112. The Parable of the Pounds

[11]As they heard these things, he proceeded to tell a parable, because he was near to Jerusalem, and because they supposed that the kingdom of God was to appear immediately. [12]He said therefore, "A nobleman went into a far country to receive a kingdom and then return. [13]Calling ten of his servants,[a] he gave them ten pounds, and said to them, 'Trade with these till I come.' [14]But his citizens hated him and sent an embassy after him, saying, 'We do not want this man to reign over us.'"[b]

[15]"When he returned, having received the kingdom, he commanded these servants, to whom he had given the money, to be called to him, that he might know what they had gained by trading. [16]The first came before him, saying, 'Lord, your pound has made ten pounds more.' [17]And he said to him, 'Well done, good servant! Because you have been faithful in a very little, you shall have authority over ten cities.' [18]And the second came, saying, 'Lord, your pound has made five pounds.' [19]And he said to him, 'And you are to be over five cities.' [20]Then another came, saying, 'Lord, here is your pound, which I kept laid away in a napkin; [21]for I was afraid of you, because you are a severe man; you take up what you did not lay down, and reap what you did not sow.'"

[22]"He said to him, 'I will condemn you out of your own mouth, you wicked servant! You knew that I was a severe man, taking up what I did not lay down and reaping what I did not sow? [23]Why then did you not put my money into the bank, and at my coming I should have collected it with interest?' [24]And he said to those who stood by, 'Take the pound from him, and give it to him who has the ten pounds.' [25](And they said to him, 'Lord, he has ten pounds!') [26]I tell you, that to everyone who has will more be given; but from him who has not, even what he has will be taken away."

[28]And when he had said this, he went on ahead, going up to Jerusalem.　(Lk. 19:11–26, 28)

---

a "Calling ten of his servants"—Jesus is here speaking especially to his chosen apostles; he is urging them to justify their stewardship of the gospel by being faithful in their efforts.

b "We do not want this man to reign over us."—The apostles falsely believe that Jesus is going up to Jerusalem to receive a kingdom. (Lk. 19:11) Jesus is seeking to prepare them for the reality of his impending rejection. He tells a parable in which the citizens reject a nobleman as their earthly ruler just as the Jews are about to reject Jesus as their spiritual ruler.

(171:8/1875–7)

XXVIII. Entry into Jerusalem

113. Danger of the Jerusalem Visit; Arrival in Bethany

[55]Now the Passover of the Jews was at hand, and many went up from the country to Jerusalem before the Passover to purify themselves. [56]They were looking for Jesus and saying to one another as they stood in the temple, "What do you think? That he will not come to the feast?" [57]Now the chief priests and the Pharisees had given orders that if anyone knew where he was, he should let them know, so that they might arrest him.[a]

[1]Six days before the Passover Jesus came to Bethany where Lazarus was, whom Jesus had raised from the dead. [9]When the great crowd of the Jews learned that he was there, they came, not only on account of Jesus but also to see Lazarus, whom he had raised from the dead. [10]So the chief priests planned to put Lazarus also to death, [11]because on account of him many of the Jews were going away and believing in Jesus. (Jn. 11:55–57; 12:1, 9–11)

---

[a] "Now the chief priests and the Pharisees had given orders that if anyone knew where he was, he should let them know, so that they might arrest him."—The Sanhedrin has decreed Jesus' death (Ch. 104), and now issues orders calling upon all of Jewry to deliver him into their hands.

(172:0,1/1878)

114. Mary Anoints Jesus

²At the house of Simon in Bethany they made him a supper; Martha served, and Lazarus was one of those at table with him. ³Mary*a* took an alabaster flask of costly ointment of pure nard and poured it over his head, and anointed the feet of Jesus and wiped his feet with her hair; and the house was filled with the fragrance of the ointment. ⁴But there were some who said to themselves indignantly, "Why was the ointment thus wasted?" ⁵And they reproached her.

⁴Judas Iscariot, one of his disciples (he who was to betray him), said, ⁵"Why was this ointment not sold for three hundred denarii and given to the poor?"

⁶But Jesus said, "Let her alone; why do you trouble her? She has done a beautiful thing to me. ⁷For you always have the poor with you, and whenever you will, you can do good to them; but you will not always have me. ⁸She has done what she could; she has anointed my body beforehand for burying.*b* ⁹And truly, I say to you, whenever the gospel is preached in the whole world, what she has done will be told in memory of her."

(Jn. 12:2–3; Mk. 14:4–5; Jn. 12:4–5; Mk. 14:6–9)

---

a   "Mary"—the sister of Lazarus.

b   "she has anointed my body beforehand for burying."—By this act Mary demonstrates her faith in Jesus and his teaching that he would be given over into the hands of the gentiles, be condemned and killed, and on the third day rise. (See Ch. 109.) Few of his followers are willing to accept or believe that this could really happen. But Mary does believe Jesus. She is anointing him before his death with ointment that was intended to be used after his death.

This ointment was quite expensive—equal in value to a year's labor (300 denarii). Judas and others object to what appears to them to be an extravagance and a waste. But Jesus rebukes them and honors Mary's act. And just as he prophesied, this story of Mary is "told in memory of her."

Jn. 12:2   At the house of Simon in Bethany they (Mk. 14:3) / There they (RSV)
Jn. 12:3   took an alabaster flask of (Mk. 14:3) / took a pound of (RSV) • nard and poured it over his head, and (Mk: 14:3) / nard and (RSV)
Mk. 14:4   Judas / But Judas (RSV) (172:1/1879)

115. Triumphal Entry into Jerusalem

12The next day a great crowd who had come to the feast heard that Jesus was coming to Jerusalem.

1And when Jesus and the apostles drew near to Jerusalem, to Bethphage and Bethany, at the Mount of Olives, he sent two of his apostles, 2and said to them, "Go into the village opposite you, and immediately as you enter it you will find a colt tied; untie it and bring it. 3If anyone says to you, 'Why are you doing this?' say, 'The Lord has need of it and will send it back here immediately.'"

4And they went away, and found a colt tied at the door out in the open street; and they untied it. 5And those who stood there said to them, "What are you doing, untying the colt?"

6And they told them what Jesus had said; and they let them go. 7And they brought the colt to Jesus, and threw their garments on it; and he sat upon it; 14as it is written, 15"Fear not, daughter of Zion; behold, your king is coming, sitting on an ass's colt!"[a]

16His apostles did not understand this at first; but when Jesus was glorified, then they remembered that this had been written of him and had been done to him.

8And many spread their garments on the road, and others spread leafy branches which they had cut from the fields. 9And those who went before and those who followed cried out, "Hosanna! Blessed is he who comes in the name of the Lord! 10Blessed is the kingdom of our father David that is coming! Hosanna in the highest!"

(Jn. 12:12; Mk. 11:1–7; Jn. 12:14–16; Mt. 11:8–10)

(continued)

---

a   "Fear not, daughter of Zion; behold, your king is coming, sitting on an ass's colt!"—This phrase is a quotation from Zechariah 9:9, "Rejoice greatly, O daughter of Zion; shout, O daughter of Jerusalem. Behold, your king comes to you. He is just and brings salvation. He is lowly, riding upon an ass, upon a colt, the foal of an ass." (KJV)

A warrior entered a city on a horse. A king on a mission of peace entered riding upon an ass. Jesus would not enter as the warrior king and ruling Messiah expected by the Jews, but rather as a man of peace, fulfilling the spiritual concept of the Messiah. Here, Jesus once more seeks to demonstrate to his followers that his kingdom is not of this world; it is a purely spiritual affair involving the rule of God in the hearts of his earth children.

Mk. 11:1   when Jesus and the apostles drew / when they drew (RSV) • his apostles, and (Ch. 22, fn. *a*) / his disciples, and (RSV)
Mk. 11:2   tied; untie / tied on which no one has ever sat; untie (RSV)
Jn. 12:16   His apostles did (Ch. 22, fn. *a*) / His disciples did (RSV) (172:3/1880–2)

115. Triumphal Entry into Jerusalem (continued)

[37]As he was now drawing near, at the descent of the Mount of Olives, the whole multitude of the disciples began to rejoice and praise God with a loud voice for all the mighty works that they had seen, [38]saying, "Blessed is the King who comes in the name of the Lord! Peace in heaven and glory in the highest!"

[39]And some of the Pharisees in the multitude said to him, "Teacher, rebuke your disciples."

[40]He answered, "I tell you, if these were silent, the very stones would cry out."

[41]And when he drew near and saw the city he wept over it, [42]saying, "Would that even today you knew the things that make for peace! But now they are hid from your eyes. [43]For the days shall come upon you, when your enemies will cast up a bank about you and surround you, and hem you in on every side, [44]and dash you to the ground, you and your children within you, and they will not leave one stone upon another in you; because you did not know the time of your visitation."[b]

[19]The Pharisees then said to one another, "You see that you can do nothing; look, the world has gone after him."

(Lk. 19:37–44; Jn. 12:19)

---

b "For the days shall come upon you, when your enemies will cast up a bank about you and surround you, and hem you in on every side, and dash you to the ground, you and your children within you, and they will not leave one stone upon another in you; because you did not know the time of your visitation."—This prophecy was swiftly fulfilled. In AD 70 the Roman army leveled Jerusalem, destroyed the temple, and dispersed the Jews living there.

The following description of this event is found on page 195 of *Civilization Past and Present*, a standard college history text: "During centuries of tribulation, the Prophets had taught that God would one day create a new Israel where righteousness prevailed under a divinely appointed leader, a Messiah. But groups concerned less with a spiritual kingdom than with an independent political state called for rebellion. In AD 66 violence erupted. The Roman garrison at Jerusalem was massacred, and the revolt spread beyond the walls of the city. Rome met the challenge with a large army commanded by Vespasian. When in AD 69 Vespasian was proclaimed emperor and went to Rome, his son Titus completed the siege of Jerusalem. The siege was recorded in all its horror by the Jewish historian Josephus: 'While the [temple] was on fire, everything was plundered that came to hand, and ten thousand of those that were caught were slain: nor was there a commiseration of any age, or any reverence of gravity, but children, and old men . . . and priests, were slain in the same manner.'" (*The Genuine Works of Flavius Josephus*, III Bk. 4, Ch. 5)

"Although other revolts were attempted later and Roman armies devastated Palestine even more completely, the wholesale destruction of Jerusalem in AD 70 spelled the end of the ancient Hebrew state. The Jews' dream of an independent political state was to remain unrealized for almost nineteen centuries, until, as a result of United Nations action, the republic of Israel was proclaimed in 1948."

(172:3/1881–3)

116. Visiting the Temple; The Widow's Mites

[10]And when he entered Jerusalem, all the city was stirred, saying, "Who is this?" [11]And the crowds said, "This is the prophet Jesus from Nazareth of Galilee."

[11]And he entered Jerusalem and went into the temple.

[41]And he sat down opposite the treasury, and watched the multitude putting money into the treasury. Many rich people put in large sums. [42]And a poor widow came, and put in two mites, which make a penny.

[43]And he called his apostles to him, and said to them, "Truly, I say to you, this poor widow has put in more than all those who are contributing to the treasury. [44]For they all contributed out of their abundance; but she out of her poverty has put in everything she had, her whole living."

[11]And when he had looked round at everything, as it was already late, he went out to Bethany with the twelve.

(Mt. 21:10–11; Mk. 11:11; 12:41–44; 11:11)

Mk. 12:42 two mites, which (KJV) / two copper coins, which (RSV)
Mk. 12:43 his apostles to (Ch. 22, fn. *a*) / his disciples to (RSV) (172:4/1883)

XXIX. The First Day in Jerusalem

117. Cleansing the Temple

¹³The Passover of the Jews was at hand, and Jesus went up to Jerusalem. ¹⁴In the temple he found those who were selling oxen and sheep and pigeons, and the money-changers at their business. ¹⁵And making a whip of cords, he drove them all, with the sheep and oxen, out of the temple, ¹²and he overturned the tables of the money-changers and the seats of those who sold pigeons.

¹⁶And he told those who sold the pigeons, "Take these things away; you shall not make my Father's house a house of trade." ¹⁶And he would not allow anyone to carry anything through the temple. ¹³He said to them, "It is written, 'My house shall be called a house of prayer'; but you make it a den of robbers."

¹⁵But when the chief priests and the scribes saw the wonderful things that he did, and the children crying out in the temple, "Hosanna to the Son of David!" they were indignant; ¹⁶and they said to him, "Do you hear what these are saying?"

And Jesus said to them, "Yes; have you never read, 'Out of the mouth of babes and sucklings thou hast brought perfect praise'?"

⁴⁷And he was teaching daily in the temple. The chief priests and the scribes and the principal men of the people sought to destroy him; ⁴⁸but they did not find anything they could do, for all the people hung upon his words.

(Jn. 2:13–15; Mt. 21:12; Jn. 2:16; Mk. 11:16; Mt. 21:13, 15–16; Lk. 19:47–48)

(continued from following page)

Increasingly yielding the fruits of the spirit in our daily lives is the law of the kingdom. It is the universal aspect of God's will for us; it applies to each and every individual. The Father would have us all bear spirit fruit—thereby developing our spiritual character along the perfected lines taught and exemplified by Jesus.

The Father also has a personal and specific will for each individual that is different for every personality. For example, the Father's special mission for Jesus was that he establish the kingdom of heaven on earth.

The Father's unique and personal will for us is his plan for our ideal lives and careers. This is our call to service, the part that God would have us play in life's drama. As we grow closer to him, we are increasingly able to discern the Father's plan for our lives. His spirit lives within us, constantly seeking to guide us forward through the maze of living towards the goal of destiny.

Mt. 21:13   Isaiah 56:7
Mt. 21:16   Psalms 8:2   (173:1/1888–91)

118. Challenging Jesus' Authority to Teach

23The chief priests and the elders of the people came up to him as he was teaching, and said, "By what authority are you doing these things, and who gave you this authority?"

24Jesus answered them, "I also will ask you a question; and if you tell me the answer, then I also will tell you by what authority I do these things. 25The baptism of John, whence was it? From heaven or from men?"

And they argued with one another, "If we say 'From heaven,' he will say to us, 'Why then did you not believe him?' 26But if we say, 'From men,' we are afraid of the multitude; for all hold that John was a prophet." 27So they answered Jesus, "We do not know."

And he said to them, "Neither will I tell you by what authority I do these things." (Mt. 21:23–27)

Mt. 21:23 The / And when he entered the temple, the (RSV) (173:2/1891–2)

119. Parable of the Two Sons

28Jesus asked the Jewish leaders, "What do you think? A man had two sons; and he went to the first and said, 'Son, go and work in the vineyard today.' 29And he answered, 'I will not'; but afterward he repented and went. 30And he went to the second and said the same; and he answered, 'I go, sir'; but did not go. 31Which of the two did the will of his father?"*a*

They said, "The first."

Jesus said to them, "Truly, I say to you, the tax collectors and the harlots go into the kingdom of God before you. 32For John came to you in the way of righteousness, and you did not believe him, but the tax collectors and the harlots believed him." (Mt. 21:28–32)

a "Which of the two did the will of his father?"—Saying we will do the will of God is not enough; we must actually do our Father's will. This is Jesus' fundamental teaching. The kingdom he taught is the will of the Father dominant in the heart of the believer. This kingdom is composed of those individuals who have faith in the Fatherhood of God and are dedicated to doing his will.

The will of God for us, his earth children, is that we increasingly yield the fruits of the spirit in our daily lives. These character fruits of the spirit are most clearly seen in the life of Jesus. They include: love, joy, peace, long-suffering, gentleness, goodness, faith, meekness, temperance, patience, kindness, and self-control.

(continued on preceding page)

Mt. 21:28 Jesus asked the Jewish leaders, "What / "What (RSV) (173:3/1893)

120. Parable of the Absent Landlord

33"Hear another parable. There was a householder who planted a vineyard, and set a hedge around it, and dug a wine press in it, and built a tower, and let it out to tenants, and went into another country. 34When the season of fruit drew near, he sent his servants to the tenants, to get his fruit; 35and the tenants took his servants and beat one, killed another, and stoned another. 36Again he sent other servants, more than the first; and they did the same to them. 37Afterward he sent his son to them, saying, 'They will respect my son.' 38But when the tenants saw the son, they said to themselves, 'This is the heir; come, let us kill him and have his inheritance.' 39And they took him and cast him out of the vineyard, and killed him. 40When therefore the owner of the vineyard comes, what will he do to those tenants?"

41They said to him, "He will put those wretches to a miserable death, and let out the vineyard to other tenants who will give him the fruits in their seasons." 16When they heard this, they said, "God forbid!"

42Jesus said to them, "Have you never read in the scriptures: 'The very stone which the builders rejected has become the head of the corner; this was the Lord's doing, and it is marvelous in our eyes'? 43Therefore I tell you, the kingdom of God will be taken away from you and given to a people producing the fruits of it. 44And he who falls on this stone, while he is thereby broken in pieces, will be saved; but when it falls on anyone, it will crush him."

45When the chief priests and the Pharisees heard his parables, they perceived that he was speaking about them.[a] 46But when they tried to arrest him, they feared the multitudes, because they held him to be a prophet.

(Mt. 21:33–41; Lk. 20:16; Mt. 21:42–46)

---

a   "When the chief priests and the Pharisees heard his parables, they perceived that he was speaking about them."—In this parable, God is the householder, the tenants are the Jewish nation, and the servants sent by the householder are the Jewish prophets. The son whom the tenants rejected and killed represents Jesus and his gospel of the kingdom.

Mt. 21:42   Psalms 118:22–23
Mt. 21:43   a people producing (Rieu) / a nation producing (RSV)
Mt. 21:44   stone, while he is thereby broken in pieces, will be saved; / stone will be broken to pieces; (RSV) (173:4/1893–4)

121. Parable of the Marriage Feast

[1]And again Jesus spoke to them in parables, saying, [2]"The kingdom of heaven may be compared to a king who gave a marriage feast for his son, [3]and sent his servants to call those who were invited to the marriage feast; but they would not come. [4]Again he sent other servants, saying, 'Tell those who are invited, Behold, I have made ready my dinner, my oxen and my fat calves are killed, and everything is ready; come to the marriage feast.' [5]But they made light of it and went off, one to his farm, another to his business, [6]while the rest seized his servants, treated them shamefully, and killed them. [7]The king was angry, and he sent his troops and destroyed those murderers and burned their city. [8]Then he said to his servants, 'The wedding is ready, but those invited were not worthy. [9]Go therefore to the thoroughfares, and invite to the marriage feast as many as you can find.' [10]And those servants went out into the streets and gathered all whom they found, both bad and good; so the wedding hall was filled with guests. [11]But when the king came in to look at the guests, he saw there a man who had no wedding garment; [12]and he said to him, 'Friend, how did you get in here without a wedding garment?' And he was speechless. [13]Then the king said to the attendants, 'Bind him hand and foot, and cast him into the outer darkness; there men will weep and gnash their teeth.' [14]For many are called, but few are chosen." (Mt. 22:1–14)

(173:5/1894–5)

122. The Request for a Sign

[18]The Jews said to him, "What sign have you to show us for doing this?"

[19]Jesus answered them, "Destroy this temple, and in three days I will raise it up."

[20]The Jews then said, "It has taken forty-six years to build this temple, and will you raise it up in three days?"

[21]But he spoke of the temple of his body. [22]When therefore he was raised from the dead, his disciples remembered that he had said this; and they believed the word which Jesus had spoken. (Jn. 2:18–22)

Jn. 2:22 believed the word / believed the scripture and the word (RSV) (173:5/1895)

XXX. The Second Day in Jerusalem

123. The Attempt to Entrap Jesus

¹³And they sent to him some of the Pharisees*a* and some of the Herodians,*b* to entrap him in his talk. ¹⁴And they came and said to him, "Teacher, we know that you are true, and care for no man; for you do not regard the position of men, but truly teach the way of God. Is it lawful to pay taxes to Caesar, or not? ¹⁵Should we pay them, or should we not?"*c*

But knowing their hypocrisy, he said to them, "Why put me to the test? Bring me a coin, and let me look at it." ¹⁶And they brought one. And he said to them, "Whose likeness and inscription is this?"

They said to him, "Caesar's."

¹⁷Jesus said to them, "Render to Caesar the things that are Caesar's, and to God the things that are God's."

And they were amazed at him. ²⁶And they were not able in the presence of the people to catch him by what he said; but marveling at his answer they were silent.

(Mk. 12:13–17; Lk. 20:26)

---

a   "Pharisees"—The Pharisees consisted of the scribes and rabbis taken together.

b   "Herodians"—The Herodians were a political party that sought emancipation from direct Roman rule through the restoration of the Herodian dynasty.

c   "Is it lawful to pay taxes to Caesar, or not? Should we pay them, or should we not?"— Jesus' enemies probably reasoned something like this: If he advised against paying taxes, he could be brought before the Roman authorities for sedition. On the other hand, if he affirmed the payment of tribute to Rome, he would lose favor with the Jewish people who hated the Roman overrule.

(174:2/1899)

124. The Sadducees and the Resurrection

[23]The same day Sadducees,[a] who say that there is no resurrection, came to him; and they asked him a question, [24]saying, "Teacher, Moses said, 'If a man dies, having no children, his brother must marry the widow, and raise up children for his brother.' [25]Now there were seven brothers among us; the first married, and died, and having no children left his wife to his brother. [26]So too the second and third, down to the seventh. [27]After them all, the woman died. [28]In the resurrection, therefore, to which of the seven will she be wife? For they all had her."

[29]But Jesus answered them, "You are wrong, because you know neither the scriptures nor the power of God. [30]For in the resurrection they neither marry nor are given in marriage, but are like angels in heaven. [31]And as for the resurrection of the dead, have you not read what was said to you by God, [32]'I *am* the God of Abraham, and the God of Isaac, and the God of Jacob'? He is not God of the dead, but of the living."[b]

[33]And when the crowd heard it, they were astonished at his teaching. [39]And some of the scribes answered, "Teacher, you have spoken well." [40]For they no longer dared to ask him any question.

(Mt. 22:23–33; Lk. 20:39–40)

---

a "Sadducees"—the Sadducees consisted of the priesthood and certain wealthy Jews.

b "And as for the resurrection of the dead, have you not read what was said to you by God, 'I *am* the God of Abraham, and the God of Isaac, and the God of Jacob'? He is not God of the dead, but of the living."—If God says I *am* the God of Abraham, Isaac, and Jacob, it means that Abraham, Isaac, and Jacob are still in existence, still living. Thus, Jesus uses this statement by God (speaking to Moses) as evidence that there is a resurrection after mortal death. Otherwise God would have said, "I *was* the God of Abraham, Isaac, and Jacob."

Mt. 22:23 Sadducees, who say there is no resurrection, came to him; / Sadducees came to him, who say there is no resurrection; (RSV)
Mt. 22:32 Ex. 3:6 • I *am* the / I am the (RSV) (174:3/1900)

125. The Great Commandment

[34]But when the Pharisees heard that he had silenced the Sadducees, they came together. [35]And one of them, a lawyer, asked him a question, to test him, [36]"Teacher, which is the greatest commandment in the law?"[a]

[29]Jesus answered, "The first is, 'Hear, O Israel; The Lord our God, the Lord is one; [30]and you shall love the Lord your God with all your heart, and with all your soul, and with all your mind, and with all your strength.' [39]And a second is like it, You shall love your neighbor as yourself. [40]On these two commandments depend all the law and the prophets."

[32]And the scribe said to him, "You are right, Teacher; you have truly said that he is one, and there is no other but he; [33]and to love him with all the heart, and with all the understanding, and with all the strength, and to love one's neighbor as oneself, is much more than all whole burnt offerings and sacrifices."

[34]And when Jesus saw that he answered wisely, he said to him, "You are not far from the kingdom of God."

And after that no one dared to ask him any question.

(Mt. 22:34–36; Mk. 12:29–30; Mt. 22:39–40; Mk. 12:32–34)

---

a "Teacher, which is the greatest commandment in the law?"—Here this question is clearly answered. Jesus quotes Dt. 6:4–5, which commands us to love God supremely and to love our neighbor as ourselves. He then goes on to say, "On these two commandments depend all the law and the prophets." *The commandment to love is "the greatest commandment."*

In 1 Corinthians, Paul gives this beautiful description of the nature and import of love: "If I speak in the tongues of men and of angels, but have not love, I am a noisy gong or a clanging cymbal. And if I have prophetic powers, and understand all mysteries and all knowledge, and if I have all faith, so as to remove mountains, but have not love, I am nothing. If I give away all I have, and if I deliver my body to be burned, but have not love, I gain nothing. Love is patient and kind, love is not jealous or boastful; it is not arrogant or rude. Love does not insist on its own way; it is not irritable or resentful; it does not rejoice at wrong, but rejoices in the right. Love bears all things, believes all things, hopes all things, endures all things. So faith, hope, love abide, these three; but the greatest of these is love." (1 Cor. 13:1–7, 13)

Mt. 22:36 the greatest commandment / the great commandment (RSV)
Mk. 12:29 Dt. 6:4
Mk. 12:30 Dt. 6:4 (174:4/1901)

126. Jesus Questions the Pharisees

⁴¹Now while the Pharisees were gathered together, Jesus asked them a question, ⁴²saying, "What do you think of the Deliverer? Whose son is he?"

They said to him, "The son of David."

⁴³He said to them, "How is it then that David, in the spirit, calls him Lord, saying in the book of Psalms, ⁴⁴'The Lord said to my Lord, Sit at my right hand, till I put thy enemies under thy feet'? ⁴⁵If David thus calls him Lord, how is he his son?"ᵃ

⁴⁶And no one was able to answer him a word, nor from that day did anyone dare to ask him any more questions.

(Mt. 22:41–46)

---

a "If David thus calls him Lord, how is he his son?"—The Pharisees said that the promised Deliverer is the "son [offspring] of David." How then is it that David, the supposed author of Psalm 101, refers to this coming Messiah as "my Lord"? How can the Lord of David be his son?

Mt. 22:42 the Deliverer? Whose (Ch. 13, fn. *c*) / the Christ? Whose (RSV)
Mt. 22:43 David, in the (RSV alt. trans.) / David, inspired by the (RSV) • saying in the book of Psalms, 'The (Lk. 20:42) / saying, 'The (RSV)
Mt. 22:44 Psalms 110:1 (174:4/1901–2)

127. Before the Greeks

20Now among those who went up to worship at the feast were some Greeks. 21So these came to Philip, who was from Bethsaida in Galilee, and said to him, "Sir, we wish to see Jesus."

22Philip went and told Andrew; Andrew went with Philip and they told Jesus.

23And Jesus answered them, "The hour has come for the Son of Man to be glorified. 24Truly, truly, I say to you, unless a grain of wheat falls into the earth and dies, it remains alone; but if it dies, it bears much fruit. 25He who loves his life loses it, and he who hates his life in this world will keep it for eternal life. 26If anyone serves me, he must follow me; and where I am, there shall my servant be also; if anyone serves me, the Father will honor him."

27"Now is my soul troubled. And what shall I say? 'Father, save me from this hour'? No, for this purpose I have come to this hour. 28Father, glorify your name."

Then a voice came from heaven, "I have glorified it, and I will glorify it again." 29The crowd standing by heard it and said that it had thundered. Others said, "An angel has spoken to him."

30Jesus answered, "This voice has come for your sake, not for mine. 31Now is the judgment of this world, now shall the ruler of this world be cast out; 32and I, when I am lifted up from the earth, will draw all men to myself."

34The crowd answered him, "We have heard from the law that the Christ*a* remains forever. How can you say that the Son of Man must be lifted up?*b* Who is this Son of Man?"

35Jesus said to them, "The light is with you for a little longer. Walk while you have the light, lest the darkness overtake you; he who walks in the darkness does not know where he goes. 36While you have the light, believe in the light, that you may become sons of light."*c*   (Jn. 12:20–32, 34–36)

---

a   "Christ"—[from Greek *Christos*, literally, anointed, translation of Hebrew anointed, Messiah] 1: one who is accepted as the Messiah (this Jesus, whom I proclaim to you, is the Christ—Ac. 17:3). (*Webster's Unabridged*) (See also Ch. 13, fn. *c*.)

b   "We have heard from the law that the Christ remains forever. How can you say that the Son of Man must be lifted up?"—*Christ* is the Greek translation of the Hebrew *Messiah*, and means literally "anointed" or "anointed one." The followers of Jesus came to regard him as "the Christ," by which they affirmed that he was the Messiah, the anointed one from God. It was believed that this long-awaited deliverer would remain on the earth forever. Therefore, the Greeks are shocked when Jesus declares that he will be "lifted up" (be crucified and ascend to heaven). They reply that "the Christ remains on earth forever. How can you say that the Son of Man must be lifted up?"

c   "believe in the light, that you may become sons of light"—We are not born knowing that we are sons and daughters of God. By believing Jesus' gospel that we are all children of a loving heavenly Father and then living in this faith we may actually realize and experience this great truth. In this way we may truly become *faith sons of God.*

Jn. 12:28   glorify your name / glorify thy name (RSV)   (174:5/1902–4)

XXXI. The Last Discourse at the Temple

128. Jesus' Indictment of His Jerusalem Enemies

¹Then said Jesus to the crowds and to his disciples, ²"The scribes and the Pharisees sit on Moses' seat; ³so practice and observe whatever they tell you, but do not what they do; for they preach, but do not practice.*a* ⁴They bind heavy burdens, hard to bear, and lay them on men's shoulders; but they themselves will not move them with their finger."

⁵"They do all their deeds to be seen by men; for they make their phylacteries*b* broad and their fringes long, ⁶and they love the place of honor at feasts and the best seats in the synagogues, ⁷and salutations in the market places, and being called rabbi by men."

⁹"And call no man your father on earth, for you have one Father, who is in heaven.*c* ¹¹He who is greatest among you shall be your servant; ¹²whoever exalts himself will be humbled, and whoever humbles himself will be exalted."

¹³"But woe to you, scribes and Pharisees, hypocrites! because you shut the kingdom of heaven against men; for you neither enter yourselves, nor allow those who would enter to go in. ¹⁴Woe to you, scribes and Pharisees, hypocrites! for you devour widows' houses and for a pretense you make long prayers; therefore you will receive the greater condemnation. ¹⁵Woe to you, scribes and Pharisees, hypocrites! for you traverse sea and land to make a single proselyte, and when he becomes a proselyte, you make him twice as much a child of hell as yourselves."

¹⁶"Woe to you, blind guides, who say, 'If anyone swears by the temple, it is nothing; but if anyone swears by the gold of the temple, he is bound by his oath.' ¹⁷You blind fools! For which is greater, the gold or the temple that has made the gold sacred? ¹⁸And you say, 'If anyone swears by the altar, it is nothing; but if anyone swears by the gift that is on the altar, he is bound by his oath.' ¹⁹You blind men! For which is greater, the gift or the altar that makes the gift sacred?"

(Mt. 23:1–7, 9, 11–19) *(continued)*

---

a "they preach, but do not practice"—The true follower of Jesus will *practice the principles* of the gospel of the kingdom. Jesus calls us not merely to espouse his teachings but rather to *live* the teachings ("not in word only but also in power and in the Holy Spirit"). (1 Thes. 1:5)

b "phylacteries"—(phy•lac•ter•ies) Phylacteries are small square leather boxes containing verses from scripture; traditionally these were worn on the left arm and forehead by Jewish men during the morning weekday prayers.

c "you have one Father, who is in heaven"—Here is a simple and clear declaration of the central truth of Jesus' gospel: God is our loving heavenly *Father.* From the Fatherhood of God everything else flows, e.g., sonship, brotherhood, faith, will, love, service, forgiveness, birth of the spirit, fellowship with God, fruit of the spirit, righteousness, and salvation.

(175:1/1906–7)

149

128. Jesus' Indictment of His Jerusalem Enemies (continued)

[23]"Woe to you, scribes and Pharisees, hypocrites! for you tithe mint and dill and cumin, and have neglected the weightier matters of the law, justice and mercy and faith; these you ought to have done, without neglecting the others. [24]You blind guides, straining out a gnat and swallowing a camel!"

[25]"Woe to you, scribes and Pharisees, hypocrites! for you cleanse the outside of the cup and of the plate, but inside they are full of extortion and rapacity. [26]You blind Pharisee! first cleanse the inside of the cup and of the plate, that the outside may be clean."

[27]"Woe to you, scribes and Pharisees, hypocrites! for you are like whitewashed tombs, which outwardly appear beautiful, but within they are full of dead men's bones and all uncleanness. [28]So you also outwardly appear righteous to men, but within you are full of hypocrisy and iniquity."

[29]"Woe to you, scribes and Pharisees, hypocrites! for you build the tombs of the prophets and adorn the monuments of the righteous, [30]saying, 'If we had lived in the days of our fathers, we would not have taken part with them in shedding the blood of the prophets.' [31]This you witness against yourselves, that you are sons of those who murdered the prophets. [32]Fill up, then, the measure of your fathers."

[33]"You serpents, you brood of vipers, how are you to escape being sentenced to hell?[c]

[34]My Father has sent you prophets and wise men, some of whom you have killed, and some you have persecuted, [35]and so upon you may come all the righteous blood shed on earth, from the blood of innocent Abel to the blood of Zechariah, whom you murdered between the sanctuary and the altar. [36]Truly, I say to you, all this will come upon this generation."

[37]"O Jerusalem, Jerusalem, killing the prophets and stoning those who are sent to you! How often would I have gathered your children together as a hen gathers her brood under her wings, but you would not! [38]Behold, your house is forsaken and desolate."

(Mt. 23:23–38)

---

c "You serpents, you brood of vipers, how are you to escape being sentenced to hell?"— These words are reminiscent of John the Baptist's earlier indictment of the Jewish religious leaders at the river Jordan: "But when he saw many of the Pharisees and Sadducees come for baptism, he said to them: 'You brood of vipers! Who warned you to flee from the wrath to come? Bring forth fruit that befits repentance. Even now the ax is laid to the root of the trees. Every tree therefore that does not bear good fruit is cut down and thrown into the fire.'" (See Ch. 13, Mt. 3:7–8, 10.)

Mt. 23:34 My Father has sent you / Therefore I send you (RSV) • men, some / men and scribes, some (RSV) • you have killed, and / you will kill and crucify, and (RSV) • you have persecuted, / you will scourge in your synagogues and persecute from town to town, (RSV)
Mt. 23:35 and so upon (NEB) / that upon (RSV) • Zechariah, whom / Zechariah the son of Bachariah, whom (RSV)
Mt. 23:37 wings, but you / wings, and you (RSV) (175:1/1908)

150

XXXII. The Discussion on the Mount of Olives

129. The Destruction of Jerusalem

[1]And as he came out of the temple, one of his disciples said to him, "Look, Teacher, what wonderful stones and what wonderful buildings!"

[2]And Jesus said to him, "Do you see these great buildings? There will not be left here one stone upon another, that will not be thrown down."

[3]As he sat on the Mount of Olives opposite the temple, the apostles [7]asked him, "Teacher, when will this be, and what will be the sign when this is about to take place?"[a]

[4]And Jesus answered them, "Take heed that no one leads you astray. [5]For many will come in my name, saying, 'I am the Deliverer,' and they will lead many astray. [6]And you will hear of wars and rumors of wars; see that you are not alarmed; for this must take place, but the end is not yet. [7]There will be famines and earthquakes in various places; [9]they will deliver you up to councils; and you will be beaten in synagogues; and you will stand before governors and kings for my sake, to bear testimony before them. [11]And when they bring you to trial and deliver you up, do not be anxious beforehand what you are to say; but say whatever is given you in that hour, for it is not you who speak, but the Holy Spirit. [12]And brother will deliver up brother to death, and the father his child, and children will rise against parents and have them put to death; [13]and you will be hated by all for my name's sake."

(Mk. 13:1–3; Lk. 21:7; Mt. 24:4–7; Mk. 13:9, 11–13) *(continued)*

---

a "Teacher, when will this be, and what will be the sign when this is about to take place?"— Tell us what will be the time of the destruction of Jerusalem, and how shall we (the apostles) know when these events are about to take place?

Mk. 13:3   temple, the apostles asked (Mt. 24:3) / temple, Peter and James and John and Andrew asked (RSV)
Mt. 24:5   the Deliverer,' and (Ch. 13, fn. *c*) / the Christ,' and (RSV)
Mt. 24:7   There / For nation shall rise against nation, and kingdom against kingdom and there (RSV)
Mk. 13:9   they / for they (RSV) (176:0–1/1912–3)

129. The Destruction of Jerusalem (continued)

²⁰"But when you see Jerusalem surrounded by armies, then know that its desolation has come near. ²¹Then let those who are in Judea flee to the mountains, and let those who are inside the city depart, and let not those who are out in the country enter it; ²²for these are days of vengeance. ²⁴This people will fall by the edge of the sword, and be led captive among all nations; and Jerusalem will be trodden down by the Gentiles.*[b]*

²¹And if anyone says to you, 'Look, here is the Deliverer!' or 'Look, there he is!' believe it not. ²²False Messiahs and false prophets will arise and show signs and wonders, to lead astray, if possible, the elect. ²³But take heed; I have told you all things beforehand."

³⁰"Truly I say unto you, this generation will not pass away before all these things take place."

(Lk. 21:20–22, 24; Mk. 13:21–23, 30)

---

b   "and Jerusalem will be trodden down by the Gentiles"—Jesus was crucified in April, AD 30 (time of the Passover). Less than 40 years later, in AD 66, there was a revolt of the Jews seeking to throw off the Roman yoke. The Roman army came against them and in AD 70 they broke through the walls, leveled Jerusalem, and killed many of its inhabitants. This they did in response to the revolts led by so-called "deliverers." The Jewish historian Josephus recorded the scene: ". . . one would have thought that the hill itself, on which the temple stood, was seething hot . . . the blood was larger in quantity than the fire . . . the ground did nowhere appear visible, for the dead bodies that lay on it, but the soldiers went over heaps of those bodies, as they ran upon such as fled from them." Quoted from *The Genuine Works of Flavius Josephus,* III, Book VI, Ch. 5, trans. by W. Whiston (Philadelphia: Johnson & Warner, and Worcester, Mass.: Isaiah Thomas, 1809). (See also Ch. 115, fn. *b* and Ch. 160, fn. *a*.)

Lk. 21:22   vengeance. / vengeance, to fulfill all that is written. (RSV)
Lk. 21:24   This people will (Lk. 21:23) / they will (RSV) • Gentiles. / Gentiles, until the times of the Gentiles are fulfilled. (RSV)
Mk. 13:21   And if / And then if (RSV) • the Deliverer!' or (Ch. 13, fn. c) / the Christ!' or (KJV) • is!' believe it not. (KJV) / is!' do not believe it. (RSV)
Mk. 13:22   False Messiahs and (Ch. 13, fn. c) / False Christs and (RSV) (176:1/1913)

130. Jesus' Second Coming

³As he sat on the Mount of Olives the apostles came to him privately, saying, "Tell us, when will this be, and what will be the sign of your coming and of the end of the world?"*ᵃ*

²⁷He answered them, saying, "Then they will see the Son of Man coming with power and great glory."

³⁶"But of that day and hour no one knows, not even the angels of heaven, nor the Son, but the Father only. ²⁸From the fig tree learn its lesson: as soon as its branch becomes tender and puts forth its leaves, you know that summer is near.*ᵇ* ²⁹So also, when you see these things taking place, you know that he is near, at the very gates."

(Mt. 24:3; Lk. 21:27; Mt. 24:36; Mk. 13:28–29)

---

a "Tell us, when will this be, and what will be the sign of your coming and of the end of the world?"—In their own minds the apostles connected the destruction of the temple at Jerusalem with the "end of the world" and Jesus' second coming. Thus two questions are being asked and answered in this discussion on the Mount of Olives: (1) When will Jerusalem be destroyed? and (2) When will Jesus return to consummate the kingdom? The first question (Jerusalem's destruction) was addressed in Chapter 129, and the second question (Jesus' second coming) is discussed here. It should be noted that although the apostles connected Jesus' second coming with the "end of the world," Jesus did not teach this doctrine. In fact he specifically taught only three things concerning his return: (1) that he definitely would one day return, (2) that when he returned it would be in power and glory, and (3) that no one in heaven or on earth knows when this return will take place except the Father.

b "From the fig tree learn its lesson: as soon as its branch becomes tender and puts forth its leaves, you know that summer is near."—In the winter the fig tree is dormant and barren; in the spring it puts forth its first tender shoots; while in the summertime it comes to full fruit. Here Jesus seems to associate his return with the summertime. Summertime of what?

The kingdom of heaven taught by Jesus is an inner spiritual dominion—the rule of God in the hearts and minds of his earth children. Since the time of Jesus the world has known little of this spiritual kingdom, but much of materialism. From the standpoint of the kingdom this materialistic age is a spiritual wintertime, a time when Jesus' inner kingdom is alive yet dormant.

He tells us to look for the springtime when the "branch becomes tender and puts forth its leaves." Perhaps he means that when we see the rebirth of his spiritual kingdom in the world, we can then look to the summertime of his next visitation.

Mt. 24:3   the apostles came (Ch. 22, fn. *a*) / the disciples came (RSV) • the end of the world?" (KJV) / the close of the age?" (RSV)
Lk. 21:27   He answered them, saying, "Then / "And then (RSV) • coming with / coming in a cloud with (RSV) (176:1–2/1913–5)

153

131. Parable of the Talents

[14]"For it will be as when a man going on a journey called his servants and entrusted to them his property;[a] [15]to one he gave five talents, to another two, to another one, to each according to his ability. Then he went away. [16]He who had received the five talents went at once and traded with them; and he made five talents more. [17]So also, he who had the two talents made two talents more. [18]But he who had received the one talent went and dug in the ground and hid his master's money. [19]Now after a long time the master of those servants came and settled accounts with them. [20]And he who had received the five talents came forward, bringing five talents more, saying, 'Master, you delivered to me five talents; here I have made five talents more.' [21]His master said to him, 'Well done, good and faithful servant; you have been faithful over a little, I will set you over much; enter into the joy of your master.' [22]And he also who had the two talents came forward, saying, 'Master, you delivered to me two talents; here I have made two talents more.' [23]His master said to him, 'Well done, good and faithful servant; you have been faithful over a little, I will set you over much; enter into the joy of your master.' [24]He also who had received one talent came forward, saying, 'Master, I knew you to be a hard man, reaping where you did not sow, and gathering where you did not winnow; [25]so I was afraid, and I went and hid your talent in the ground. Here you have what is yours.' [26]But his master answered him, 'You wicked and slothful servant! You knew that I reap where I have not sowed, and gather where I have not winnowed? [27]Then you ought to have invested my money with the bankers, and at my coming I should have received what was my own with interest. [28]So take the talent from him, and give it to him who has the ten talents. [29]For to everyone who has will more be given, and he will have abundance; but from him who has not, even what he has will be taken away.'"

[37]And every day he was teaching in the temple, but at night he went out and lodged on the mount called Olivet.   (Mt. 25:14–29; Lk. 21:37)

---

a   "For it will be as when a man going on a journey called his servants and entrusted to them his property"—In this parable a man going on a journey entrusts his property to his servants; in a like manner, Jesus is leaving this world and is entrusting his property—his truth—to his apostles and believers. The faithful servants use the talents given them to create new wealth for their master; likewise Jesus' apostles and believers are called to use the truths he taught to grow in truth and to minister this truth in others. As new wealth was produced from the old, so new spiritual gains should be the result of our stewardship of Jesus' truth.

(continued next page)

(176:3/1916–8)

XXXIII. The Third Day in Jerusalem

132. Judas Conspires to Betray Jesus

¹It was now two days before the Passover and the feast of Unleavened Bread.

³The chief priests and the elders of the people gathered in the palace of the high priest, who was called Caiaphas, ⁴and took counsel together in order to arrest Jesus by stealth and kill him. ⁵But they said, "Not during the feast, lest there be a tumult among the people."

¹⁴Then one of the twelve, who was called Judas Iscariot, went to the chief priests ¹⁵and said, "What will you give me if I deliver him to you?"

¹¹And when they heard it they were glad, and promised to give him a reward. ⁶So he agreed, and sought an opportunity to betray him to them in the absence of the multitude.

(Mk. 14:1; Mt. 26:3–5, 14–15; Mk. 14:11; Lk. 22:6)

(continued from previous page)

The Parable of the Talents also teaches us that, in accordance with the truths we receive, we will one day face a reckoning. We must grow in the knowledge of truth and increasingly give forth the fruits of the spirit in our daily lives. And we must grow in our devotion to the unselfish service of others. In this way we are worthy stewards of Jesus' truth and will be abundantly rewarded. If, however, we are like the unworthy servant who hid his talent in the ground, if we are selfish and slothful stewards of truth, we must also face the just consequences of our actions. Jesus' truth is living, it must grow in us and through us in the world.

(175:1/1906–7)

XXXIV. The Fourth Day

133. Preparation for the Passover

[17]Now the apostles came to Jesus, saying, "Where will you have us prepare for you to eat the Passover?"[a]

[13]And he sent two of his disciples, Peter and John, and said to them, "Go into the city, and a man carrying a jar of water will meet you; follow him, [14]and wherever he enters, say to the householder, 'The Teacher says, "Where is the guest room, where I am to eat the Passover with my apostles?"' [12]And he will show you a large upper room furnished; there make ready."

[13]And they went, and found it as he had told them; and they prepared the Passover.

(Mt. 26:17; Mk. 14:13–14; Lk. 22:12–13)

---

a   "Where will you have us prepare for you to eat the Passover?"—The Passover was a part of the Jews' commemoration of the time of their escape from Egypt under Moses. The Passover meal took place on the fourteenth day of the first month (Nisan) of the Jewish calendar (middle of March). The feast of Unleavened Bread began the next day and lasted for seven days. (Leviticus 23:5–6)

The Passover was celebrated in remembrance of the original Passover meal in Egypt. This was the time when Moses directed the Hebrew slaves to slaughter a lamb, put its blood on their doorposts, and then to eat the lamb. That night, according to tradition, the Lord "passed over" the Hebrew households while the first born of all the Egyptians died. Because of this, Pharaoh summoned Moses and "urged the people to hurry and leave Egypt." The feast of Unleavened Bread was celebrated in remembrance of this hasty exit from Egypt. (See Exodus 12:1–33.)

Mt. 26:17   Now the / Now on the first day of Unleavened Bread the • the apostles came (Ch. 22, fn. *a*) / the disciples came (RSV)
Mk. 14:13   disciples, Peter and John, and (Lk. 22:8) / disciples and (RSV)
Mk. 14:14   my apostles?" (Ch. 22, fn. *a*) / my disciples." (RSV) (178:2/1933)

XXXV. The Last Supper

134. At the Start of the Supper

[17]And when it was evening he came with the twelve. [24]A dispute arose among them, which of them was to be regarded as the greatest.

[14]And when the hour came, he sat at table, and the apostles with him. [15]And he said to them, "I have earnestly desired to eat this Passover with you before I suffer; [16]for I tell you I shall not eat it again until it is fulfilled in the kingdom of God."[a] [17]And he took a cup, and when he had given thanks he said, "Take this, and divide it among yourselves; [18]for I tell you that from now on I shall not drink of the fruit of the vine until the kingdom of God comes."

(Mk. 14:17; Lk. 22:24, 14–18)

---

a   "I have earnestly desired to eat this Passover with you before I suffer; for I tell you I shall not eat it again until it is fulfilled in the kingdom of God."—Jesus knows that he is about to suffer and die at the hands of the Jerusalem religious leaders and tells the apostles that he will not eat with them again until they sit together in the kingdom of God in heaven.

Jesus taught two distinct concepts of the kingdom of God:

(1) The kingdom of God on earth—In all his teachings Jesus gave first emphasis to the kingdom within. ("The kingdom of God is within you." Ch. 107, Lk. 17:21) This is the kingdom of God on earth; it exists in the hearts and minds of each individual who has chosen to abide by his Father's will—to do the will of God. This is the kingdom that Jesus came to establish on our world.

(2) The kingdom of God in heaven—Jesus also taught another phase of the kingdom, the kingdom of God in heaven. This is the goal of gospel believers, to survive death and ascend to the heavenly mansion worlds. ("In my Father's house are many mansions." Ch. 140, Jn. 14:2) This is the salvation—the eternal survival—we attain by choosing and doing the Father's will while on earth.

Lk. 22:16   it again until (RSV alt. trans.) / it until (RSV)   (179:0–2/1936–8)

135. Jesus Washes the Apostles' Feet

³Jesus, knowing that the Father had given all things into his hands, and that he had come from God and was going to God, ⁴rose from supper, laid aside his garments, and girded himself with a towel. ⁵Then he poured water into a basin, and began to wash the disciples' feet, and to wipe them with the towel with which he was girded.

⁶He came to Simon Peter; and Peter said to him, "Lord, do you wash my feet?"

⁷Jesus answered him, "What I am doing you do not know now, but afterward you will understand."

⁸Peter said to him, "You shall never wash my feet."

Jesus answered him, "If I do not wash you, you have no part in me."

⁹Simon Peter said to him, "Lord, not my feet only but also my hands and my head!"

¹⁰Jesus said to him, "He who has bathed does not need to wash, except for his feet, but he is clean all over; and you are clean, but not everyone of you." ¹¹(For he knew who was to betray him; that was why he said, "You are not all clean.")

¹²When he had washed their feet, and taken his garments, and resumed his place, he said to them, "Do you know what I have done to you? ¹³You call me Teacher and Lord; and you are right, for so I am. ¹⁴If I then, your Lord and Teacher, have washed your feet, you also ought to wash one another's feet. ¹⁵For I have given you an example, that you also should do as I have done to you. ¹⁶Truly, truly, I say to you, a servant is not greater than his master; nor is he who is sent greater than he who sent him. ¹⁷If you know these things, blessed are you if you do them."

²⁵And he said to them, "The kings of the Gentiles exercise lordship over their subjects; and those in authority over them are called benefactors. ²⁶But not so with you; rather let the greatest among you become as the youngest, and the leader as one who serves. ²⁷For which is the greater, one who sits at table, or one who serves? Is it not the one who sits at table? But I am among you as one who serves."

(Jn. 13:3–17; Lk. 22:25–27)

Lk. 22:25 over their subjects; and (NEB) / over them; and (RSV) (179:3/1938–40)

158

136. Jesus' Last Words to Judas

¹⁴And when the hour came, he sat at table, and the apostles with him. ¹⁵And he said to them, "I have earnestly desired to eat this Passover with you before I suffer." ²¹When Jesus had thus spoken, he was troubled in spirit, and testified, "Truly, truly, I say to you, one of you will betray me."

²²And they were very sorrowful, and began to say to him one after another, "Is it I, Lord?"

²³He answered, "He who has dipped his hand in the dish with me will betray me."

²⁵Judas, who betrayed him, said, "Is it I, Master?"

He said to him, "You have said so."

²³One of his apostles, whom Jesus loved,ᵃ was lying close to the breast of Jesus; ²⁴so Simon Peter beckoned to him and said, "Tell us who it is of whom he speaks." ²⁵So lying thus, close to the breast of Jesus, he said to him, "Lord, who is it?"

²⁶Jesus answered, "It is he to whom I shall give this morsel when I have dipped it." So when he had dipped the morsel, he gave it to Judas, the son of Simon Iscariot.

²⁷Jesus said to him, "What you are going to do, do quickly."

²⁸Now no one at the table knew why he said this to him. ²⁹Some thought that, because Judas had the money box, Jesus was telling him, "Buy what we need for the feast"; or, that he should give something to the poor. ³⁰So, after receiving the morsel, he immediately went out; and it was night.

(Lk. 22:14–15; Jn. 13:21; Mt. 26:22–23, 25; Jn. 13:23–30)

---

a "One of his apostles, whom Jesus loved"—The apostle John Zebedee, the writer of this gospel according to John.

Jn. 13:23 his apostles, whom (Ch. 22, fn. *a*) / his disciples, whom (RSV) (179:4/1940–1)

159

137. Jesus Establishes the Remembrance Supper

27And he took a cup, and, when he had given thanks, he gave it to them, saying, "Drink of it, all of you. 25Do this, as often as you drink it, in remembrance of me.*a* 29I tell you I shall not drink again of this fruit of the vine until that day when I drink it new with you in my Father's kingdom."

19And he took bread, and when he had given thanks he broke it and gave it to them, saying, "This is my body.*b* Do this in remembrance of me."

(Mt. 26:27; 1 Cor. 11:25; Mt. 26:29; Lk. 22:19)

---

a   "Do this . . . in remembrance of me"—This remembrance supper is the believer's symbolic rendezvous with the Master, wherein the bread and wine are partaken in remembrance of him.

The Jewish Passover celebrated the Jews' emergence from a state of racial slavery into individual freedom. Jesus is here instituting a new Passover symbolizing a new dispensation of spiritual freedom in the kingdom of heaven.

b   "And he took bread . . . and gave it to them, saying, 'This is my body.' "—Here Jesus identifies the bread with his body, his life and teachings in the flesh.

On another occasion Jesus declared, "I am the bread of life." (Ch. 56, Jn. 6:35) He also explained what he meant by "bread": "The bread of God is that which comes down from heaven and gives life to the men of the world." (Ch. 56, Jn. 6:33) This bread of life is the word of the Father as revealed in the Son.

Jesus also declared: "I am this living bread, and if any man eats of this bread, he shall live forever." (Ch. 56, Jn. 6:51) In his earth life, Jesus brought to mankind the gift of the living word of truth incarnated in the likeness of mortal flesh. Our faith acceptance of his truth gives us eternal life.

Here Jesus is instituting a new sacrament in which the bread is partaken in remembrance of his life on earth and the words of truth he spoke.

Lk. 22:19 body. (Mt. 26:26) / body which is given for you. (RSV) (179:5/1941–3)

XXXVI. The Farewell Discourse

138. The Commandment to Love

³⁵And he said to them, "When I sent you out with no purse or bag or sandals, did you lack anything?"

They said, "Nothing."

³⁶He said to them, "But now, let him who has a purse take it, and likewise a bag. ³¹Now is the Son of Man glorified, and in him God is glorified. ³³Little children, yet a little while I am with you. You will seek me; but, where I am going you cannot come. ³⁶Where I am going you cannot follow me now; but you shall follow afterward."

³⁴"A new commandment I give to you, that you love one another even as I have loved you.ᵃ ³⁵By this all men will know that you are my disciples, if you have love for one another."ᵇ

¹¹"These things I have spoken to you, that my joy may be in you, and that your joy may be full."

¹²"This is my commandment, that you love one another as I have loved you. ¹³Greater love has no man than this, that a man lay down his life for his friends. ¹⁴You are my friends if you do what I command you. ¹⁵I do not call you servants; but I have called you friends, and all that I have heard from my Father I have made known to you. ¹⁶You did not choose me, but I chose you, and appointed you that you should go and bear fruit and that your fruit should abide. ¹⁷This I command you, to love one another."ᶜ

(Lk. 22:35–36; Jn. 13:31,33,36,34–35; 15:11–17)

---

a "A new commandment I give to you, that you love one another even as I have loved you."—The older commandments to "love one another" and to "love your neighbor as yourself" are raised to greater heights in this new commandment to love others even as Jesus loves us.

b "By this all men will know that you are my disciples, if you have love for one another."—The way of Jesus is the way of love. It is the rule of living within the kingdom. If we would be his disciples, we must love one another.

c "This I command you, to love one another"—This commandment to love is the greatest commandment in Jesus' teachings. It is the only command that Jesus clearly emphasizes to his disciples. The true follower will make love a priority of life.

Love is the desire to do good to others.
Love identifies the will of God.

Jn. 13:31   "Now / When he had gone out, Jesus said, "Now (RSV)
Jn. 13:33   me; but, where / me, and as I said to the Jews so now I say to you, 'Where (RSV)
Jn. 13:36   Where / Jesus answered, 'Where (RSV)
Jn. 13:34   you. / you, that you also love one another. (RSV)
Jn. 15:15   I do not call / No longer do I call (RSV) • servants; / servants, for the servant does not know what his master is doing; • friends, and all / friends, for all (RSV) (180:0–1/1944–5)

139. "I Am the Vine, You Are the Branches"

[1]"I am the true vine, and my Father is the vine dresser. [2]Every branch of mine that bears no fruit, he takes away, and every branch that does bear fruit he prunes, that it may bear more fruit.[a] [3]You are already made clean by the word which I have spoken to you. [4]Abide in me, and I in you. As the branch cannot bear fruit by itself unless it abides in the vine, neither can you unless you abide in me. [5]I am the vine, you are the branches.[b] He who abides in me, and I in him, he it is that bears much fruit, for apart from me you can do nothing. [6]If a man does not abide in me, he is cast forth as a branch and withers; and the branches are gathered, thrown into the fire and burned. [7]If you abide in me, and my words abide in you, ask whatever you will, and it shall be done for you. [8]By this my Father is glorified, that you bear much fruit, and so prove to be my disciples."[c]

[9]"As the Father has loved me, so have I loved you; abide in my love. [10]If you keep my commandments, you will abide in my love, just as I have kept my Father's commandments and abide in his love." (Jn. 15:1–10)

---

a "Every branch of mine that bears no fruit, he takes away, and every branch that does bear fruit he prunes, that it may bear more fruit."—When we enter the kingdom, we have only begun our efforts to perfect ourselves in the doing of our Father's will. We enter the kingdom as little children, but the Father requires that we grow up by grace to spiritual adulthood. When we follow in the way of the spirit we *increasingly* give forth the fruit of the spirit in our daily lives. Spiritual fruit bearing is the proof that we are living in the kingdom—doing the Father's will. The Father requires that we bear much fruit, and he prunes away our unfruitful branches.

The fruits of the spirit are simply the character traits that Jesus manifested in his life on earth; thus he is our ideal example.

b "I am the vine, you are the branches."—This is a wonderful thought for meditation.

c "By this my Father is glorified, that you bear much fruit, and so prove to be my disciples." —To increasingly and spontaneously give forth the fruit of the spirit in our daily lives is the test and measure of our following in the way of Jesus—doing the Father's will. Some of the fruits of the spirit are love, joy, peace, long-suffering, gentleness, goodness, faith, meekness, temperance, patience, and kindness. Of these love is the greatest.

(180:2/1945–6)

140. The Hatred of the World

[18]"If the world hates you, know that it has hated me before it hated you. [19]If you were of the world, the world would love its own; but because you are not of the world, the world hates you. I chose you out of the world. [20]Remember the word that I said to you, 'The servant is not greater than his master.' If they persecuted me, they will persecute you. [21]But all this they will do to you on my account, because they do not know him who sent me. [22]If I had not come and spoken to them, they would not have sin; but now they have no excuse for their sin.[a] [23]He who hates me hates my Father. [26]But when the Comforter comes, whom I shall send to you from the Father, even the Spirit of Truth, he will bear witness to me."[b]

(Jn. 15:18–23, 26) *(continued)*

---

a "If I had not come and spoken to them, they would not have sin; but now they have no excuse for their sin."—Evil is an unconscious or unintended transgression of God's will, but sin represents a conscious and knowing choice to do wrong.

b "But when the Comforter comes, whom I shall send to you from the Father, even the Spirit of Truth, he will bear witness to me."—Before this time we have heard of the Father's Spirit of Love and the Holy Spirit, but this is the first mention of the Spirit of Truth. This is a new spiritual endowment that is to be sent into the world by Jesus. This Spirit of Truth is a joint bestowal of the Father and the Son, and it bears witness to Jesus and his teachings.

Jn. 15:19 world, the world hates you. I chose you out of the world. / world, but I chose you out of the world, therefore the world hates you. (RSV)
Jn. 15:20 you, 'The servant (KJV) / you, 'A servant (RSV)
Jn. 15:23 Father. / Father also. (RSV)
Jn. 15:26 the Comforter comes, (KJV) / the Counselor comes, (RSV) • Truth, he / Truth, who proceeds from the Father, he (RSV) (180:3/1946–7)

140. The Hatred of the World (continued)

[1]"Let not your hearts be troubled; believe in God, believe also in me. [2]In my Father's house are many mansions;[c] if it were not so, I would not have told you that I go to prepare a place for you. [3]And when I go and prepare a place for you, I will come again and will take you to myself, that where I am you may be also."

[5]Thomas said to him, "Lord, we do not know where you are going; how can we know the way?" [6]Jesus said to him, "I am the way, and the truth, and the life. No one comes to the Father, except through me. [7]If you know me, you know my Father also; henceforth you know him and have seen him."

[8]Philip said to him, "Lord, show us the Father, and we shall be satisfied."

[9]Jesus said to him, "Have I been with you so long, and yet you do not know me, Philip? He who has seen me has seen the Father. How can you then say, 'Show us the Father'? [10]Do you not believe that I am in the Father and the Father in me? The words that I say to you I do not speak on my own authority; but the Father who dwells in me does his works. [11]Believe me that I am in the Father and the Father in me; or else believe me for the work's sake."

(Jn. 14:1–3, 5–11)

---

c   "In my Father's house are many mansions"—Heavenly worlds to which believers ascend after death.

Jn. 14:2   many mansions; (KJV) / many rooms; (RSV) • so, I would not have / so, would I have (RSV) • you / you? (RSV)
Jn. 14:6   Father, except through me. (Wms) / Father, but by me. (RSV)
Jn. 14:7   you know me, / you had known me, (RSV) • you know my / you would have known my (RSV)
Jn. 14:9   you then say, (KJV) / you say, (RSV)
Jn. 14:11   the work's sake." (KJV) / the sake of the works themselves." (RSV) (180:3/1947–8)

141. The Spirit of Truth

[16]"And I will pray the Father, and he will give you another Counselor to be with you for ever, [17]even the Spirit of Truth, whom the world cannot receive; you shall know him, and he will dwell with you, and will be in you."[a]

[18]"I will not leave you desolate; I will come to you.[b] [19]Yet a little while, and the world will see me no more, but you will see me. [20]In that day you will know that I am in my Father, and you in me, and I in you. [21]He who has my commandments and keeps them, he it is who loves me; and I will love him and manifest myself to him."

[25]"These things I have spoken to you while I am still with you. [26]But the Counselor, the Holy Spirit,[c] whom the Father will send in my name, he will teach you all things, and bring to your remembrance all that I have said to you."[d]

[22]Judas (not Iscariot) said to him, "Lord, how is it that you will manifest yourself to us, and not to the world?"

[23]Jesus answered him, "If a man loves me, he will keep my word, and my Father and I will come to him and make our home with him."[e]

(Jn. 14:16–21, 25–26, 22–23)

---

a   "the Spirit of Truth, whom the world cannot receive; you shall know him, and he will dwell with you, and will be in you."—The reception and function of the Spirit of Truth is limited by the individual's spiritual capacity and love of truth. The world has not yet come to accept the truths of Jesus' teaching and cannot receive his Spirit of Truth, but believers may know this Spirit in their own inner experience.

b   "I will not leave you desolate; I will come to you."—Jesus is returning to the Father but he assures the apostles and believers that he is not leaving us alone. In his place he is sending his personal spirit, the Spirit of Truth, to be with us, guide us, and comfort us.

c   "But the Counselor, the Holy Spirit"—In John's recital of Jesus' words, the apostle here associates the "Counselor" with the Holy Spirit. However, the Counselor Jesus is referring to is the same Counselor mentioned earlier—the Spirit of Truth. (See Jn. 14:16 above.) Why then does John identify the Counselor with the Holy Spirit? Perhaps it is because the Spirit of Truth, when it comes, works as one with the Holy Spirit.

d   "he will teach you all things, and bring to your remembrance all that I have said to you."—The Spirit of Truth functions in us to restate the words of Jesus and to lead us into all truth. (See also Jn. 16:13, Ch. 142.)

e   "my father and I will come to him and make our home with him"—Jesus' Spirit of Truth will come and live (with the Father's Spirit) in the souls of those who follow in the Master's way.

Jn. 14:17   receive; / receive, because it neither sees him nor knows him; (RSV) • you shall know / you know (RSV) • him, and he will dwell with / him, for he dwells with (RSV)
Jn. 14:21   and / and he who loves me will be loved by my Father, and (RSV)
Jn. 14:23   Father and I will / Father will love him, and we will (RSV)   (180:4/1948–9)

142. The Necessity for Leaving

[1]"I have said all this to you to keep you from falling away. [2]They will put you out of the synagogues; indeed, the hour is coming when whoever kills you will think he is offering service to God. [3]And they will do this because they have not known the Father. [4]But I have said these things to you, that when the hour comes you may remember that I told you."

[5]"Now I am going to him who sent me, yet none of you asks me, 'Why are you going?' [7]Nevertheless I tell you the truth; it is to your advantage that I go away.[a] For if I do not go away the Comforter will not come to you; but if I go, I will send him to you. [8]And when he comes he will make the world conscious of sin and righteousness and judgment."[b]

[12]"I have yet many things to say to you, but you cannot bear them now. [13]When the Spirit of Truth comes, he will guide you into all truth. He will not speak of himself, but whatever he hears he will speak, and he will declare to you the things that are to come. [14]He will glorify me. He will draw on my truth and declare it to you.[c] [15]All that the Father has is mine; therefore I said that he will take what is mine and declare it to you." (Jn. 16:1–5, 7–8, 12–15) *(continued)*

---

a   "it is to your advantage that I go away"—Here Jesus makes a startling statement. How could his leaving the apostles alone in the world be to their advantage?

Jesus is to die, but in his stead he is sending a new spirit that will take the place of his personal presence and teaching. This new spirit endowment is the Spirit of Truth; it is a joint bestowal of the Father and the Son, and it functions to foster truth in the individual. This spirit comforter destroys the believer's sense of isolation and loss due to Jesus leaving the world. It helps men recall his words and illuminates his life on earth, and it provides new power for the believer to witness to the truths of Jesus' gospel (as was seen at Pentecost). Eventually it leads the believer into all truth.

b   "he will make the world conscious of sin and righteousness and judgment"—The Spirit of Truth in us makes clear the difference between sin and righteousness, and helps us to choose wisely concerning them.

c   "He will not speak of himself, but whatever he hears he will speak. . . . He will draw on my truth and declare it to you."—The Spirit of Truth comes from Jesus and reveals Jesus' truth to us.

Jn. 16:3   Father. / Father, nor me. (RSV)
Jn. 16:4   when the hour (KJV) / when their hour (RSV) • you. / you of them. (RSV)
Jn. 16:5   Now / But now (RSV) • me, 'Why are (Tay) / me, 'Where are (RSV)
Jn. 16:7   the Comforter will (KJV) / the Counselor will (RSV)
Jn. 16:8   will make the world conscious of sin (Bas) / will convince the world concerning sin (RSV) • and judgment." / and judgment: concerning sin because they do not believe in me. (RSV)
Jn. 16:13   all truth. (KJV) / all the truth; (RSV) • He / for he (RSV) • speak of himself, but (KJV) / speak on his own authority, but (RSV)
Jn. 16:14   me. He / me, for he (RSV) • will draw on my truth and (Phi) / will take what is mine and (RSV)
(180:6/1951–2)

142. The Necessity for Leaving (continued)

16"A little while, and you will see me no more; again a little while, and you will see me."

17Some of his apostles said to one another, "What is this that he says to us, 'A little while and you will not see me, and again a little while and you will see me,' and 'because I go to the Father'?" 18They said, "What does he mean by 'a little while'? We do not know what he means."

19Jesus knew that they wanted to ask him, so he said to them, "Is this what you are asking yourselves, what I meant by saying, 'A little while and you will not see me, and again a little while and you will see me'? 20You will be sorrowful, but your sorrow will turn into joy. 21When a woman is in travail she has sorrow because her hour has come, but when she is delivered of the child she no longer remembers the anguish for joy that a child is born into the world. 22So you have sorrow now, but I will see you again and your hearts will rejoice, and no one will take your joy from you. 23In that day if you ask anything of the Father, he will give it to you in my name. 24Hitherto you have asked nothing in my name; ask, and you will receive that your joy may be full."

25"I have said this to you in proverbs. The hour is coming when I shall no longer speak to you in parables but tell you plainly of the Father, 27for the Father himself loves you. 28I came from the Father and have come into the world."

29His apostles said, "Ah, now you are speaking plainly, not in any figure! 30By this we believe that you came from God."

(Jn. 16:16–25, 27–30)

Jn. 16:17   his apostles said (Ch. 22, fn. *a*) / his disciples said (RSV)
Jn. 16:23   day if / day you will ask nothing of me. Truly, truly, I say to you, if (RSV)
Jn. 16:25   in proverbs. (KJV) / in figures; (RSV) • in parables but (KJV) / in figures but (RSV)
Jn. 16:27   you. / you, because you have loved me and have believed that I came from the Father. (RSV)
Jn. 16:29   His apostles said (Ch. 22, fn. *a*) / His disciples said (RSV) (180:6/1952)

XXXVII. Final Admonitions and Warnings

143. Last Words of Peace and Comfort

[27]"Peace I leave with you; my peace I give to you; not as the world gives do I give to you. Let not your hearts be troubled, neither let them be afraid. [28]You heard me say to you, 'I go away, and I will come to you.' [29]And now I have told you before it takes place, so that when it does take place, you may believe."[a]

[32]"The hour is coming, indeed it has come, when you will be scattered, every man to his home, and will leave me alone; yet I am not alone, for the Father is with me. [33]I have said this to you, that in me you may have peace. In the world you have tribulation; but be of good cheer, I have overcome the world." (Jn. 14:27–29; 16:32–33)

---

a   "You heard me say to you, 'I go away, and I will come to you.' And now I have told you before it takes place, so that when it does take place, you may believe."—Here Jesus once again prophesies his own death. What is the purpose of this prophecy? It is to enable the apostles not to be dismayed, but rather to grow stronger in their faith when they witness its fulfillment (Jesus' crucifixion). And it is to enable them to know peace, the peace of Jesus, in the midst of their coming tribulation. ("I have said this to you, that in me you may have peace.") (Jn. 16:33 above)

Prophecy strengthens our faith and prepares us for the future. It enables us to face even great tribulation with faith, peace, and assurance.

(181:1/1953–4)

144. Warning the Apostles and Peter

[31]Then Jesus said to them, "You will all fall away because of me this night; it is written, 'Smite the shepherd, and the sheep of the flock will be scattered.' [32]But after I am raised up, I will go before you to Galilee."

[33]Peter declared to him, "Though they all fall away because of you, I will never fall away. [35]Even if I must die with you, I will not deny you."

[34]Jesus said to him, "Truly, I say to you, this very night, before the cock crows, you will deny me three times."

[26]And when they had sung a hymn, they went out to the Mount of Olives. (Mt. 26:31–33, 35, 34; Mk. 14:26)

Mt. 26:31 Zechariah 13:7 • it / for it (RSV) • Smite the (Zh. 13:7; KJV) / I will strike the (RSV)
Mt. 26:35 Even / Peter said to him, "Even (RSV) (181:2/1962)

XXXVIII. Back at the Gethsemane Camp

145. Jesus Prays for His Apostles

[39]And he came out and went, as was his custom, to the Mount of Olives; and the apostles followed him.

[1]Jesus lifted up his eyes to heaven and said, "Father, the hour has come; glorify your Son that the Son may glorify you. [2]You have given him power over all flesh, to give eternal life to all whom you have given him. [3]And this is eternal life, that they know you the only true God, and him whom you have sent. [4]I glorify you on earth, having accomplished the work which you gave me to do. [5]And now, Father, glorify me with the glory which I had with you before the world was made."

[6]"I have manifested your name[a] to the men whom you gave me out of the world. Yours they were, and you gave them to me, and they have kept your word. [7]Now they know that everything that you have given me is from you. [8]I have given them the words which you gave me. They have received them and know in truth that I came from you; and they have believed that you did send me. [9]I am praying for them. I am not praying for the world but for those whom you have given me. [10]All mine are yours and yours are mine, and I am glorified in them. [11]And now I am no more in the world, and I am coming to you, but they are in the world. Holy Father, keep them in your name, that they may be one even as we are one. [12]While I was with them, I kept them in your name."

(Lk. 22:39; Jn. 17:1–12) *(continued)*

---

a   "I have manifested your name"—What is the name of God that Jesus manifested to the apostles? It is *Father*. Throughout his life Jesus consistently taught us to look to God as our Father, our loving heavenly Father.

Lk. 22:39   the apostles followed (Ch. 22, fn. *a*) / the disciples followed (RSV)
Jn. 17:1–12   you (NRSV) / thee, thou (RSV) • your, yours (NRSV) / thy, thine (RSV) • are (NRSV) / art (RSV) • have, gave, did (NRSV) / hast, gavest, didst (RSV)
Jn. 17:1   Jesus lifted / When Jesus had spoken these words, he lifted (RSV)
Jn. 17:2   You / since you (RSV)
Jn. 17:3   and him whom / and Jesus Christ whom (RSV)
Jn. 17:5   glorify me with / glorify thou me in thy own presence with (RSV)
Jn. 17:8   I / for I (RSV) • me. They / me and they (RSV)
Jn. 17:9   me. / me, for they are yours; (RSV)
Jn. 17:11   world, and I am coming to you, but they are in the world. / world, but they are in the world, and I am coming to you. (RSV) • name, that / name which you have given me, that (RSV) (182:1/1963–4)

145. Jesus Prays for His Apostles (continued)

12"I have guarded them, and none of them is lost but the son of perdition. 14I have given them your word, and the world has hated them. 15I do not pray that you should take them out of the world, but that you should keep them from evil. 17Sanctify them in the truth; your word is truth. 18As you did send me into the world, so I have sent them into the world. 19And for their sake I consecrate myself, that they also may be consecrated in truth."

20"I do not pray for these only, but also for those who believe in me through their word, 21that they may all be one. You, Father, are in me and I in you, that they also may be in us, so that the world may believe that you have sent me. 22The glory which you have given me I have given to them. May they be one even as we are one, 23I in them and you in me, so that the world may know that you have sent me and have loved them even as you have loved me. 24Father, I desire that they also behold my glory which you have given me before the foundation of the world. 25O righteous Father, the world has not known you, but I have known you, and these know that you have sent me. 26I made known to them your name."

(Jn. 17:12, 14–15, 17–26)

Jn. 17:12   perdition. / perdition, that scripture might be fulfilled. (RSV)
Jn. 17:14   them. / them because they are not of the world, even as I am not of the world. (RSV)
Jn. 17:21   You, Father, are in me and I in you; / even as thou, Father, art in me and I in thee, (RSV)
Jn. 17:22   them. May they be / them, that they may be (RSV)
Jn. 17:23   me, so / me, that they may become perfectly one, so (RSV)
Jn. 17:24   also behold / also, whom you have given me, may be with me where I am, to behold (RSV) • me before / me in your love for me before (RSV)
Jn. 17:26   name." / name, and I will make it known, that the love with which you have loved me may be in them, and I in them." (RSV) (182:1/1964–5)

170

146. Jesus Prays in Gethsemane

32And they went to a place which was called Gethsemane; and he said to his apostles, "Sit here, while I pray." 33And he took with him Peter and James and John, and began to be greatly distressed and troubled. 34And he said to them, "My soul is very sorrowful, even to death; remain here, and watch." 41And he withdrew from them about a stone's throw, and knelt down and prayed, 42"Father, if you are willing, remove this cup from me; nevertheless not my will, but yours, be done."[a]

40And he came to the apostles and found them sleeping; and he said to Peter, "So, could you not watch with me one hour? 41Watch and pray that you may not enter into temptation; the spirit indeed is willing, but the flesh is weak."

42Again, for the second time, he went away and prayed, "My Father, if this cannot pass unless I drink it, your will be done."[b] 44And his sweat became like great drops of blood falling down upon the ground. 43And there appeared to him an angel from heaven, strengthening him.

43And again he came and found them sleeping, for their eyes were heavy.

44So, leaving them again, he went away and prayed for the third time, saying the same words. 45Then he came to the apostles and said to them, "Are you still sleeping and taking your rest? Behold, the hour is at hand, and the Son of Man is betrayed into the hands of sinners. 46Rise, let us be going, see, my betrayer is at hand." (Mk. 14:32–34; Lk. 22:41–42; Mt. 26:40–42; Lk. 22:44, 43; Mt. 26:43–46)

---

a "not my will, but yours, be done."—In this time of his great earth crisis Jesus resorts to his favorite prayer, "Not my will, but yours, be done." This prayer, along with its positive form, "Your will be done" (Mt. 26:42 above) should be the habitual practice and constant guide of the true follower of Jesus. This prayer of faith submission to the Father's will is right in *all* life situations.

b "your will be done."—Jesus is now convinced that it is his Father's will that he submit to the natural course of human events. He is living the earth life to the full, and he accepts the death that is a part of this life. An ordinary human being cannot have his death removed through divine intervention, so Jesus refuses to use his heavenly powers to free himself—even though it means death on the cross.

Mk. 14:32   his apostles, "Sit (Ch. 22, fn. *a*) / his disciples, "Sit (RSV)
Lk. 22:42   if you are willing, (NIV) / if thou art willing, (RSV) • but yours, be (NIV) / but thine, be (RSV)
Mt. 26:40   the apostles and (Ch. 22, fn. *a*) / the disciples and (RSV)
Mt. 26:42   it, your will (NIV) / it, thy will (RSV)
Lk. 22:44   And / and (RSV)
Mt. 26:45   the apostles and (Ch. 22, fn. *a*) / the disciples and (RSV)   (182:3/1968–70)

XXXIX. The Betrayal and Arrest of Jesus

147. The Arrest of Jesus

2Now Judas, who betrayed him, also knew the place; for Jesus often met there with his disciples. 3So Judas, procuring a band of soldiers and some officers from the chief priests and Pharisees, went there with lanterns and torches and weapons.

43And Judas came, and with him a crowd with swords and clubs from the chief priests and the scribes and the elders. 44Now the betrayer had given them a sign, saying, "The one I shall kiss is the man; seize him and lead him away under guard."

4Then Jesus, knowing all that was to befall him, came forward and said to them, "Whom do you seek?"

5They answered him, "Jesus of Nazareth."

Jesus said to them, "I am he." 6When he said to them, "I am he," they drew back and fell to the ground.

47Judas was leading them. He drew near to Jesus to kiss him. 45And when he came, he went up to him at once, and said, "Master!" And he kissed him.

48Jesus said to him, "Judas, would you betray the Son of Man with a kiss?"

7Again he asked them, "Whom do you seek?"

And they said, "Jesus of Nazareth."

8Jesus answered, "I told you that I am he; so, if you seek me, let these men go."

(Jn. 18:2–3; Mk. 14:43–44; Jn. 18:4–6; Lk. 22:47; Mk. 14:45; Lk. 22:48; Jn. 18:7–8) *(continued)*

Mk. 14:43 And Judas / And immediately, while he was still speaking, Judas (RSV) • came, and / came, one of the twelve, and (RSV)

Lk. 22:47 Judas was / While he was still speaking, there came a crowd, and the man called Judas, one of the twelve, was (RSV)

Lk. 22:48 Jesus / but Jesus (RSV) (183:2–3/1972–4)

⁵⁰Then they came up and laid hands on Jesus. ¹⁰Simon Peter, having a sword, drew it. ¹¹Jesus said to Peter, "Put your sword into its sheath; ⁵²for they who take the sword will perish by the sword. ¹¹Shall I not drink the cup which the Father has given me? ⁵³Do you think I cannot appeal to my Father, and he will at once send me more than twelve legions of angels?"

¹²So the band of soldiers and their captain and the officers of the Jews seized Jesus and bound him. ⁵⁵At that hour Jesus said to the crowds, "Have you come out as against a robber, with swords and clubs to capture me? Day after day I sat in the temple teaching, and you did not seize me."

⁵⁶Then all the disciples forsook him and fled.

⁵¹And a young man followed him, with nothing but a linen coat about his body. They seized him, ⁵²but he left the linen coat and ran away naked.

(Mt. 26:50; Jn. 18:10–11; Mt. 26:52; Jn. 18:11; Mt. 26:53; Jn. 18:12; Mt. 26:55–56; Mk. 14:51–52)

Mt. 26:50 Jesus. / Jesus and seized him. (RSV)
Jn. 18:10 Simon / Then Simon (RSV) • it. / it and struck the high priest's slave and cut off his right ear. (RSV)
Mt. 26:52 for they who (KJV) / for all who (RSV)
Mk. 14:51 linen coat about / linen cloth about (RSV) • They / and they (RSV)
Mk. 14:52 linen coat and / linen cloth and (RSV) (183:3/1974–5)

XL. Jesus Goes before the Sanhedrin Court

148. The Private Examination by Annas

¹³First they led him to Annas; he was the father-in-law of Caiaphas, who was high priest that year. ¹⁴It was Caiaphas who had given counsel to the Jews that it was expedient that one man should die for the people.

¹⁹Annas then questioned Jesus about his disciples and his teaching. ²⁰Jesus answered him, "I have spoken openly to the world. I have always taught in synagogues and in the temple, where all Jews come together. I have said nothing secretly. ²¹Why do you ask me? Ask those who have heard me, what I said to them; they know what I said."

²²When he had said this, one of the officers standing by struck Jesus with his hand, saying, "Is that how you answer the high priest?"

²³Jesus answered him, "If I have spoken wrongly, bear witness to the wrong; but if I have spoken rightly, why do you strike me?"

²⁴When day came Annas sent him bound to Caiaphas, the high priest; ⁵³and all the chief priests and the elders and the scribes were assembled.

(Jn. 18:13–14, 19–24; Mk. 14:53)

Jn. 18:13   he / for he (RSV)
Jn. 18:19   Annas then / The high priest then (RSV)
Jn. 18:24   When day came Annas sent (Lk. 22:60) / Annas then sent (RSV) (184:0–1/1978–80)

149. In The Courtyard of Annas; Peter's Denial

[15]Simon Peter followed Jesus, and so did another disciple. As this disciple was known to the high priest, he entered the court of the high priest along with Jesus, [16]while Peter stood outside at the door. So the other disciple, who was known to the high priest, went out and spoke to the maid who kept the door, and brought Peter in.

[18]Now the servants and officers had made a charcoal fire, because it was cold, and they were standing and warming themselves; Peter also was with them, standing and warming himself. [17]The maid who kept the door said to Peter, "Are not you also one of this man's disciples?"

He said, "I am not."

[26]One of the servants of the high priest asked, "Did I not see you in the garden with him?" [27]Peter again denied it.

[69]And the maiden began again to say, "This man is one of them."

[71]But he began to invoke a curse on himself and to swear, "I do not know this man of whom you speak."

[59]And after an interval of about an hour still another insisted saying, "Certainly this man also was with him; for he is a Galilean."

[60]But Peter said, "I do not know what you are saying."

And immediately, while he was still speaking, the cock crowed. [61]And the Lord turned and looked at Peter.[a] And Peter remembered the word of the Lord, how he had said to him, "Before the cock crows today, you will deny me three times." [62]And he went out and wept bitterly.

(Jn. 18:15–16, 18, 17, 26–27; Mk. 14:69, 71; Lk. 22:59–62)

---

a "And the Lord turned and looked at Peter."—Perhaps this took place as Jesus was being led from Annas' house to the home of Caiaphas and his "trial" before the Sanhedrin court.

Jn. 18:26   priest asked / priest, a kinsman of the man whose ear Peter had cut off, asked (RSV)
Mk. 14:69   maiden began / maiden saw him and began (RSV) • say, "This / say to the bystanders, "This (RSV)
Lk. 22:60   said, "I / said, "Man, I (RSV) (184:2/1980–2)

150. Before the Sanhedrin Court

59Now the chief priests and the whole council sought false testimony against Jesus that they might put him to death. 60But they found none, though many false witnesses came forward. At last two came forward 61and said, "This fellow said, 'I am able to destroy the temple of God, and to build it in three days.'"

62And the high priest stood up and said, "Have you no answer to make? What is it that these men testify against you?" 63But Jesus was silent. And the high priest said to him, "I adjure you by the living God, tell us if you are the Deliverer, the Son of God."*a*

62And Jesus said, "I am; and presently shall the Son of Man be seated at the right hand of Power, and reign over the hosts of heaven."

63And the high priest tore his garments, and said, "Why do we still need witnesses? 64You have heard his blasphemy. What is your decision?"

66They answered, "He deserves death." 67Then they spat in his face and struck him, and some slapped him.

(Mt. 26:59–63; Mk. 14:62–64; Mt. 26:66–67)

---

a   "I adjure you by the living God, tell us if you are the Deliverer, the Son of God."—Caiaphas identifies the Jewish Deliverer-Messiah as the Son of God. Jesus, without hesitation, affirms that he is the Son of God.

Mt. 26:63   the Deliverer, the (Ch. 13, fn. *c*) / the Christ, the (RSV)
Mk. 14:62   and presently shall the Son of Man be seated / and you will see the Son of Man seated (RSV) • and reign over the hosts of / and coming with the clouds of (RSV) (184:3/1982–4)

151. The Time of Humiliation

63Now the men who were holding Jesus mocked him and beat him; 64they also blindfolded him and asked him, "Prophesy! Who is it that struck you?" 65And they spoke many other words against him, reviling him.

66And they said, 67"If you are the Messiah, tell us."

But he said to them, "If I tell you, you will not believe; 68and if I ask you, you will not answer."

(Lk. 22:63–68)

Lk. 22:66   And / ; and they led him away to their council, and (RSV)
Lk. 22:67   the Messiah, tell (Ch. 13, fn. *c*) / the Christ, tell (RSV) (184:4/1984–5)

XLI. Trial before Pilate

152. The Sanhedrin Brings Charges against Jesus

²⁸Then they led Jesus from the house of Caiaphas to the praetorium. It was early. They themselves did not enter the praetorium, so that they might not be defiled, but might eat the passover.ᵃ ²⁹So Pilateᵇ went out to them and said, "What accusation do you bring against this man?"

³⁰They answered him, "If this man were not an evildoer, we would not have handed him over."

³¹Pilate said to them, "Take him yourselves and judge him by your own law."

The Jews said to him, "It is not lawful for us to put any man to death."

²And they began to accuse him, saying, "We found this man perverting our nation, and forbidding us to give tribute to Caesar, and saying that he himself is a king."

¹²But when he was accused by the chief priests and elders, he made no answer. ¹³Then Pilate said to him, "Do you not hear how many things they testify against you?" ¹⁴But he gave him no answer, not even to a single charge, so that the governor wondered greatly.

(Jn. 18:28–31; Lk. 23:2; Mt. 27:12–14)

---

a   "They themselves did not enter the praetorium, so that they might not be defiled, but might eat the passover."—The praetorium was an addition to the Roman fortress of Antonia, where Pilate and his wife resided during his visits to Jerusalem. The praetorium was a gentile building; the Jews would not enter it because it would render them ceremonially unclean and would bar them from participating in the Passover feast.

b   "Pilate"—Pilate was the Roman procurator who governed Judea, Samaria, and Idumea.

Lk. 23:2   is a king. / is Christ a king. (RSV)   (185:0,2/1987,89–90)

153. Pilate Examines Jesus Privately

33Pilate entered the praetorium again and called Jesus, and said to him, "Are you the King of the Jews?"

34Jesus answered, "Do you say this of your own accord, or did others say it to you about me?"

35Pilate answered, "Am I a Jew? Your own nation and the chief priests have handed you over to me; what have you done?"

36Jesus answered, "My kingdom is not of this world. If my kingdom were of this world, then would my servants fight, that I should not be delivered to the Jews."

37Pilate said to him, "So you are a king?"

Jesus answered, "I am, as you say, a king. For this I was born, and for this I have come into the world, to bear witness to the truth. Everyone who loves the truth hears my voice."

38Pilate said to him, "What is truth?"*a*

After he had said this, he went out to the Jews again, and told them, "I find no fault in him."

5But they were urgent, saying, "He stirs up the people, teaching throughout all Judea, from Galilee even to this place."

(Jn. 18:33–38; Lk. 23:5)

---

a "What is truth?"—That is: Who knows what truth is?

Jn. 18:36 (KJV)
Jn. 18:37 "I am, as you say, a (NOR) / "You say that I am a (RSV) • who loves the (Phi) / who is of the (RSV)
Jn. 18:38 no fault in (KJV) / no crime in (RSV) (185:3/1991–2)

154. Jesus before Herod

[6]When Pilate heard this,[a] he asked whether the man was a Galilean. [7]And when he learned that he belonged to Herod's jurisdiction, he sent him over to Herod, who was himself in Jerusalem at that time. [8]When Herod saw Jesus, he was very glad, for he had long desired to see him, because he had heard about him, and he was hoping to see some sign done by him. [9]So he questioned him at some length; but he made no answer. [10]The chief priests and the scribes stood by, vehemently accusing him. [11]And Herod with his soldiers treated him with contempt and mocked him. Then, arraying him in gorgeous apparel, he sent him back to Pilate. [12]And Herod and Pilate became friends with each other that very day, for before this they had been at enmity with each other. (Lk. 23:6–12)

---

a "When Pilate heard this"—When Pilate heard that Jesus taught "throughout all Judea, from *Galilee* even to this place." (Ch. 153; italics added)

(185:3–4/1992–3)

155. Jesus Appears before Pilate Again

¹³Pilate then called together the chief priests and the rulers and the people, ¹⁴and said to them, "You brought me this man as one who was perverting the people. After examining him I did not find this man guilty of any of your charges. ¹⁵Neither did Herod, for he sent him back to us. Behold, nothing deserving death has been done by him. ¹⁶I will therefore chastise him and release him."

⁸And the crowd came up and began to ask Pilate to do as he was wont to do for them. ¹⁵Now at the feast the governor was accustomed to release for the crowd any one prisoner whom they wanted. ¹⁶And they had then a notorious prisoner, called Barabbas, ¹⁹a man who had been thrown into prison for an insurrection started in the city, and for murder. ¹⁷So when they gathered, Pilate said to them, "Whom do you want me to release for you, Barabbas or Jesus?"

¹¹But the chief priests stirred up the crowd to have him release for them Barabbas instead. ¹⁰Pilate perceived that it was out of envy that the chief priests had delivered him up. ¹⁸But they all cried out together, "Away with this man, and release to us Barabbas."

(Lk. 23:13–16; Mk. 15:8; Mt. 27:15–16; Lk. 23:19; Mt. 27:17; Mk. 15:11, 10; Lk. 23:18)

(continued)

Lk. 23:14 After / and after (RSV) • him I / him before you, behold, I (RSV) • charges. / charges against him. (RSV)
Mt. 27:17 Jesus?" / Jesus who is called Christ?" (RSV)
Mk. 15:10 Pilate perceived / He perceived (RSV) (185:5/1993–4)

155. Jesus Appears before Pilate Again (continued)

¹⁹While he was sitting on the judgment seat, his wife sent word to him, "Have nothing to do with this innocent man, for I have suffered much over him in a dream last night."

²⁰Now the chief priests and the elders persuaded the people to ask for Barabbas and destroy Jesus. ²⁰Pilate addressed them once more, desiring to release Jesus: ¹²"Then what shall I do with the man whom you call the King of the Jews?"

²¹But they shouted out, "Crucify him, crucify him!"

¹⁴And Pilate said to them, "Why, what evil has he done?"

They shouted all the more, "Crucify him."

²¹The governor again said to them, "Which of the two do you want me to release for you?"

And they said, "Barabbas."

²²Pilate said to them, "Then what shall I do with Jesus?"

They all said, "Let him be crucified."

(Mt. 27:19–20; Lk. 23:20; Mk. 15:12; Lk. 23:21; Mk. 15:14; Mt. 27:21–22)

Mt. 27:19 While / Besides while (RSV) • with this innocent man (Knox) / with that righteous man (RSV) • him in / him today in (RSV) • dream last night." (NEB) / dream." (RSV)
Mk. 15:12 "Then / And Pilate again said to them, "Then (RSV)
Lk. 23:21 "Crucify him, crucify (KJV) / "Crucify, crucify (RSV)
Mt. 27:22 Jesus?" / Jesus who is called Christ?" (RSV) (185:5/1994)

181

156. Pilate's Last Appeal to the Crowd

¹Then Pilate took Jesus and scourged him. ²⁷The soldiers of the governor took Jesus into the praetorium, and they gathered the whole battalion before him. ¹⁷And they clothed him in a purple cloak, ²⁹and plaiting a crown of thorns they put it on his head, and put a reed in his right hand. And kneeling before him they mocked him, saying, "Hail, King of the Jews!" ³⁰And they spat upon him, and took the reed and struck him on the head.

⁴Pilate went out again and said to them, "See, I am bringing him out to you, that you may know that I find no crime in him." ⁵So Jesus came out, wearing the crown of thorns and the purple robe. Pilate said to them, "Behold the man!"

⁶When the chief priests and the officers saw him, they cried out, "Crucify him, crucify him!"

Pilate said to them, "I find no crime in him."

⁷The Jews answered him, "We have a law, and by that law he ought to die, because he has made himself the Son of God." ⁸When Pilate heard these words, he was the more afraid.

(Jn. 19:1; Mt. 27:27; Mk. 15:17; Mt. 27:29–30; Jn. 19:4–8)

Mt. 27:27 The / Then the (RSV)
Jn. 19:6 them, "I / them, "Take him yourselves and crucify him, for I (RSV) (185:6/1994–5)

157. Pilate's Last Interview with Jesus

⁹He entered the praetorium again and said to Jesus, "Where do you come from?" But Jesus gave no answer. ¹⁰Pilate therefore said to him, "Do you refuse to speak to me? Do you not know that I have power to release you, and power to crucify you?"

¹¹Jesus answered him, "You could have no power over me unless it were permitted from above. He who delivered me to you has the greater sin."

(Jn. 19:9–11)

Jn. 19:9 "Where do you come from?" (Mof) / "Where are you from?" (RSV)
Jn. 19:10 "Do you refuse to speak (Wms) / "You will not speak (RSV)
Jn. 19:11 "You could have (KJV) / "You would have (RSV) • it were permitted from / it had been given you from (RSV) (185:7/1994–5)

158. Pilate Surrenders to the Jews

12Upon this Pilate sought to release him, but the Jews cried out, "If you release this man, you are not Caesar's friend."

13When Pilate heard these words, he brought Jesus out and sat down on the judgment seat at a place called The Pavement. 14Now it was the day of preparation of the Passover; it was about the sixth hour.*a* He said to the Jews, "Behold your King!"

15They cried out, "Away with him, crucify him!"

Pilate said to them, "Shall I crucify your King?"

The chief priests answered, "We have no king but Caesar."

23They were urgent, demanding with loud cries that he should be crucified. And their voices prevailed. 24So Pilate gave sentence that their demand should be granted. 25He released the man who had been thrown into prison for insurrection and murder, whom they asked for; but Jesus he delivered up to their will.

24So when Pilate saw that he was gaining nothing, but rather that a riot was beginning, he took water and washed his hands before the crowd, saying, "I am innocent of this man's blood; see to it yourselves."

25And all the people answered, "His blood be on us and on our children!"

(Jn. 19:12–15; Lk. 23:23–25; Mt. 27:24–25)

---

a "the sixth hour"—6 A.M. (*Master Study Bible*, p. 1114)

Jn. 19:13 Pavement. / Pavement, and in Hebrew, Gabbatha. (RSV)
Jn. 19:15 him, crucify / him, away with him, crucify (RSV)
Lk. 23:23 They / But they (RSV) (185:7–8/1996)

159. The Death of Judas

3When Judas, his betrayer, saw that Jesus was condemned, he repented and brought back the thirty pieces of silver to the chief priests and the elders, 4saying, "I have sinned in betraying innocent blood."

They said, "What is that to us? See to it yourself."

5And throwing down the pieces of silver in the temple, he departed; and he went and hanged himself.

(Mt. 27:3–5)

Mt. 27:3 that Jesus was / that he was (RSV) (186:1/1998)

XLII. The Time of the Cross

160. On the Way to the Crucifixion

[17]So they took Jesus, and he went out, bearing his own cross. [32]Two others also, who were criminals, were led away to be put to death with him.

[19]Pilate also wrote a title and put it on the cross. It read, "Jesus of Nazareth—the King of the Jews." [20]Many of the Jews read this title, for the place where Jesus was crucified was near the city; and it was written in Hebrew, in Latin, and in Greek. [21]The chief priests of the Jews then said to Pilate, "Do not write, 'The King of the Jews,' but, 'This man said, I am King of the Jews.'"

[22]Pilate answered, "What I have written I have written."

[27]And there followed him a great multitude of the people, and of women who bewailed and lamented him. [28]But Jesus turning to them said, "Daughters of Jerusalem, weep not for me, but weep for yourselves and for your children. [29]For behold, the days are coming when they will say, 'Blessed are the barren, and the breasts that never nursed.' [30]Then they will begin to say to the mountains, 'Fall on us.'"[a]

[21]And they compelled a passer-by, Simon of Cyrene, who was coming in from the country, the father of Alexander and Rufus, to carry his cross.

(Jn. 19:17; Lk. 23:32; Jn. 19:19–22; Lk. 23: 27–30; Mk. 15:21)

---

a "Daughters of Jerusalem, weep not for me, but weep for yourselves and for your children. For behold, the days are coming when they will say, 'Blessed are the barren, and the breasts that never nursed.' Then they will begin to say to the mountains, 'Fall on us.'"—Here Jesus is referring to the coming destruction of Jerusalem in AD 70 when the Romans destroyed the city in response to a violent revolt of Jews seeking political independence. (See Ch. 129, fn. *b*, for a fuller discussion of Jerusalem's destruction.)

Jn. 19:17 cross. / cross, to the place called the place of the skull, which is called in Hebrew Golgotha. (RSV)
Lk. 23:28 Jerusalem, weep not for (KJV) / Jerusalem, do not weep for (RSV)
Lk. 23:29 barren, and / barren, and the wombs that never bore, and (RSV) • never nursed." (NRSV) / never gave suck." (RSV) (187:1/2004–6)

161. The Crucifixion

²²And they brought him to the place called Golgotha. ³³There they crucified him, and the criminals, one on the right and one on the left. ³⁴And Jesus said, "Father, forgive them; for they know not what they do."

³⁴They offered him wine to drink, mingled with gall;ᵃ but when he tasted it, he would not drink it. ³⁷And over his head they put the charge against him, which read, "This is Jesus—the King of the Jews."

²³When the soldiers had cruci-fied Jesus they took his garments and made four parts, one for each soldier; also his tunic. But the tunic was without seam, woven from top to bottom. ²⁴So they said to one another, "Let us not tear it, but cast lots for it to see whose it shall be." Thus was fulfilled the scripture, "They parted my garments among them, and for my clothing they cast lots." ²⁵So the soldiers did this.

(Mk. 15:22; Lk. 23:33–34; Mt. 27:34, 37; Jn. 19:23–25)

---

a "They offered him wine to drink, mingled with gall;"—This drugged wine was intended to help lessen the suffering, but Jesus refused to drink it.

Mk. 15:22 Golgotha. / Golgotha (which means the place of a skull). (RSV)
Lk. 23:33 There / And when they came to the place which is called The Skull, there (RSV)
Jn. 19:24 Ps. 22:18 • Thus was fulfilled the / This was to fulfill the (RSV) (187:2/2006–8)

162. Those Who Were Present

²⁵And it was the third hour,^{*a*} when they crucified him.

²⁵Standing by the cross of Jesus were his mother, and his mother's sister, Mary, the wife of Clopas,^{*b*} and Mary Magdalene, ⁴¹and also many other women who came up with him to Jerusalem.

³⁹And those who passed by derided him, wagging their heads ⁴⁰and saying, "You who would destroy the temple and build it in three days, save yourself! If you are the Son of God, come down from the cross."

⁴¹So also the chief priests and the scribes and elders mocked him, saying, ⁴²"He saved others; himself he cannot save. If he is the King of Israel, let him now come down now from the cross, and we will believe in him. ⁴³He trusts in God. Let God deliver him now. He said, 'I am the Son of God.'" ⁴⁴And the robbers who were crucified with him also reviled him in the same way.

³⁶Then the soldiers sat down and kept watch over him there. ³⁶The soldiers also mocked him, coming up and offering him sour wine.

(Mk. 15:25; Jn 19:25; Mk. 15:41; Mt. 27:39–44, 36; Lk. 23:36)

---

a   "the third hour"—The third hour after sunrise. (*New Oxford Annotated Bible*, p. 1237) This would be around 9 o'clock Friday morning.

b   "his mother's sister, Mary, the wife of Clopas"—It would appear that Jesus' mother, Mary, had a sister (also named Mary), identified here as "the wife of Clopas."

Jn. 19:25   Standing / But standing (RSV)
Mt. 27:42   (KJV) • he is the (RSV) / he be the (KJV)
Mt. 27:43   He said / for he said (RSV)
Mt. 27:36   Then the soldiers sat / then they sat (RSV)
Lk. 23:36   him sour wine. (Phi) / him vinegar. (RSV) (187:3/2008)

163. The Criminal on the Cross

39One of the criminals who were hanged railed at him, saying, "Are you not the Son of God? Save yourself and us!"

40But the other rebuked him, saying, "Do you not fear God, since you are under the same sentence of condemnation? 41And we indeed justly, for we are receiving the due reward of our deeds; but this man has done nothing wrong." 42And he said, "Lord, remember me when you come into your kingdom."

43And he said to him, "Verily, I say to you, today you will be with me in Paradise."

26When Jesus saw his mother, and the disciple whom he loved[a] standing near, he said to his mother, "Woman, behold your son!" 27Then he said to the disciple, "Behold your mother!"

And from that hour the disciple took her to his own home.

(Lk. 23:39–43; Jn. 19:26–27)

---

a   "the disciple whom he loved"—John, the writer of this gospel, is here referring to himself. It was John who cared for Jesus' mother, Mary, at this tragic time of her son's crucifixion, and then took her to live at his home.

Lk. 23:39   the Son of God? / the Christ? (RSV)
Lk. 23:42   said, "Lord, remember (KJV) / said, "Jesus, remember (RSV)
Lk. 23:43   him, "Verily, I (KJV) / him, "Truly, I (RSV) (187:4/2008–10)

164. Jesus' Last Hour on the Cross

[45]Now from the sixth hour there was darkness over all the land until the ninth hour.[a] [46]And about the ninth hour Jesus cried, "Eli, Eli, lama sabachthani?" that is, "My God, my God, why hast thou forsaken me?"[b]

[28]After this Jesus said, "I thirst." [29]A bowl full of common wine stood there; so they put a sponge full of the wine on a javelin and held it to his mouth.

[46]Then Jesus, crying with a loud voice, said, "It is finished; Father, into your hands I commend my spirit!" [30]And he bowed his head and gave up his spirit.

[39]And when the centurion, who stood facing him, saw that he thus breathed his last, he said, "Certainly this man was innocent. Truly this man was a Son of God!"

[49]And all his acquaintances and the women who had followed him from Galilee stood at a distance and saw these things.

(Mt. 27:45–46; Jn. 19:28–29; Lk. 23:46; Jn. 19:30; Mk. 15:39; Lk. 23:49)

---

a "Now from the sixth hour there was darkness over all the land until the ninth hour."—This was probably due to a sandstorm from the Arabian Desert. "From the sixth . . . until the ninth hour" (after sunrise) would be from around noon till 3 P.M. (*New Oxford Annotated Bible*, p. 1211) Thus Jesus probably died on Friday afternoon around 3 o'clock.

b "My God, my God, why hast thou forsaken me?"—This is the first line of Psalm 22. In his final hours of consciousness perhaps Jesus' human mind here returns to the repetition of Psalms memorized in childhood.

Mt. 27:46 cried, "Eli / cried with a loud voice, "Eli (RSV)
Jn. 19:28 Jesus said, / Jesus, knowing that all was now finished, said (RSV) • said, "I / said (to fulfill the scripture), "I (RSV)
Jn. 19:29 of common wine stood (TCNT) / of vinegar stood (RSV) • the wine on (Phi) / the vinegar on (RSV) • on a javelin and (NEB) / on hyssop and (RSV)
Lk. 23:46 said, "It is finished; Father, (Jn. 19:30) / said, "Father, (RSV) • into your hands (NAB) / into thy hands (RSV) • I commend my (KJV) / I commit my (RSV)
Mk. 15:39 said, "Certainly this man was innocent. Truly (Lk. 23:47) / said, "Truly (RSV) • was a Son (Gspd) / was the Son (RSV) (187:5/2010–1)

165. After Jesus' Death

³¹Since it was the day of Preparation, in order to prevent the bodies from remaining on the cross on the Sabbath (for that Sabbath was a high day), the Jews asked Pilate that their legs might be broken, and that they might be taken away. ³²So the soldiers came and broke the legs of the first, and of the other who had been crucified with him; ³³but when they came to Jesus and saw that he was already dead, they did not break his legs. ³⁴But one of the soldiers pierced his side with a spear, and at once there came out blood.

³⁵He who saw it[a] has borne witness—his testimony is true, and he knows that he tells the truth—that you also may believe.

(Jn. 19:31–35)

---

a   "He who saw it"—John Zebedee (the author of this gospel of John).

Jn. 19:34   blood. / blood and water. (RSV) (187:5/2011)

XLIII. Burial in Joseph's Tomb

166. Joseph and Nicodemus Bury Jesus

[42]And when evening had come, since it was the day of Preparation, that is, the day before the Sabbath, [43]Joseph of Arimathea, a respected member of the council[a] who was also himself looking for the kingdom of God,[b] took courage and went to Pilate, and asked for the body of Jesus. [58]Then Pilate ordered it to be given to him.

[38]So he came and took away his body. [39]Nicodemus also, who had at first come to him by night, came bringing a mixture of myrrh and aloes, about a hundred pounds' weight. [40]They took the body of Jesus, and bound it in linen cloths with the spices, as is the burial custom of the Jews.

[41]Now in the place where he was crucified there was a garden, and in the garden a new tomb where no one had ever been laid. [42]So because of the Jewish day of Preparation, as the tomb was close at hand, they laid Jesus there. [60]And Joseph laid Jesus' body in his own new tomb, which he had hewn in the rock; and he rolled a great stone to the door of the tomb, and departed.

[54]It was the day of Preparation and the Sabbath was beginning.[c] [55]The women who had come with him from Galilee followed and saw the tomb and how his body was laid. [61]Mary Magdalene and the other Mary[d] were there, sitting opposite the sepulchre. [56]Then they returned, and prepared spices and ointments. On the Sabbath they rested according to the commandment. (Mk. 15:42–43; Mt. 27:58; Jn. 19:38–42; Mt. 27:60; Lk. 23:54–55; Mt. 27:61; Lk. 23:56)

---

a   "the council"—the Sanhedrin.

b   "looking for the kingdom of God"—Jesus in his kingdom teachings always emphasized the kingdom as a *present* reality—the rule of the Father in the heart of the believer. So why is Joseph "looking for the kingdom"? This is because the Jews of this period regarded the kingdom as something that was coming (in spectacular fashion) in their *future*. In this respect they looked especially to Daniel and the prophecy of the Great Image.

    In this prophecy King Nebuchadnezzar has a dream that depicts the coming of the kingdom of God to earth. Daniel volunteers to interpret the dream. It reveals that four great kingdoms will rule the (Western) world. The first kingdom is Nebuchednezzar's Babylon; it will be followed by Persia, then Greece, and finally Rome. This series of conquering world empires ends with Rome; it gradually declines and disintegrates (becomes divided) into its constituent parts, the Roman provinces, and is overrun by various barbarian tribes.   *(continued next page)*

c   "the Sabbath was beginning"—The Sabbath began at sundown on Friday evening.

d   "the other Mary"—Mary, the wife of Clopas.

Mt. 27:60   And Joseph laid Jesus' body in / and laid it in (RSV) (188:0–1/2012–3)

167. Guarding the Tomb

⁶²Next day,ᵃ that is, after the day of Preparation, the chief priests and the Pharisees gathered before Pilate ⁶³and said, "Sir, we remembered how that deceiver said, while he was still alive, 'After three days I will rise again.' ⁶⁴Therefore order the sepulchre to be made secure until the third day, lest his disciples go and steal him away, and tell the people, 'He has risen from the dead,' and the last fraud will be worse than the first."

⁶⁵Pilate said to them, "You have a guard of soldiers; go, make it as secure as you can."

⁶⁶So they went and made the sepulchre secure by sealing the stone and setting a guard.

(Mt. 27:62–66)

(continued from previous page)

These provinces (e.g., Italia, Gallia, Hispania, Britannia, Germania, Syria, Judea, and Aegyptus) form the basis for the modern nation-states of Europe, the Middle East, and North Africa. Daniel further interprets the dream, saying, "And in the days of those kings [after the Roman Empire becomes divided into various kingdoms], the God of heaven will set up a kingdom which shall never be destroyed. It shall break in pieces all these kingdoms and bring them to an end, and it shall stand forever." (Dan. 2:44)

This coming of the kingdom of God as depicted by Daniel was the concept held by the Jews at the time of Jesus. It refers to a future time when God will destroy the kingdoms of men and set up a divine world government. God, through his anointed one, the Messiah, will then rule the nations from his capital at Jerusalem, and this rule will be forever. This was the kingdom concept held by John the Baptist, the apostles, and the Jewish believers. It is why many of his followers expected Jesus' immediate return to rule the earth in power and glory.

Jesus, while he emphasized the kingdom *within*, also recognized that in the future God would bring the outer kingdom (divine world government) to our world. This is a future phase of the kingdom in which God rules the nations of the world in addition to his rule in the hearts of believers.

The center of the prayer Jesus taught his apostles is a petition for this advanced stage of the kingdom, the time when God will rule both hearts and governments (as he does in heaven)—"Your kingdom come; your will be done on earth as it is in heaven." (See also Ch. 107, fn. *b*.)

a   "Next day"—Saturday (the Sabbath).

Mt.27:63   that deceiver said (KJV) / that imposter said (RSV)   (188:2/2014)

191

PART 4

RESURRECTION AND FINAL APPEARANCES

XLIV. The Resurrection

168. The Disappearance of Jesus' Body

[2]And behold, an angel of the Lord descended from heaven and came and rolled back the stone. [4]And for fear the guards trembled and became like dead men.

[11]Some of the guards went into the city and told the chief priests all that had taken place. [12]And when they had assembled with the elders and taken counsel, they gave a sum of money to the soldiers [13]and said, "Tell people, 'His disciples came by night and stole him away while we were asleep.' [14]And if this comes to the governor's ears, we will satisfy him and keep you out of trouble." [15]So they took the money and did as they were directed.

(Mt. 28:2, 4, 11–15)

Mt. 28:2   behold, an / behold, there was a great earthquake; for an (RSV) • stone. / stone and sat upon it. (RSV)
Mt. 28:4   fear the / fear of him the (RSV)
Mt. 28:11   Some / While they were going, behold, some (RSV)   (189:2/2022–4)

169. The Women Discover the Empty Tomb

[1]And when the Sabbath was past, toward the dawn of the first day of the week,[a] Mary Magdalene, and Mary, the mother of James,[b] and Salome,[c] bought spices, so that they might go and anoint him. [3]And they were saying to one another, "Who will roll away the stone for us from the door of the tomb?"

[4]And they saw that the stone was rolled back. It was very large. [3]But when they went in they did not find the body.

(Mk. 16:1, 3–4; Lk. 24:3)

---

a   "the first day of the week"—Sunday.

b   "Mary, the mother of James"—James Alpheus, the apostle.

c   "Salome"—The mother of James and John Zebedee.

Mk. 16:1   past, toward the dawn of the first day of the week, Mary (Mt. 28:1) / past, Mary (RSV)
Mk. 16:4   And they / And looking up, they (RSV)   (189:4/2025–6)

170. Jesus' Appearance to Mary

[11]Mary Magdalene stood outside the tomb. [14]She turned round and saw Jesus standing, but she did not know that it was Jesus. [15]Supposing him to be the gardener, she said to him, "Sir, if you have carried him away, tell me where you have laid him, and I will get him."

[6]Jesus said to her, "Remember how he told you, while he was still in Galilee, [7]that the Son of Man would be delivered into the hands of sinful men, and be crucified, and on the third day rise."

[8]And they remembered his words.

[16]Jesus said to her, "Mary."

She turned and said to him, "Master!"

[17]Jesus said to her, "Touch me not.[a] I have not yet ascended to the Father. But go to my apostles —and Peter—and say to them, I am ascending to my Father and your Father."

(Jn. 20:11, 14–15; Lk. 24:6–8; Jn. 20:16–17)

---

[a]   "Touch me not"—It is a fact that Jesus' earthly body was not in the tomb; it is also a fact that the resurrected Jesus appeared to Mary (and many others). Given these two facts, it might be assumed that Jesus appeared to Mary in his (former) earthly body. However, the fact that Jesus tells Mary not to touch his body suggests otherwise.

Jesus is ascending to his Father and he tarries on earth for a time in his new heavenly body. Mary does not at first recognize Jesus in his new "ascending" form.

In this and his other appearances following his resurrection Jesus appears and disappears at will, sometimes within closed and locked rooms. This further confirms that Jesus' risen body is not earthly flesh, but composed of a more spiritual substance.

Jn. 20:11   Mary / But Mary (RSV) • Mary Magdalene stood (Jn. 20:1) / Mary stood (RSV) • stood outside / stood weeping outside (RSV) • tomb. / tomb, and as she wept she stooped to look into the tomb; (RSV)
Jn. 20:14   She / Saying this, she (RSV)
Jn. 20:15   will get him." (NIV) / will take him away." (RSV)
Lk. 24:6   Jesus said to her, "Remember / Remember (RSV)
Lk. 24:7   Man would be / Man must be (RSV)
Jn. 20:16   him, "Master!" (KJV) / him in Hebrew, "Rabboni!" (which means teacher). (RSV)
Jn. 20:17   Touch me not. (KJV) / Do not touch me, (RSV) • I / for I (RSV) • my apostles—and Peter—and (Mk. 16:7; Ch. 22, fn. a) / my brethren and (RSV) • Father." / Father, to my God and your God." (RSV) (189:4/2026–7)

171. The Women Report to the Apostles

[9]And returning from the tomb they told all this to the eleven and to all the rest. [10]Now it was Mary Magdalene and Joanna and Mary the mother of James and the other women with them who told this to the apostles. [11]But these words seemed to them an idle tale, and they did not believe them.

(Lk. 24:9–11)

(189:4/2027)

172. Peter and John Go to the Tomb

[3]Peter then came out with the other disciple,[a] and they went toward the tomb. [4]They both ran, but the other disciple outran Peter and reached the tomb first. [5]Stooping to look in, he saw the linen cloths lying there, but he did not go in. [6]Then Simon Peter came, following him, and went into the tomb; he saw the linen cloths lying, [7]and the napkin, which had been on his head, not lying with the linen cloths but rolled up in a place by itself. [8]Then the other disciple, who reached the tomb first, also went in, and he saw and believed.

[10]Then the disciples went back to their homes.

(Jn. 20:3–8, 10)

---

[a] "the other disciple"—This other disciple is John Zebedee, the author of this gospel of John. In his gospel writings John generally refers to himself in the third person (e.g., "He," "the other disciple," "the disciple whom Jesus loved," etc.).

Jn. 20:5   Stooping to / and stooping to (RSV) (189:5/2027–8)

XLV. Appearance on the Way to Emmaus

173. The Walk with Cleopas and His Brother

¹³That very day two men were going to a village named Emmaus, about seven miles from Jerusalem, ¹⁴and talking with each other about all these things that had happened. ¹⁵While they were talking and discussing together, Jesus himself drew near and went with them. ¹⁶But their eyes were kept from recognizing him. ¹⁷And he said to them, "What is this conversation which you are holding with each other as you walk?"

And they stood still, looking sad. ¹⁸Then one of them, named Cleopas, answered him, "Are you the only visitor to Jerusalem who does not know the things that have happened there in these days?"

¹⁹And he said to them, "What things?"

And they said to him, "Concerning Jesus of Nazareth, who was a prophet mighty in deed and word before God and all the people. ²⁰Our chief priests and rulers delivered him up to be condemned to death, and crucified him. ²¹But we had hoped that he was the one to redeem Israel. Yes, and besides all this, it is now the third day since this happened. ²²Moreover, some women of our company amazed us. They were at the tomb early this morning ²³and did not find his body. ²⁴Some of those who were with us went to the tomb, and found it just as the women had said, but they did not see Jesus." (Lk. 24:13–24) *(continued)*

Lk. 24:13 two men were / two of them were (RSV)
Lk. 24:20 Our / and how our (RSV)
Lk. 24:22 early this morning (NIV) / early in the morning (RSV)
Lk. 24:24 but they did not see Jesus. (NRSV) / but him they did not see. (RSV) (190:5/2034–5)

173. The Walk with Cleopas and His Brother (continued)

25And he said to them, "O slow of heart to believe all that the prophets have spoken!" 27And beginning with Moses and all the prophets, he interpreted to them what referred to him in all the scriptures.

28So they drew near to the village to which they were going. He appeared to be going further, 29but they constrained him, saying, "Stay with us, for it is toward evening and the day is now far spent." So he went in to stay with them. 30When he was at table with them, he took the bread and blessed, and broke it, and gave it to them.

31And their eyes were opened and they recognized him; and he vanished out of their sight. 32They said to each other, "Did not our hearts burn within us while he talked to us on the road, while he opened to us the scriptures?"

33And they rose that same hour and returned to Jerusalem. They found the eleven gathered together and those who were with them. 34They said, "The Lord has risen indeed, and has appeared to us!" 35Then they told what had happened on the road, and how he was known to them in the breaking of the bread. (Lk. 24:25, 27–35)

Lk. 24:25 O slow / O foolish men and slow (RSV)
Lk. 24:27 them what referred to him in (NAB) / them in (RSV) • scriptures. / scriptures the things concerning himself. (RSV)
Lk. 24:33 Jerusalem. They / Jerusalem, and they (RSV)
Lk. 24:34 They said, (NRSV) / who said, (RSV) • to us!" / to Simon!" (RSV) (190:5/2035–6)

XLVI. Jesus Appears to the Apostles

174. The First Appearance

[19]On the evening of that day, the first day of the week,[a] the doors being shut where the apostles were for fear of the Jews, Jesus came and stood among them and said to them, "Peace be with you."

[37]But they were startled and frightened, and supposed that they saw a spirit.

[38]And he said to them, "Why are you troubled, and why do doubts rise in your minds?" [14]And he upbraided them for their unbelief, because they had not believed those who saw him after he had risen. [44]"This is what I told you while I was still with you."[b]

[20]Then the apostles were glad when they saw the Lord. (Jn. 20:19; Lk. 24:37–38; Mk. 16:14; Lk. 24:44; Jn. 20:20)

(continued from following page)

Jesus' life on earth is so valuable to us because he lived his teachings. He *demonstrated* a new and higher type of faith—a *living faith* in God. This faith was wholly personal and purely spiritual. His entire life exhibited this living faith. This spiritual attitude dominated his thinking and feeling, his believing and praying, his teaching and preaching.

Jesus challenges us to achieve this faith—not only to believe *what* he believed, but also *as* he believed. This is the full meaning of his one supreme requirement to "follow me." Jesus desires that his disciples fully share his extraordinary faith. He wants us to trust in God as he trusted in God and to believe in men as he believed in men.

Jesus does not so much require his followers to believe *in* him as he requires us to believe *with* him, believe that *we are all children of a loving heavenly Father.* He wants us to believe in the reality of the love of God and, in full confidence, to accept our status and security as his sons and daughters on earth.

a   "the first day of the week"—Sunday.

b   "This is what I told you while I was still with you."—Here Jesus reminds the apostles that he clearly told them that he would be betrayed and delivered into the hands of the chief priests and the rulers of the Jews, be put to death, and on the third day rise.

Jn. 20:19   the apostles were (Ch. 22, fn. *a*) / the disciples were (RSV)
Lk. 24:38   do doubts rise (NIV) / do questions rise (RSV) • your minds?" (NIV) / your hearts?" (RSV)
Mk. 16:14   unbelief, because / unbelief and hardness of heart, because (RSV)
Lk. 24:44   "This is what I told you (AB) / Then he said to them, "These are my words which I spoke to you, (RSV) • you. / you, that everything written about me in the Law of Moses and the prophets and the Psalms must be fulfilled." (RSV)
Jn. 20:20   the apostles were (Ch. 22, fn. *a*) / the disciples were (RSV)   (191:2/2040)

175. The Second Appearance

24Now Thomas, one of the twelve, called the Twin, was not with them when Jesus came. 25So the other apostles told him, "We have seen the Lord."

But he said to them, "Unless I see in his hands the print of the nails, and place my finger in the mark of the nails, and place my hand in his side, I will not believe."

26Eight days later, his disciples were again in the house, and Thomas was with them. The doors were shut, but Jesus came and stood among them, and said, "Peace be upon you." 27Then he said to Thomas, "Be not faithless, but believing."a

28Thomas answered him, "My Lord and my God!"

29Jesus said to him, "You have believed because you have seen me. Blessed are those who believe without seeing."

(Jn. 20:24–29)

---

a   "Be not faithless, but believing."—Consider the central role that faith played in Jesus' personal religion, the gospel of the kingdom: Faith is the price we pay for admission into the kingdom. By faith we advance, make progress, in the kingdom. By faith we are justified, and gain eternal salvation. By faith we may be made whole. Jesus once said, "If you have faith . . . nothing will be impossible to you." (Ch. 28; Mt. 17:20)

Jesus lived an ideal religious life. In his faith we may discover the ideal human faith, the greatest faith our world has ever known. Jesus' faith grew to such heights of trust that it overcame all human fear and doubt. And as his followers we may learn from him, and make Jesus the "author and finisher of our faith."

The human Jesus looked upon God as our loving Father in heaven. His God is the Father of all, and he loves each human personality with an infinite Fatherly affection. Jesus looked upon men as God's children and his brethren in the flesh. He elevated the *idea* of God as a Father to a sublime *faith experience* with his teaching that every human personality is a child of this Father of love, a son of God.

Jesus trusted God as a small child trusts his earthly parent. His faith was childlike but never childish. He depended on God as a child depends upon his earthly parent. He was absolutely certain and secure in his trust in the Father's guidance, overcare, and protection. Even in the face of apparent defeat and a cruel and unjust death, he was unmoved in his faith. Faith was his spiritual anchorage, ever keeping him secure throughout the many trials and tribulations of his life.

By faith Jesus bore the transcendent fruits of the spirit. By faith he lived secure in the presence of his heavenly Father. And by faith he achieved his one great purpose in life—the knowing and doing of the Father's will.

(continued on preceding page)

Jn. 20:25   other apostles told (Ch. 22, fn. *a*) / other disciples told (RSV)
Jn. 20:26   be upon you." (KJV) / be with you." (RSV)
Jn. 20:27   Be not faithless (KJV) / Do not be faithless (RSV)
Jn. 20:29   You have believed (NIV) / Have you believed (RSV) • who believe without seeing." (Ber) / who have not seen yet believe." (RSV) (191:5/2042–3)

XLVII. Appearances in Galilee

176. Appearance by the Sea of Galilee

[1]After this Jesus revealed himself again to the apostles by the Sea of Tiberias,[a] and he revealed himself in this way. [2]Simon Peter, Thomas called the Twin, Nathaniel of Cana in Galilee, the sons of Zebedee, and his other apostles were together. [3]Simon Peter said to them, "I am going fishing." They said to him, "We will go with you." They went out and got into the boat; but that night they caught nothing.

[4]Just as day was breaking, Jesus stood on the beach; yet the apostles did not know that it was Jesus. [5]Jesus said to them, "Lads, have you any fish?"

They answered him, "No."

[6]He said to them, "Cast the net on the right side of the boat, and you will find some." So they cast it, and now they were not able to haul it in, for the quantity of fish. [7]That disciple whom Jesus loved[b] said to Peter, "It is the Lord!" When Simon Peter heard that it was the Lord, he put on his clothes, for he was stripped for work, and sprang into the sea. [8]But the other apostles came in the boat, dragging the net full of fish, for they were not far from land, but about a hundred yards off.

[9]When they got out on land, they saw a charcoal fire there, and bread. [10]Jesus said to them, "Bring some of the fish." [11]So Simon Peter went aboard and hauled the net ashore, full of large fish, a hundred and fifty-three of them; and although there were so many, the net was not torn. [12]Jesus said to them, "Come and have breakfast." [13]Jesus came and took the bread and gave it to them, and so with the fish. [14]This was now the third time that Jesus was revealed to the apostles after he was raised from the dead.

(Jn. 21:1–14)

---

a   "the Sea of Tiberias"—the Sea of Galilee.

b   "That disciple whom Jesus loved"—John Zebedee. See Ch. 172, fn. a.

Jn. 21:1   the apostles by (Ch. 22, fn. a) / the disciples by (RSV)
Jn. 21:2   and his other apostles were (Ch. 22, fn. a) / and two others of his disciples were (RSV)
Jn. 21:4   the apostles did (Ch. 22, fn. a) / the disciples did (RSV)
Jn. 21:5   them, "Lads, have (Wms) / them, "Children, have (RSV)
Jn. 21:8   other apostles came (Ch. 22, fn. a) / other disciples came (RSV)
Jn. 21:9   there, and / there, with fish lying on it, and (RSV)
Jn. 21:10   fish." / fish that you have just caught." (RSV)
Jn. 21:14   the apostles after (Ch. 22, fn. a) / the disciples after (RSV) (192:1/2045–7)

177. The Visit with Peter

[15]When they had finished breakfast, Jesus said to Simon Peter, "Simon, son of John, do you love me?"

He said to him, "Yes, Lord; you know that I love you."

He said to him, "Feed my lambs."

[16]A second time he said to him, "Simon, son of John, do you love me?"

He said to him, "Yes, Lord; you know that I love you."

He said to him, "Tend my sheep."

[17]He said to him a third time, "Simon, do you love me?"

Peter was grieved because he said to him the third time, "Do you love me?" And he said to him, "Lord, you know everything; you know that I love you."

Jesus said to him, "Feed my sheep." [19]And after this he said to him, "Follow me."

[20]Peter turned and saw John following them. [21]When Peter saw him, he said to Jesus, "Lord, what about this man?"

[22]Jesus said to him, "If it is my will that he remain until I come back, what is that to you? Follow me!"

[23]The saying spread abroad among the brethren that this apostle was not to die [before the Master's return]; yet Jesus did not say to him that he was not to die, but, "If it is my will that he remain until I come, what is that to you?"   (Jn. 21:15–17, 19–23)

Jn. 21:15   me?" / me more than these?" (RSV)
Jn. 21:17   Simon, do / Simon, son of John, do (RSV)
Jn. 21:20   saw John following them. / saw following them the disciple whom Jesus loved, who had lain close to his breast at the supper and had said, "Lord, who is it that is going to betray you?" (RSV)
Jn. 21:22   come back, what / come, what (RSV)
Jn. 21:23   this apostle was (Ch. 22, fn. *a*) / this disciple was (RSV) • die [before the Master's return]; / die; (RSV) (192:2/2047–8)

---

178. Appearance on the Mountain

[16]The eleven apostles went to Galilee, to the mountain to which Jesus had directed them. [17]And when they saw him they worshiped him.   (Mt. 28:16–17)

Mt. 28:16   The eleven / Now the eleven (RSV) • eleven apostles went (Ch. 22, fn. *a*) / eleven disciples went (RSV) (192:3/2050)

XLVIII. Jesus' Ascension
and Bestowal of the Spirit of Truth

179. The Last Appearance

³To the apostles Jesus presented himself alive after his passion by many proofs, appearing to them during forty days, and speaking of the kingdom of God.*ᵃ* ⁴And being assembled together with them he charged them not to depart from Jerusalem, but to wait for the promise of the Father.*ᵇ* ⁴⁹"And behold, I send the promise of my Father upon you; but stay in the city, until you are clothed with power from on high."

⁶So when they had come together, they asked him, "Lord, will you at this time restore the kingdom to Israel?"*ᶜ*

⁸He said, "You shall receive power when the Holy Spirit has come upon you,*ᵈ* and you shall be my witnesses in Jerusalem and in all Judea and Samaria and to the end of the earth."

(Ac. 1:3–4; Lk. 24:49; Ac. 1:6, 8)

---

a "speaking of the kingdom of God."—After his death Jesus continues to emphasize the central concept of his ministry—the kingdom of God (the rule of God in the heart of the individual believer).

b "the promise of the Father"—the Spirit of Truth. "But when the Comforter comes, whom I shall send to you from the Father, even the Spirit of Truth. . . ." (Ch. 140, Jn. 15:26)

c "will you at this time restore the kingdom to Israel?"—The apostles still cling to their long-nourished concepts of a Jewish Messiah who restores Israel's political kingdom. But Jesus was not a material Messiah coming to reestablish the political power of the Jewish state. He responds by promising that new *spiritual* power will come upon the apostles, and that they will then go into all the world preaching the gospel of the kingdom.

d "you shall receive power when the Holy Spirit has come upon you"—Here again the influence and activity of the Holy Spirit is closely associated with the coming of the "new Counselor," the Spirit of Truth. (See Ch. 140, fn. *b* and Ch. 141, fn. *c*.)

Ac. 1:3   To the apostles Jesus presented (Ch. 22, fn. *a*) / To them he presented (RSV)
Ac. 1:4   And being assembled together with (KJV) / And while staying with (RSV) • Father. / Father, which he said, "you heard from me, (RSV)
Ac. 1:8   He said, "You / But you (RSV)   (193:3/2055)

180. Jesus' Ascension

⁵⁰He led them out as far as Bethany, and lifting up his hands he blessed them. ¹⁹Then the Lord Jesus, after he had spoken to them, parted from them and was taken up into heaven and sat down at the right hand of God.

(Lk. 24:50; Mk. 16:19)

Mk. 16:19   Then / So then (RSV) • them, parted from them and was (Lk. 24:51) / them, was (RSV)   (193:5/2057)

181. The Disciples Meet in the Upper Room

[12]Then they returned to Jerusalem from the mount called Olivet, which is near Jerusalem, a Sabbath day's journey away; [13]and when they had entered, they went up to the upper room where they were staying, Peter and John and James and Andrew, Philip and Thomas, Bartholomew and Matthew, James the son of Alpheus and Simon the Zealot and Judas the brother of James.

[15]Peter stood up among the brethren (the company of persons was in all about a hundred and twenty), and said, [16]"Brethren, the scripture has been fulfilled concerning Judas who was guide to those who arrested Jesus. [17]For he was numbered among us, and was allotted his share in this ministry."

[20]"It is written in the book of Psalms, 'His office let another take.' [21]So one of the men who have accompanied us during all the time that the Lord Jesus went in and out among us, [22]beginning from the baptism of John until the day when he was taken up from us—one of these men must become with us a witness to his resurrection." [23]And they put forward two, Joseph called Barsabbas, who was surnamed Justus, and Matthias. [26]And they cast lots for them, and the lot fell to Matthias; and he was enrolled with the eleven apostles.

(Ac. 1:12–13, 15–17, 20–23, 26)

Ac. 1:13 Judas the brother of (KJV) / Judas, the son of (RSV)
Ac. 1:15 Peter / In those days Peter (RSV)
Ac. 1:16 scripture has been fulfilled / scripture had to be fulfilled (RSV) • fulfilled concerning / fulfilled, which the Holy Spirit spoke beforehand by the mouth of David, concerning (RSV)
Ac. 1:20 "It / For it (RSV) • Psalms, 'His / Psalms, 'Let his habitation become desolate, and let there be no one to live in it'; and 'His (RSV) (193:6/2057–8)

---

182. Bestowal of the Spirit of Truth

[14]All these with one accord devoted themselves to prayer, together with the women and Mary the mother of Jesus, and with his brothers.

[2]And suddenly a sound came from heaven like the rush of a mighty wind, and it filled all the house where they were sitting. [4]And they were all filled with the Holy Spirit[a] and began to speak in other tongues, as the Spirit gave them utterance.

(Ac. 1:14; 2:2, 4)

---

a "they were all filled with the Holy Spirit"—In response to the coming of the Spirit of Truth, the spirit counselor Jesus promised to send after his death. (See Ch. 140, fn. b, Ch. 141, fns. a−e, and Ch. 142, fn. a.)

(194:0/2059)

Index
Verse Citations

208

Index
Biblical Text

A

Abel, 150
Abiatar, 52
abide, 161, 162
abides, 162
abiding, 8
Abilene, 17
ability, 154
abolish, 32
Abraham, 18, 94, 95, 116, 120, 133,
  145
Abraham's, 94
absence, 155
abundance, 61, 74, 111, 139, 154
abundantly, 109
acceptable, 58
accompanied, 131, 204
accomplish, 39
accomplished, 7, 113, 169
accord, 94, 109, 126, 178, 204
accordance, 90
account, 27, 125, 129, 133, 135, 163
accounts, 86, 154
accursed, 91
accusation, 18, 177
accuse, 54, 177
accused, 177
accusers, 92
accusing, 179
accustomed, 180
acknowledge, 110
acknowledges, 110
acquaintances, 13, 188
act, 92
add, 112
added, 27, 33
addressed, 181
adjure, 176
adorn, 150
adulterers, 122
adultery, 32, 73, 92, 98
advantage, 166
adversaries, 120
adversary, 41
afflicted, 47, 55
afraid, 12, 64, 65, 80, 132, 134, 141,
  154, 168, 182
afterward, 41, 48, 56, 141, 142, 158,
  161
age, 23, 67, 105
agree, 85, 100
agreed, 105, 155
agreeing, 100
air, 62, 98

alabaster, 51, 136
alarmed, 151
Alexander, 184
alike, 119
alive, 112, 128, 191, 203
allotted, 204
allow, 140, 149
allowed, 67, 123
alms, 32
aloes, 190
alone, 55, 73, 85, 92, 93, 96, 117,
  136, 148, 168
Alphaeus, 204
Alpheus, 26
already, 32, 39, 64, 74, 105, 106,
  124, 139, 162, 189
altar, 149, 150
always, 41, 65, 84, 93, 118, 125, 128,
  136, 174
amazed, 13, 45, 55, 74, 82, 132,
  144, 197
amazement, 67
ample, 111
Andrew, 23, 26, 28, 46, 148, 204
angel, 4, 7, 148, 171, 194
angels, 14, 83, 84, 110, 127, 145,
  153, 173
anger, 86, 119
angry, 32, 90, 128, 143
anguish, 167
Anna, 11
Annas, 17, 174
anoint, 51, 194
anointed, 51, 58, 104, 121, 136
answer, 18, 110, 116, 141, 144, 147,
  174, 176, 177, 179, 182
answering, 51
answers, 13, 40
anxious, 33, 34, 96, 110, 112, 151
anxiously, 13
apart, 65, 80, 162
apostle, 202
apostles, 26, 39, 64, 68, 69, 73, 75,
  78, 83, 112, 137, 139, 151, 153,
  156, 157, 159, 167, 169, 171, 195,
  196, 199, 200, 201, 202, 203,
  204
apparel, 179
appeal, 173
appear, 134, 150
appearances, 90
appeared, 10, 17, 62, 76, 80, 171, 198
appearing, 203
appears, 90, 91

appointed, 18, 97, 161
approaches, 112
Archelaus, 12
argued, 141
arguing, 82
Arimathea, 190
arise, 48, 67, 115, 128, 152
arisen, 48
armies, 152
arms, 11, 84, 123
arose, 6, 64, 82, 128, 157
arrayed, 112
arraying, 179
arrest, 91, 107, 135, 142, 155
arrested, 93, 204
ascended, 195
ascending, 75, 195
ascertained, 10, 12
Aser, 11
ashamed, 83, 129
ashes, 101
ashore, 63, 68, 201
aside, 158
ask, 18, 21, 32, 37, 40, 41, 43, 85,
  105, 124, 141, 145, 146, 147, 162,
  167, 174, 176, 180, 181
asked, 18, 21, 37, 39, 43, 44, 48, 51,
  61, 72, 77, 78, 81, 82, 84, 104, 105,
  114, 128, 130, 132, 141, 145, 146,
  147, 151, 167, 172, 175, 176, 179,
  183, 189, 190, 203
asking, 13, 49, 76, 123, 130, 167
asks, 40, 41, 131, 166
asleep, 64, 121, 194
ass, 120
ass's, 137
assembled, 174, 194, 203
assembling, 9
astonished, 13, 44, 45, 59, 99, 114,
  145
astray, 85, 90, 91, 151, 152
ate, 52, 68, 70, 71, 72, 116, 128
attendant, 58
attendants, 143
Augustus, 7
authorities, 91, 110
authority, 34, 45, 49, 55, 90, 130,
  134, 141, 158, 164
avail, 75
awake, 113, 121
awe, 64
awoke, 64
ax, 18

B

babe, 6
babes, 42, 140
bag, 34, 97, 161
band, 172, 173
bandages, 125
bank, 65, 134, 138
bankers, 154
banquet, 43, 118, 119
baptism, 17, 18, 113, 141, 204
baptist, 17, 42, 43, 78
baptize, 19, 21
baptized, 17, 18, 20, 37, 107, 113
baptizing, 18, 21, 22, 37
Barabbas, 180, 181
barn, 62, 112
barns, 111
barren, 184
Barsabbas, 204
Bartholomew, 26, 204
Bartimaeus, 132
basin, 158
baskets, 68
bathed, 158
battalion, 182
beach, 201
bearers, 48
bearing, 93, 184
beast, 103
beasts, 14
beat, 64, 103, 122, 142, 176
beaten, 151
beautiful, 136, 150
beckoned, 44, 159
bed, 40, 50, 55
Beelzebub, 57, 74
befall, 172
befits, 18
beg, 65, 104, 129
beggar, 104
begged, 48, 65
begging, 132
begrudge, 100
beheaded, 43, 76
beheld, 2, 101
behold, 6, 9, 13, 17, 20, 22, 23, 26,
   34, 42, 76, 77, 80, 84, 98, 102, 116,
   118, 130, 132, 133, 137, 143, 150,
   170, 171, 180, 182, 183, 184, 187,
   194, 203
believe, 2, 36, 39, 48, 67, 70, 75,
   82, 88, 93, 95, 105, 106, 107, 121,
   124, 125, 126, 141, 148, 152, 164,
   167, 168, 170, 176, 186, 189, 196,
   198, 200
believed, 2, 6, 25, 35, 39, 48, 75, 91,
   93, 94, 109, 125, 141, 143, 169,
   196, 199, 200
believes, 27, 50, 70, 71, 82, 124

believing, 135, 200
belly, 74
belong, 107
belonged, 118, 179
belongs, 27, 100
beloved, 20, 80
belts, 34
benefactors, 158
bent, 92, 120
beseech, 65
beseeching, 47
besought, 39, 49, 66, 86
best, 128, 149
Bethany, 18, 121, 124, 135, 136, 137,
   139, 203
Bethesda, 50
Bethlehem, 7, 9, 10, 12
Bethphage, 137
Bethsaida, 23, 101, 148
betray, 75, 136, 155, 158, 159, 172
betrayed, 26, 159, 171, 172
betrayer, 171, 172, 183
betraying, 183
better, 66, 84
bewailed, 184
beware, 31, 34, 77, 110, 111
beyond, 18, 27, 47, 107, 123
bid, 89, 111
bier, 48
bill, 129
bind, 62, 65, 85, 149
binds, 74
birds, 60, 62, 98, 112
birth, 7, 104
birthday, 43
bitterly, 175
blade, 61
blasphemes, 110
blaspheming, 107
blasphemy, 55, 74, 107, 176
bless, 30
blessed, 6, 11, 42, 68, 76, 101, 113,
   118, 119, 123, 137, 138, 158, 198,
   200, 203
blind, 30, 50, 58, 73, 74, 104, 105,
   106, 108, 109, 118, 119, 125, 132,
   149, 150
blindfolded, 176
blood, 2, 66, 78, 114, 117, 150, 171,
   183, 189
blowing, 69
blows, 36
boat, 28, 44, 60, 64, 65, 66, 68, 69,
   201
boats, 44, 70
bodies, 189
body, 33, 43, 57, 66, 90, 110, 112,
   136, 143, 160, 173, 190, 194, 197
bond, 120

bondage, 94
bones, 150
book, 58, 147, 204
booths, 80
bore, 2, 22, 27, 62, 76
born, 2, 7, 9, 35, 36, 42, 104, 105,
   106, 167, 178
borne, 22, 100, 189
bosom, 2
bottom, 185
bought, 63, 119, 194
bound, 43, 65, 85, 103, 120, 125,
   149, 173, 174, 190
bowed, 188
bowl, 188
box, 159
boy, 13, 82
branch, 153, 162
branches, 62, 137, 162
bread, 40, 41, 52, 68, 70, 71, 119,
   128, 155, 160, 198, 201
break, 43, 189
breakfast, 201, 202
breaking, 44, 198, 201
breast, 122, 159
breasts, 76, 184
breathed, 188
brethren, 202, 204
bride, 27
bridegroom, 25, 27, 53
bridegroom's, 27
broad, 149
broke, 65, 68, 160, 189, 198
broken, 113, 142, 189
bronze, 72
brood, 18, 74, 150
brother, 17, 23, 26, 28, 30, 32, 34,
   43, 67, 76, 85, 86, 111, 121, 124,
   128, 145, 151, 204
brother's, 27, 30, 43
brothers, 28, 59, 76, 88, 99, 118, 130,
   131, 145, 204
brow, 59
bruising, 65
build, 78, 111, 114, 131, 143, 150,
   176, 186
builders, 142
buildings, 151
built, 31, 49, 59, 142
bundles, 62
burden, 100
burdens, 114, 149
burial, 190
burn, 19, 198
burned, 62, 143, 162
burning, 113
burnt, 146
burst, 53
bury, 98

burying, 136
bushel, 29
business, 140, 143
buy, 37, 68, 159
buys, 63

C

Caesar, 7, 17, 144, 177, 183
Caesarea, 78
Caesarea Philippi, 78
Caiaphas, 17, 126, 155, 174, 177
calf, 128
calm, 64
calves, 143
camel, 99, 150
Cana, 25, 48, 201
Canaanite, 77
candle, 29
candlestick, 29
Capernaum, 25, 44, 48, 49, 55, 59,
   66, 69, 71, 77, 84, 101
captain, 173
captive, 152
captives, 58
capture, 173
care, 64, 96, 103, 144
cares, 109
carpenter's, 59
carried, 48, 55, 195
carry, 97, 140, 184
carrying, 156
cast, 29, 30, 31, 70, 74, 82, 95, 106,
   138, 142, 143, 148, 162, 185, 201,
   204
castigate, 34
casting, 28, 87
casts, 74
catch, 44, 114, 144
cattle, 37
caught, 92, 201
cause, 22, 123
causes, 84
cave, 125
ceased, 40, 44, 51, 64, 66
Centurion, 49, 188
Cephas, 23
ceremonial, 25
certificate, 123
chaff, 19
chain, 65
chains, 65
chance, 103
charcoal, 175, 201
charge, 92, 109, 177, 185
charged, 47, 67, 81, 203
charges, 129, 180
charging, 34
chastise, 180
cheek, 30

cheer, 168
chief, 9, 83, 91, 126, 132, 133, 135,
   140, 141, 142, 155, 172, 174, 176,
   177, 178, 179, 180, 181, 182, 183,
   184, 186, 191, 194, 197
child, 6, 7, 10, 11, 12, 13, 48, 67, 82,
   84, 123, 149, 151, 167
child's, 67
childhood, 82
children, 12, 18, 40, 41, 42, 84, 86,
   94, 99, 101, 123, 126, 131, 138,
   140, 145, 150, 151, 161, 183, 184
choked, 60
choose, 100, 161
chooses, 101
Chorazin, 101
chose, 118, 161, 163
chosen, 74, 96, 143
Christ, 2, 23, 38, 148
church, 78
Chuza, 56
circumcise, 6, 90
circumcised, 7
cities, 46, 56, 134
citizens, 128, 134
city, 4, 6, 7, 12, 23, 29, 37, 39, 41,
   44, 46, 48, 51, 59, 65, 74, 119,
   138, 139, 143, 152, 156, 180, 184,
   194, 203
claim, 95, 108
clay, 104, 105
clean, 47, 150, 158, 162
cleanse, 114, 150
cleansed, 115
cleansing, 47
clear, 19
clearly, 30
Cleopas, 197
climbed, 133
climbs, 108
cloak, 30, 182
Clopas, 186
close, 159, 190
closed, 58, 61
cloth, 53, 125,
clothe, 112
clothed, 42, 65, 182, 203
clothes, 112, 201
clothing, 31, 112, 185
cloths, 7, 190, 196
cloud, 80
clubs, 172, 173
coat, 30, 173
coats, 18
cock, 168, 175
coin, 127, 144
coins, 127
cold, 175
collect, 18

collected, 134
collector, 26, 85, 122, 133
collectors, 18, 26, 127, 141
colt, 137
comforted, 29
Comforter, 163, 166
coming, 2, 11, 19, 22, 23, 38, 41,
   68, 81, 109, 113, 124, 130, 134,
   137, 153, 154, 166, 167, 168, 169,
   184, 186
command, 82, 123, 128, 130, 161
commanded, 47, 68, 72, 92, 119,
   132, 134
commandment, 72, 146, 161, 190
commandments, 98, 146, 162, 165
commands, 45
commend, 188
commended, 129
commit, 32, 98
commits, 94
committed, 32
common, 188
companies, 68
company, 13, 197, 204
compare, 42
compared, 62, 143
compassion, 47, 48, 68, 86, 103, 128
compel, 119
compelled, 184
complete, 131
conceived, 4
concerning, 42, 48, 124, 197, 204
condemn, 92, 132, 134
condemnation, 149, 187
condemned, 92, 183, 197
confess, 105
confessed, 21
confessing, 17
confirmed, 85
congregation, 85
conscious, 166
consecrate, 170
consecrated, 170
consent, 114
consented, 20
consider, 112
considered, 4
consist, 111
consolation, 11
console, 124
consoling, 124
constrained, 198
consume, 89
contempt, 179
content, 18
continual, 41
continue, 94
continues, 94
contributed, 139

212

dinner, 114, 118, 143
dipped, 159
directed, 194, 202
discern, 77
disciple, 57, 106, 131, 175, 187, 196, 201
disciples, 25, 26, 27, 28, 37, 39, 40, 42, 43, 48, 52, 53, 57, 61, 63, 66, 68, 70, 71, 72, 75, 76, 77, 78, 82, 88, 89, 94, 99, 101, 104, 106, 110, 121, 123, 126, 129, 136, 138, 143, 149, 151, 156, 161, 162, 172, 173, 174, 175, 191, 194, 196, 200
discussed, 84
discussing, 82, 84, 197
disease, 47, 66
diseases, 46, 47
dish, 114, 159
dishonest, 129
dishonor, 95
disobeyed, 128
dispute, 157
disregard, 83
distance, 115, 128, 188
distracted, 96
distressed, 86, 171
district, 12, 77, 78
divide, 111, 157
divided, 68, 74, 113, 128
divider, 111
division, 105, 109, 113
divorce, 123
doers, 31
dogs, 30
door, 32, 40, 41, 46, 55, 108, 109, 116, 137, 175, 190, 194
doors, 199, 200
doubtless, 59
doubts, 199
dove, 20, 22
doves, 34
dragging, 201
drank, 37, 116
draw, 37, 38, 148, 166
drawing, 113, 127, 138
dream, 10, 181
dresser, 162
drew, 48, 63, 75, 89, 128, 132, 137, 138, 142, 172, 173, 197, 198
drink, 33, 37, 53, 87, 111, 112, 113, 130, 157, 160, 171, 173, 185
drinking, 42, 97
drinks, 38
drops, 171
dropsy, 118
drove, 14, 140
drowned, 65, 84
drunk, 25
drunken, 113

due, 187
dug, 142, 154
dull, 61
dumb, 74
dunghill, 131
duties, 113
dwell, 165
dwells, 164
dwelt, 2, 12, 25, 117
dying, 125

E
ear, 61
early, 92, 100, 177, 197
earnestly, 49, 157, 159
ears, 42, 60, 61, 131, 194
earth, 8, 27, 28, 29, 32, 40, 42, 55, 61, 74, 85, 101, 113, 148, 149, 150, 169, 203
earthquakes, 151
ease, 111
easier, 55, 99
east, 9, 10, 116
easy, 116
eat, 26, 33, 39, 51, 53, 67, 68, 70, 71, 72, 73, 111, 113, 119, 128, 156, 157, 159, 177
eating, 42, 97
eats, 71, 127
edge, 59, 152
effect, 41
Egypt, 12
elder, 128
elders, 49, 72, 83, 141, 155, 172, 174, 177, 181, 183, 186, 194
eldest, 92
elect, 152
Eli, Eli, lama sabachthani, 188
Elijah, 21, 76, 78, 80, 81
Elizabeth, 4, 6
embassy, 131, 134
embraced, 128
eminent, 118
emmaus, 197
enclosed, 44
encounter, 131
end, 4, 7, 151, 153, 203, 262
ended, 13, 49
endures, 70
enemies, 30, 138, 147
enemy, 62
enmity, 179
enrolled, 7, 204
enrollment, 7
enter, 31, 32, 36, 47, 74, 82, 84, 97, 99, 108, 109, 114, 116, 123, 137, 149, 152, 154, 171, 177
entered, 6, 39, 45, 46, 49, 51, 52, 54, 67, 77, 89, 96, 115, 123, 133, 139,

175, 178, 182, 204
entering, 114
enters, 108, 109, 156
entrap, 144
entreated, 128
entrust, 129
entrusted, 154
envy, 180
epileptics, 47
equal, 100
escape, 150
escaped, 107
estate, 6
eternal, 27, 38, 39, 50, 70, 71, 75, 83, 98, 102, 107, 129, 148, 169
evening, 46, 69, 77, 100, 157, 190, 198, 199
everlasting, 99
everyone, 27, 31, 32, 36, 38, 40, 46, 71, 94, 110, 113, 118, 122, 126, 134, 154, 158, 178
everything, 44, 63, 86, 99, 101, 108, 128, 139, 143, 169, 202
everywhere, 34, 45, 57
evidence, 85
evil, 29, 30, 31, 40, 41, 73, 74, 77, 82, 87, 120, 170, 181
evildoer, 177
exalted, 118, 122, 149
exalts, 118, 122, 149
examine, 119
examining, 180
example, 158
exceedingly, 10, 29, 43, 80
exceeds, 32
except, 27, 35, 36, 67, 71, 74, 101, 115, 158, 164
exchange, 83
exclaimed, 6
excuse, 163
excused, 119
excuses, 119
exercise, 130, 158
expect, 113
expectantly, 19
expedient, 126, 174
explain, 73
explained, 63
extortion, 114, 150
extortioners, 122
eye, 30, 33, 84, 99
eyes, 11, 39, 58, 61, 101, 104, 105, 106, 109, 122, 125, 138, 169, 171, 197, 198

F
face, 42, 77, 80, 89, 115, 125,
faces, 84
facing, 188

214

215

healed, 46, 47, 49, 50, 56, 66, 74, 77, 115, 118, 120
healing, 34, 47
hearing, 49, 61, 91, 132
hears, 27, 31, 50, 95, 97, 166, 178
heart, 13, 28, 32, 41, 61, 73, 74, 102, 112, 146, 198
hearts, 19, 55, 94, 164, 167, 168, 198
heat, 100
heathen, 85
heaven, 17, 20, 22, 27, 28, 29, 30, 31, 32, 34, 40, 41, 42, 61, 63, 68, 70, 71, 76, 77, 78, 84, 85, 89, 98, 101, 122, 123, 127, 128, 138, 141, 143, 145, 148, 149, 153, 169, 171, 176, 194, 203, 204
heavenly, 8, 30, 36, 73, 84
heavens, 20
heavy, 42, 149, 171
Hebrew, 50, 184
hedge, 142
hedges, 119
heed, 32, 77, 80, 109, 111, 151, 152
heir, 142
held, 54, 142, 188
hell, 149, 150
help, 44, 82, 96, 114
hem, 66, 138
hemorrhage, 66
hen, 150
henceforth, 6, 29, 113, 164
herd, 65
herdsmen, 65
Herod, 9, 10, 12, 17, 27, 43, 76, 179, 180
Herod's, 56, 179
Herodians, 54, 144
Herodias, 27, 43
hewn, 31, 190
hid, 29, 62, 77, 95, 132, 138, 154
hidden, 42, 57, 63, 101, 110
high, 4, 17, 43, 52, 80, 126, 155, 174, 175, 176, 189, 203
higher, 118
highest, 8, 137, 138
highway, 17, 18
highways, 119
hill, 6, 29, 59
hillside, 65
hindered, 114
hire, 97, 100
hired, 100, 128
hireling, 109
hitherto, 167
hold, 72, 141
holding, 25, 176, 197
holds, 39
holes, 98
holy, 6, 11, 19, 30, 43, 45, 75, 83,

101, 126, 151, 165, 169, 203, 204
Holy Spirit, 6, 11, 19, 101, 151, 165, 203, 204
home, 6, 55, 65, 98, 113, 127, 165, 168, 187
homes, 196
honey, 17
honor, 59, 72, 95, 98, 118, 148, 149
honored, 118
hoped, 197
hoping, 179
Hosanna, 137, 140
host, 8, 118
hosts, 84, 176
hour, 11, 34, 37, 38, 48, 68, 91, 100, 101, 110, 113, 148, 151, 153, 157, 159, 166, 167, 168, 169, 171, 173, 175, 183, 186, 187, 188, 198
hours, 121
house, 6, 7, 10, 13, 26, 29, 31, 46, 49, 51, 52, 57, 67, 74, 77, 84, 94, 96, 97, 99, 113, 118, 119, 122, 124, 127, 128, 133, 136, 140, 150, 164, 177, 200, 204
household, 48, 57
householder, 62, 100, 113, 116, 119, 142, 156
houses, 42, 129, 149
housetops, 57, 110
humble, 28
humbled, 118, 122, 149
humbles, 84, 118, 122, 149
hundred, 51, 68, 85, 86, 127, 129, 136, 190, 201, 204
hundredfold, 60
hundreds, 68
hung, 140
hunger, 28, 70, 128
hungry, 52
hurried, 43
husband, 38
hymn, 168
hypocrisy, 110, 144, 150
hypocrites, 120, 149, 150

I
idle, 100, 196
ignoring, 67
ill, 48, 50, 121
illness, 121
immediately, 28, 43, 46, 47, 54, 55, 60, 66, 67, 82, 118, 120, 132, 134, 137, 159, 175
imploring, 86
importunity, 40
impossible, 41, 99
increase, 27
increased, 13
increasing, 60

indignant, 120, 123, 130, 140
indignantly, 136
infirmity, 47, 120
inherit, 28, 102
inheritance, 111, 142
iniquity, 116, 150
inn, 7, 103
innkeeper, 103
innocent, 150, 181, 183, 188
inquired, 9, 132
inscription, 144
insisted, 175
inspired, 11
instantly, 77
insurrection, 180, 183
intend, 91
interest, 154
interpreted, 198
interval, 175
invalids, 50
invested, 154
invite, 118, 143
invited, 25, 51, 118, 119, 143
invoke, 175
inwardly, 31
Isaac, 116, 145
Isaiah, 17, 18, 25, 58, 61
Iscariot, 26, 136, 155, 159, 165
Israel, 6, 9, 11, 12, 22, 36, 49, 146, 186, 197, 203
Israelite, 23
Ituraea, 17

J
Jacob, 37, 116
jailers, 86
Jairus, 66
James, 26, 28, 46, 59, 67, 80, 89, 171, 194, 196, 204
jar, 39, 156
javelin, 188
Jeremiah, 78
Jericho, 103, 132, 133
Jerusalem, 9, 11, 13, 17, 18, 21, 35, 38, 47, 50, 72, 89, 90, 103, 107, 116, 117, 124, 132, 134, 135, 137, 139, 140, 150, 152, 179, 184, 186, 197, 198, 203, 204
Jew, 37, 178
Jewish, 141, 190
Jews, 9, 18, 21, 25, 35, 37, 38, 49, 50, 71, 72, 88, 90, 91, 92, 94, 95, 105, 107, 109, 121, 124, 125, 126, 135, 140, 143, 173, 174, 177, 178, 181, 182, 183, 184, 185, 189, 190, 199
Joanna, 56, 196
John, 2, 6, 17, 18, 19, 20, 21, 22, 23, 26, 27, 28, 37, 40, 42, 43, 46, 53, 67, 76, 78, 80, 87, 89, 107, 108,

217

moored, 69
morning, 46, 77, 92, 100, 197
morrow, 33, 103
morsel, 159
moses, 2, 11, 23, 47, 70, 80, 90, 92,
  106, 123, 145, 198
Most High, 4
moth, 112
mother, 6, 10, 11, 12, 13, 25, 43, 46,
  48, 57, 59, 67, 71, 72, 76, 98, 123,
  130, 131, 186, 187, 194, 196, 204
mother-in-law, 46
mount, 137, 138, 151, 153, 154, 168,
  169, 204
Mount of Olives, 137, 138, 151, 153,
  168, 169
mountain, 28, 38, 41, 69, 80, 81, 202
mountains, 65, 85, 152, 184
mourn, 29, 42
mouth, 28, 58, 73, 74, 82, 134, 140,
  188
multitude, 8, 49, 50, 110, 111, 132,
  138, 139, 141, 155, 184
multitudes, 18, 131, 142
murder, 73, 180, 183
murdered, 150
murderers, 143
murmur, 71
murmured, 71, 75, 127, 133
music, 128
mustard, 62
muttering, 90, 91
myrrh, 10, 190
mysteries, 61

N
nails, 200
Nain, 48
naked, 173
name, 2, 4, 6, 7, 11, 31, 35, 40, 66,
  85, 87, 101, 107, 108, 137, 138,
  148, 151, 165, 167, 169, 170
Naphtali, 25
napkin, 134, 196
nard, 136
narrow, 116
Nathaniel, 23, 26, 201
nation, 49, 126, 177, 178
nations, 112, 152
Nazareth, 4, 7, 12, 13, 23, 45, 58,
  132, 139, 172, 184, 197
neck, 84
need, 20, 26, 32, 52, 72, 112, 127,
  137, 158, 159, 176
needed, 35
needful, 96
needle, 99
neglected, 150
neglecting, 150

neighbor, 102, 103, 146
neighborhood, 65
neighbors, 6, 104, 118, 127
nests, 62, 98
net, 28, 63, 201
nets, 28, 44
new, 45, 53, 160, 161, 190
news, 46, 47, 56
Nicodemus, 35, 36, 190
night, 8, 11, 12, 35, 44, 61, 65, 104,
  111, 121, 154, 159, 168, 181, 190,
  194, 201
nights, 74
nobleman, 48, 134
north, 116
noticed, 72, 118
notorious, 180
numbered, 57, 110, 204
nursed, 184

O
oath, 43, 149
obedient, 13
obey, 45, 64
observe, 72, 105, 149
observed, 98, 130
observing, 72
obtain, 29
odor, 125
offended, 73
offenders, 117
offense, 42, 59, 75
offer, 11, 47, 53
offered, 10, 185
offering, 166, 186
offerings, 146
office, 26, 204
officers, 43, 91, 172, 173, 174, 175,
  182
officials, 43
oil, 51, 103, 129
ointment, 51, 121, 136
ointments, 190
old, 12, 13, 36, 53, 76, 95, 112
olives, 137, 138, 151, 153, 168, 169
Olivet, 154, 204
oneself, 146
open, 106, 109, 113, 116, 137
opened, 20, 28, 40, 58, 104, 105,
  106, 125, 198
opening, 10, 55
openly, 47, 88, 90, 126, 174
opens, 11, 108
opportunity, 43, 155
opposite, 137, 139, 151, 190
oppressed, 58
ordained, 26
order, 155, 189, 191
ordered, 86, 190

orders, 12, 43, 64, 135
ought, 38, 41, 110, 120, 150, 154,
  158, 182
outer, 143
outran, 196
outside, 67, 76, 114, 116, 150, 175,
  195
outwardly, 150
overcome, 67, 168
overshadow, 4
overshadowed, 80
overtake, 148
overturned, 140
owe, 129
owed, 51, 86
own, 2, 7, 10, 30, 57, 59, 63, 71, 83,
  90, 94, 95, 103, 108, 109, 126, 129,
  131, 134, 154, 163, 164, 177, 178,
  184, 187, 190
owner, 100, 142
ox, 118, 120
oxen, 119, 140, 143

P
painfully, 69
pains, 47
pair, 11
palace, 155
parable, 62, 63, 73, 108, 111, 113,
  117, 118, 122, 127, 134, 142
parables, 60, 61, 63, 142, 143, 167
paradise, 187
paralytic, 55
paralytics, 47
paralyzed, 50
parents, 11, 13, 99, 104, 105, 151
part, 150, 158
parted, 185, 203
partners, 44
parts, 185
pass, 37, 133, 152, 171
passed, 50, 84, 103, 104, 186
passerby, 184
passes, 73
passing, 59, 132, 133
passion, 203
Passover, 13, 35, 135, 140, 155, 156,
  157, 159, 177, 183
past, 194
pasture, 109
patch, 53
path, 60
patience, 86
pavement, 183
pay, 51, 86, 100, 144
payment, 86
peace, 8, 11, 51, 64, 66, 97, 113, 131,
  138, 168, 199, 200
peacemakers, 29

pearl, 63
pearls, 30, 63
pennies, 110
penny, 57, 139
people, 9, 11, 19, 25, 39, 44, 47, 48,
  49, 65, 67, 68, 69, 70, 73, 74, 76,
  89, 90, 91, 92, 119, 120, 125, 126,
  129, 132, 139, 140, 141, 142, 144,
  152, 155, 174, 178, 180, 181, 183,
  184, 191, 194, 197
people's, 61
peoples, 11
perceive, 38, 61
perceived, 142, 180
perceiving, 55, 66, 69
perdition, 170
perfect, 30, 140
perform, 70
performs, 126
perish, 64, 85, 107, 126, 128, 173
perishes, 70
permitted, 182
perplexed, 43, 76
persecute, 29, 163
persecuted, 29, 50, 150, 163
persons, 127, 204
persuaded, 181
perverting, 177, 180
Peter, 23, 26, 28, 67, 73, 75, 78, 80,
  83, 86, 99, 113, 156, 158, 159,
  168, 171, 173, 175, 195, 196, 201,
  202, 204
Phanuel, 11
Pharisee, 51, 114, 122, 150
Pharisee's, 51
Pharisees, 18, 21, 26, 32, 35, 37, 51,
  52, 53, 54, 72, 73, 74, 77, 91, 93,
  105, 110, 114, 118, 123, 125, 126,
  127, 129, 135, 138, 142, 144, 146,
  147, 149, 150, 172, 191
Philip, 17, 23, 26, 148, 164, 204
Philip's, 43
Philippi, 78
phylacteries, 149
physician, 26
physicians, 66
piece, 53
pieces, 65, 142, 183
pierced, 189
pigeons, 11, 140
Pilate, 17, 117, 177, 178, 179, 180,
  181, 182, 183, 184, 189, 190, 191
piped, 42
pit, 30, 73
pity, 82
places, 42, 118, 149, 151
placing, 92
plainly, 83, 107, 121, 167
plaiting, 182

plan, 114
planned, 135
plant, 73
planted, 73, 117, 142
plants, 62
plate, 150
platter, 43
playmate, 42
pleased, 20, 43, 81
pleasing, 93, 101
pleasure, 112
plenteous, 57
plentiful, 97
plentifully, 111
plow, 98
pluck, 52
plunder, 74
pods, 128
point, 48, 49, 66
Pontius Pilate, 17
pool, 50, 104
poor, 25, 28, 42, 58, 98, 118, 119,
  133, 136, 139, 159
porches, 50
portico, 107
portion, 96
position, 144
possess, 98
possessed, 77
possessions, 98, 111, 113
possible, 82, 99, 152
possibly, 19
pots, 25, 72
pound, 134
pounds, 134
poured, 136, 158
pouring, 103
poverty, 139
power, 2, 4, 34, 66, 109, 145, 153,
  169, 176, 182, 203
powers, 78
practice, 149
praetorium, 177, 178, 182
praise, 105, 115, 132, 138
praised, 120
praising, 8, 115
pray, 30, 32, 40, 41, 57, 97, 119, 122,
  165, 170, 171
prayed, 46, 122, 171
prayer, 11, 204
prayers, 53, 149
praying, 32, 40, 41, 169
preach, 26, 34, 46, 58, 149
preached, 42, 136
preaching, 17, 34, 47, 55, 56, 57
preparation, 183, 189, 190, 191
prepare, 17, 42, 81, 156, 164
prepared, 11, 111, 130, 156, 190
presence, 11, 52, 116, 118, 144

present, 11, 117
presented, 203
presently, 176
press, 114, 142
pressed, 44
pressing, 66
presume, 18, 49
pretense, 149
prevail, 78
prevailed, 183
prevent, 20, 189
price, 63
priest, 47, 52, 103, 126, 155, 174,
  175, 176
priesthood, 17
priests, 9, 18, 21, 52, 83, 91, 115,
  126, 132, 135, 140, 141, 142, 155,
  172, 174, 176, 177, 178, 179, 180,
  181, 182, 183, 184, 186, 191, 194,
  197
prince, 74
principal, 140
print, 200
prison, 27, 42, 43, 86, 180, 183
prisoner, 180
private, 56, 110
privately, 63, 101, 153
proceeds, 73
proclaim, 57, 58, 65, 95, 98
proclaimed, 91, 110
procuring, 172
produces, 61
producing, 142
profit, 83
progress, 84
promise, 203
promised, 155
proofs, 203
property, 128, 154
prophecy, 31, 61
prophesied, 126
prophesy, 176
prophet, 9, 17, 18, 21, 25, 38, 42, 48,
  51, 58, 59, 69, 74, 91, 105, 114, 139,
  141, 142, 197
prophetess, 11
prophets, 23, 31, 32, 71, 76, 78, 95,
  101, 114, 116, 146, 150, 152, 198
proselyte, 149
prove, 162
proved, 103
proverb, 59
proverbs, 167
provide, 97, 112
provided, 56
provoke, 114
prunes, 162
psalms, 147, 204
public, 6

publican, 122
publicans, 42
punish, 113
pure, 28, 136
purification, 11
purify, 72, 135
purple, 182
purpose, 46, 148
purse, 97, 161
purses, 112
pursued, 46

Q
quantity, 201
quarter, 47
question, 55, 141, 145, 146, 147
questioned, 45, 55, 174, 179
questioning, 55, 81
questions, 13, 147
quickens, 75
quickly, 119, 124, 128, 129, 159
quietly, 124
Quirinius, 7
quote, 59

R
rabbi, 27, 35, 39, 121, 149
rage, 12
railed, 187
raiment, 42
rain, 30
raise, 18, 143, 145
raised, 76, 135, 143, 168, 201
ran, 65, 68, 82, 128, 133, 173, 196
ranks, 2, 22
rapacity, 150
ravenous, 31
ravens, 112
reached, 196
read, 52, 58, 92, 102, 123, 140, 142,
    145, 184, 185
ready, 17, 89, 113, 119, 143, 156
reap, 39, 112, 134, 154
reaper, 39
reapers, 62
reaping, 134, 154
reaps, 39
reason, 95, 109, 123
rebuke, 83, 138
rebuked, 82, 83, 89, 123, 132, 187
receive, 27, 89, 97, 99, 100, 123, 129,
    132, 134, 149, 165, 167, 203
received, 2, 34, 89, 96, 100, 104,
    105, 109, 128, 132, 133, 134, 154,
    169
receives, 39, 40, 84, 127
receiving, 100, 159, 187
reckoning, 86
recognized, 198

recognizing, 197
recover, 121
recovering, 58
red, 77
redeem, 197
redemption, 11
reed, 42, 182
referred, 198
refuse, 182
refused, 41, 65, 86, 128
refuses, 85
regard, 41, 144
regarded, 6, 41, 157
region, 17, 45, 77, 123
reign, 17, 134, 176
reigned, 12
rejected, 81, 83, 142
rejects, 97
rejoice, 29, 39, 101, 138, 167
rejoiced, 6, 10, 95, 101, 120
rejoices, 6, 27, 85
rejoicing, 127
release, 58, 180, 181, 182, 183
released, 86, 183
remain, 97, 171, 202
remained, 6, 12, 22, 107
remaining, 189
remains, 108, 148
remember, 163, 166, 187, 195
remembered, 137, 143, 175, 191, 195
remembers, 167
remembrance, 160, 165
remove, 171
removed, 55
rend, 30
render, 144
renounce, 131
repaid, 118
repay, 103, 118
repent, 17
repentance, 17, 18, 127
repented, 101, 141, 183
repents, 127
repetitions, 32
report, 48
reported, 55, 86, 119
reports, 66
reproach, 114
reproached, 136
reproved, 27
required, 111, 113, 114
resist, 30
respect, 142
respected, 190
responsibilities, 83
rest, 42, 68, 97, 112, 121, 143, 171, 196
rested, 190
restore, 133, 203
restored, 54

resumed, 158
resurrection, 124, 145, 204
return, 10, 97, 115, 118, 134
returned, 6, 13, 49, 55, 101, 134,
    190, 198, 204
returning, 13, 196
reveal, 101
revealed, 11, 22, 42, 57, 78, 101,
    110, 201
revelation, 11
revile, 29
reviled, 106, 186
reviling, 176
reward, 29, 41, 87, 155, 187
rich, 99, 111, 118, 129, 133, 139
riches, 99, 129
right, 30, 32, 38, 65, 90, 95, 100,
    102, 130, 146, 147, 158, 176, 182,
    185, 201, 203
righteous, 11, 26, 43, 122, 127, 150,
    170
righteousness, 28, 32, 33, 129, 141,
    166
rightly, 51, 174
rigid, 82
ring, 128
riot, 183
ripe, 61
rise, 30, 40, 50, 61, 83, 91, 124, 132,
    151, 171, 191, 195, 199
risen, 42, 76, 81, 116, 191, 198, 199
rising, 81
river, 17
road, 97, 98, 103, 132, 137, 198
roadside, 132
rob, 18
robber, 108, 173
robbers, 103, 109, 140, 186
robe, 128, 182
rock, 31, 78, 190
rocky, 60
roll, 194
rolled, 82, 190, 194, 196
Romans, 126
roof, 49, 55
room, 32, 41, 55, 119, 156, 204
rooms, 110
root, 18, 60, 62
rooted, 73
rose, 12, 26, 46, 55, 59, 60, 69, 124,
    158, 198
round, 84, 107, 139, 195
Rufus, 184
ruler, 9, 35, 67, 118, 120, 148
ruler's, 67
rulers, 9, 66, 110, 130, 180, 197
rumors, 151
rush, 204
rushed, 65

221

slow, 198
small, 112, 133
smallest, 62
smites, 30
snatch, 107
snatches, 109
soft, 42
soil, 60
sold, 57, 63, 86, 110, 136, 140
soldier, 43, 185
soldiers, 18, 49, 172, 173, 179, 182, 185, 186, 189, 191, 194
Solomon, 107, 112
son, 2, 4, 6, 7, 13, 17, 20, 22, 23, 26, 27, 28, 37, 41, 42, 48, 52, 55, 59, 70, 71, 74, 75, 78, 80, 81, 82, 83, 93, 94, 98, 101, 105, 106, 107, 110, 113, 121, 124, 128, 130, 132, 133, 140, 142, 143, 147, 148, 153, 159, 161, 169, 170, 171, 172, 176, 182, 186, 187, 188, 195, 202, 204
Son of God, 22, 106, 107, 121, 124, 176, 182, 186, 187, 188
Son of Man, 42, 52, 55, 70, 74, 75, 78, 81, 83, 93, 98, 110, 113, 130, 132, 133, 148, 153, 161, 171, 172, 176, 195
sons, 2, 29, 37, 74, 128, 129, 130, 141, 148, 150, 201
soon, 48, 56, 87, 153
sorrow, 167
sorrowful, 98, 159, 167, 171
sorry, 43
sort, 4, 51
sorted, 63
sought, 13, 88, 91, 133, 140, 155, 176, 183
soul, 6, 57, 83, 102, 111, 146, 148, 171
souls, 42
sound, 36, 128, 204
sour, 186
south, 116
sow, 60, 62, 112, 134, 154
sowed, 60, 62, 154
sower, 39, 60
sows, 39
spare, 128
sparrows, 57, 110
spat, 104, 176, 182
speak, 23, 34, 36, 38, 42, 48, 55, 61, 63, 76, 87, 93, 94, 105, 114, 151, 164, 166, 167, 175, 182, 204
speaking, 34, 44, 58, 67, 76, 90, 142, 167, 175, 203
speaks, 27, 74, 90, 106, 110, 159
spear, 189
speck, 30
speechless, 143

spend, 103
spent, 66, 128, 198
spices, 190, 194
spilled, 53
spin, 112
spirit, 6, 11, 13, 14, 19, 20, 22, 27, 28, 34, 36, 38, 45, 55, 58, 74, 75, 82, 89, 101, 110, 120, 125, 147, 151, 159, 163, 165, 166, 171, 188, 199, 203, 204
Spirit of Truth, 163, 165, 166
spirits, 45, 101
spiritual, 70
spit, 132
spittle, 104
sponge, 188
sprang, 60, 201
spread, 45, 47, 48, 137, 202
springing, 38
sprout, 61
squandered, 128
staff, 34
stand, 41, 74, 100, 116, 151
standing, 44, 51, 92, 100, 122, 125, 148, 174, 175, 186, 187, 195
stands, 21, 27
star, 9, 10
started, 69, 180
startled, 199
stature, 13, 112, 133
stay, 39, 133, 198, 203
stayed, 13, 39, 121, 126
staying, 204
steal, 98, 109, 191
stealth, 155
steep, 65
steps, 50
stern, 64
sternly, 47
steward, 25, 56, 100, 129
stewardship, 129
still, 48, 64, 67, 73, 98, 119, 124, 165, 171, 175, 176, 191, 195, 197, 199
stirred, 139, 180
stirs, 178
stole, 194
stomach, 73
stone, 25, 41, 92, 107, 121, 125, 138, 142, 151, 190, 191, 194
stone's, 171
stoned, 142
stones, 18, 65, 95, 107, 138, 151
stoning, 150
stood, 25, 48, 58, 76, 102, 115, 122, 133, 134, 135, 137, 175, 176, 179, 188, 195, 197, 199, 200, 201, 204
stooping, 196
stopped, 132

store, 111
storehouse, 112
storm, 64
story, 41
straight, 17, 18, 116, 120
straighten, 120
straining, 150
stranger, 108
strangers, 108
street, 137
streets, 116, 119, 143
strength, 65, 102, 146
strengthening, 171
stretch, 54
stretched, 47, 54
stretching, 76
strictly, 67
strike, 174
stripped, 103, 201
strong, 6, 13, 69, 74, 129
struck, 174, 176, 182
studied, 90
stumble, 84, 121
stumbles, 121
stumbling, 83
subdue, 65
subject, 101
subjects, 158
sucked, 76
sucklings, 140
suddenly, 80, 204
sue, 30
suffer, 81, 83, 123, 157, 159
suffered, 66, 117, 181
sufficient, 33
sum, 194
summer, 153
summoned, 10, 86
summoning, 129
sums, 139
sun, 30, 60, 80
sundown, 46
sung, 168
supper, 136, 158
support, 56
suppose, 40, 51
supposed, 134, 199
supposing, 13, 124, 195
surnamed, 204
Susanna, 56
suspense, 107
swaddling, 7
swallowing, 150
swear, 175
swears, 149
sweat, 171
sweep, 127
swine, 30, 65, 128
sword, 152, 173

How to Read the Numbers and Reference Notes

The basic text for this restatement comes from the first four books of the New Testament, the *Gospels* of Matthew, Mark, Luke, and John; they are abbreviated as Mt., Mk., Lk., and Jn.

On each page the chapter and verses that have been quoted are listed at the end of the text. For example, the verses quoted on page 2 are listed as (Jn. 1:1–4, 6–18). This signifies that the text appearing on page 2 is taken from the book of John, Chapter 1, verses 1 through 4 and 6 through 18.

The superscript numbers that appear at the beginning of various lines (e.g., ^{1}In) and sometimes within sentences (e.g., God, ^{13}born) are the verse numbers as they are listed in Scripture. Italicized superscript letters that appear at the end of sentences and sometimes within sentences (e.g., John.[b]) are footnote references. They refer the reader to the bottom of the page for an explanation or comment concerning the footnoted material.

The primary translation used in this work is the *Revised Standard Version* (RSV) of the Bible. However, many other versions have also been consulted and employed, especially the *King James Version* (KJV). Other translations that are quoted in the text of this restatement are listed on the next page.

Since the *Revised Standard Version* has been chosen as the primary reference text, any other translation that has been used, or any other deviation from the *Revised Standard Version* text, is shown in the small notations at the bottom of each page.

As an example of how differences from the *Revised Standard Version* are shown, consider the following notation that appears at the bottom of page 2:

Jn. 1:14   Word was made flesh (KJV) / Word became flesh (RSV)

After the chapter and verse reference (Jn. 1:14) comes any phraseology that differs from the *Revised Standard Version* ("Word was made flesh"). The source of this difference is shown in parentheses (KJV). When there is no reference listed, the source of the change is the author's restating and reworking of the Biblical text. To the right of the slash is the text as it appears in the *Revised Standard Version* ("Word became flesh") followed by (RSV). Wherever possible the first and last words on both sides of the slash are the same ("Word . . . flesh") and the different wording (was made / became) appears between them.

If there are several changes within a particular verse, these changes are listed in order and separated by a dot (•), as may be seen at the bottom of page 40:

Mt. 6:10   Your kingdom (NRSV) / Thy kingdom (RSV) • your will (NRSV) / thy will (RSV)

Sometimes an entire verse comes from another translation, especially the

227

King James Version. In such a case the change is shown in the verse notes, as at the bottom of page 26:

Mk. 3:14   KJV

If the gospel text contains a quotation or reference from the Old Testament, its Old Testament source is identified in the verse notes, as in

Mt. 2:6   Micah 5:2

at the bottom of page 9. This signifies that Mt. 2:6 is a quotation from Micah, chapter 5, verse 2.

The major purpose of the verse notes is to show any part of a sentence that has been changed or omitted. If entire sentences are left out, they are not shown; and, if only one half of a compound sentence (divided by a semicolon) is used, the other half is not listed. Numerous minor punctuation changes are not shown.

The parenthetical note at the end of the verse notes, for example (122:3/1346) on page 4, references the corresponding paper, section, and page(s) in *The Urantia Book.*

Following is a list of other translations that were used in preparing this restatement, along with their abbreviations:

AB   *The Amplified Bible*
ASV   *The American Standard Version*
Bas   *The New Testament in Basic English*
Ber   *The Berkeley Version of the New Testament* (Gerrit Verkuyl)
Gspd *The New Testament: An American Translation* (Edgar J. Goodspeed)
Knox *The Holy Bible: A Translation from the Latin Vulgate in the Light of Hebrew and Greek Originals* (Monsignor Ronald Knox)
Lam   *The New Testament According to the Eastern Texts* (George M. Lamsa)
Mof   *The New Testament: A New Translation* (James Moffatt)
Mon   *The Centenary Translation: The New Testament in Modern English* (Helen Barrett Montgomery)
NAB   *Revised New Testament of the New American Bible*
NAS   *The New American Standard Bible*
NEB   *The New English Bible: New Testament*
NIV   *The New International Version*
Nor   *The New Testament: A New Translation* (Olaf M. Norlie)
NRSV *New Revised Standard Version Bible*
Phi   *The New Testament in Modern English* (J. B. Phillips)
Rieu *The Four Gospels* (E. V. Rieu)
TCNT *The Twentieth Century New Testament*
TEV   *Today's English Version*
Wey   *The New Testament in Modern Speech* (Richard Francis Weymouth)
Wms   *The New Testament: A Translation in the Language of the People* (Charles B. Williams)

Maps and Images

The Parables of Jesus

The Miracles of Jesus

Jesus' Philosophy of Living

Bibliography

Editors of Reader's Digest. *Jesus and His Times*. Pleasantville, NY: Reader's Digest Association, 1987.

Faw, Duane L. *The Paramony*. Malibu, CA: Duane L. Faw, 1986.

Halley, H. H. *Halley's Bible Handbook, New Revised Edition*. Grand Rapids, MI: Zondervan Publishing House, 1965.

The Holy Bible, King James Version. Nashville, TN: Thomas Nelson Publishers, 1976.

Hughes, David. *The Star of Bethlehem: An Astronomer's Confirmation*. New York: Walker and Company, 1979.

Jefferson, Thomas, comp. *The Jefferson Bible*. New York: Grosset & Dunlap, 1940.

Kohlenberger, John R. *The Precise Parallel New Testament*. New York: Oxford University Press, 1995.

Master Study Bible, New American Standard. Nashville, TN: Holman Bible Publishers, 1981.

May, Herbert G., ed. *Oxford Bible Atlas*. New York: Oxford University Press, 1984.

May, Herbert G., and Bruce M. Metzger, eds. *The New Oxford Annotated Bible with the Apocrypha. Revised Standard Version*. New York: Oxford University Press, 1977.

Richards, Lawrence O., ed. *The Revell Bible Dictionary*. New York: Wynwood Press, 1990.

Robertson, A. T., and George L. Robinson. "The Gospels Paralleled." In *Master Study Bible: New American Standard*. Nashville, TN: Holman Bible Publishers, 1981.

Sinnott, Roger W. "Computing the Star of Bethlehem." *Sky and Telescope* (December 1986), p. 632–635.

Standard Bible Atlas. Cincinnati, OH: The Standard Publishing Company, 1959.

The Urantia Book. Chicago: Urantia Foundation, 1955.

Vaughn, Curtis, ed. *The Word: The Bible from 26 Translations*. Moss Point, MS: Mathis Publishers, 1988.

Wallban, Walter T., Alastair M. Taylor, and Nels M. Bailkey. *Civilization Past and Present. Volume 1, Fifth Edition*. Chicago: Scott, Foresman, 1965.

Webster's Third New International Dictionary of the English Language, Unabridged. Springfield, MA: Merriam-Webster, 2002.